AMERICA'S VIETNAM

In the series *Asian American History and Culture,* edited by Cathy Schlund-Vials, Shelley Sang-Hee Lee, and Rick Bonus. Founding editor, Sucheng Chan; editors emeriti, David Palumbo-Liu, Michael Omi, K. Scott Wong, and Linda Trinh Võ.

ALSO IN THIS SERIES:

A list of additional titles in this series appears at the back of this book.

MARGUERITE NGUYEN

AMERICA'S VIETNAM

The Longue Durée *of U.S. Literature and Empire*

TEMPLE UNIVERSITY PRESS
Philadelphia • Rome • Tokyo

TEMPLE UNIVERSITY PRESS
Philadelphia, Pennsylvania 19122
www.temple.edu/tempress

Library of Congress Cataloging-in-Publication Data

Names: Nguyen, Marguerite Bich, 1976– author.
Title: America's Vietnam : the *longue durée* of U.S. literature and empire /
    Marguerite Bich Nguyen.
Description: Philadelphia, Pennsylvania : Temple University Press, 2018. |
    Series: Asian American history & culture | Includes bibliographical
    references and index.
Identifiers: LCCN 2017053401 (print) | LCCN 2018010642 (ebook) |
    ISBN 9781439916131 (E-book) | ISBN 9781439916117 (hardback : alk. paper) |
    ISBN 9781439916124 (paper : alk. paper)
Subjects: LCSH: Vietnam War, 1961–1975—Social aspects—United States. |
    Popular culture—United States—History—20th century. | Vietnam War,
    1961–1975—Influence. | Vietnam War, 1961–1975—Literature and the war. |
    Vietnam War, 1961–1975—Mass media and the war. | War and society. |
    BISAC: LITERARY CRITICISM / American / Asian American. | LITERARY
    CRITICISM / Asian / Indic.
Classification: LCC DS559.8.S6 (ebook) | LCC DS559.8.S6 N47 2018 (print) |
    DDC 810.9/358597—dc23
LC record available at https://lccn.loc.gov/2017053401

Printed in the United States of America

9 8 7 6 5 4 3 2 1

For Luc Thach Nguyen

CONTENTS

ACKNOWLEDGMENTS

M y deepest gratitude goes to my parents, Luc Nguyen and Nga Nguyen, who showed me that an analytical mind also needs to be a compassionate one. Together, their experiences, struggles, and stories taught me critical thinking from a young age and shape the central questions and concerns that form the backbone of this book. I am also indebted to my sister, Thuy-Anh Nguyen, for her support and encouragement, and to my nieces, Isabelle, Sophie, and Josephine Tindale, for their love and affection. They remind me of how much fun it is to create and learn new things.

T. R. Johnson consistently helped me see my work with fresh, optimistic eyes, and he knew how to make me laugh when it got to be that time. His intellect and kindness have sustained me, and his faith in me and in the project kept the finish line in view along the toughest of stretches.

This project formally began at the University of California (UC), Berkeley, where I benefited greatly from a variety of intellectual relationships. Abdul JanMohamed was a generous adviser and tireless advocate. His guidance and feedback continue to inform how I think about the academic world today. I credit Nguyen Nguyet Cam and Peter Zinoman for encouraging and aiding me with Vietnamese-language studies and for creating a generative interdisciplinary space. Their instruction rerouted my intellectual path for the better. I always looked forward to their teachings and gatherings, and I cherish the lifelong friendships I gained from them.

I am also indebted to Sau-ling Cynthia Wong for opening up Asian American literary studies to me, for teaching me to approach the field with acumen and care, and for her intellectual wisdom and friendship. Conversations with Anne Cheng, Colleen Lye, Susan Schweik, and Hertha D. Sweet Wong significantly shaped my approach to the fields of American literature and Asian American studies.

This project would not have been possible without financial support from the Wesleyan University Department of English and Office of Academic Affairs; the UC Berkeley Department of English, Department of History, Center for Southeast Asia Studies, and Graduate Division; the Tulane University Department of English and School of Liberal Arts; the Andrew Mellon Postdoctoral Fellowship in the Humanities; the U.S. Department of Education Foreign Language Area Studies program; the Rockefeller Foundation; and the Leadership Alliance. I am also grateful to the organizers of programs and workshops where I had the opportunity to participate in stimulating conversations that helped to advance the project, including the Conference on Asian American Literary and Visual Culture at Wellesley College, sponsored by the Alliance to Advance Liberal Arts Colleges; the Diasporas, Exiles, and Refugees workshop at the University of California; the East of California Junior Faculty Workshop at the University of Illinois, Chicago; the Leadership Alliance National Symposium at New York University; the Southeast Asian Studies Summer Institute at the University of Wisconsin, Madison; the State of Asian American Studies workshop at the University of Connecticut, Storrs; and the Vietnamese Advanced Summer Institute in Hanoi and Ho Chi Minh City, Vietnam.

Thanks also go to the following individuals and organizations for their assistance with various archival and copyrighted materials used in this book: the Australian War Memorial, Barry Lawrence Ruderman Antique Maps, Tiffany Chung, Copper Canyon Press, the Denis Stanley Gibbons Estate, the General Sciences Library in Ho Chi Minh City, the Georgia Historical Society, Harlan Greene, Emi Kanaka, the Museum of the City of New York, the National Archives and Records Administration, the New York Public Library, and the Vietnam National Museum of History and its Documentary and Library Department.

Much appreciation goes to Temple University Press for bringing this book to completion. Sara Jo Cohen's immediate grasp of the project, astute eye, and enthusiasm made this process not only rewarding but also a pleasure. I am lucky to have worked with her as my editor. I am also indebted to Donald Goellnicht and Julia Lee for their incredibly helpful feedback, which inspired me to write a stronger book, as well as the staff at the press—especially Ann-Marie Anderson and Joan S. P. Vidal—and Susan Deeks, for their patience and for attending so closely to the production details. Dina Dineva prepared a thoughtful and thorough index.

This book bears the imprint of a number of colleagues and friends. Joel Pfister meticulously read every word of the manuscript, many times over, and his challenging questions sharpened each chapter and the book's overall scope. Mariam Beevi, Andy Curran, Chi Thuc Ha, Sean McCann, Ellen Nerenberg, Isabelle Thuy Pelaud, Suzy Taraba, Liz Tinker, Monique Truong, and Stephanie Weiner have all provided various forms of support for this project, and I am thankful to have them as colleagues.

Cathy Schlund-Vials continues to model what it means to be a colleague and mentor. She has been vital to the completion of this project and to the evolution of my thinking about Southeast Asian American studies more generally. Others have also left their mark on this book: Lisa Cohen, Rachel Ellis-Neyra, Matt Garrett, Joe Fitzpatrick, Alice Hadler, J. Kēhaulani Kauanui, Daniel Kim, Andrew Lam, Anita Mannur, Ruth Nisse, Courtney Weiss Smith, Amy Tang, and Quan Tran. I am also fortunate to count as part of my community Ilesanmi Adeboye, Melissa Fabros, Catherine Fung, Amy Lee, Emmanuel Raymundo, Fumi Showers, and Ivan Small. They have been the greatest of friends and interlocutors. Tolani Adeboye has seen this project through from its very beginnings to its end. Her camaraderie, insights, and wisdom are gifts that I value, and her humor always helps me see beyond the challenges of the present.

AMERICA'S VIETNAM

INTRODUCTION

Rethinking America's Vietnam

O
n the U.S. Department of State's current webpage, a section titled "Office of the Historian" lists finding aids, historical documents, and summaries of U.S. foreign relations with different countries. It is a gold mine for those interested in thinking critically about these topics. Selecting "Vietnam" from the drop-down menu yields a chronology of Vietnamese-American contact, which the site suggests began in the late nineteenth century: "Relations between citizens of the United States and residents of what is today the Socialist Republic of Vietnam began during the nineteenth century, when that region was a colony of the French Empire." A little farther down, we find that the United States had commercial agents in Saigon beginning in 1889, and it established its first consul in the country in 1907.[1] In light of America's longer-standing ties to other Asian countries, such as China, Japan, and the Philippines, and the transformative impact of these connections on American national identity and trade, the official start of American relations with Vietnam seems rather belated—a delayed occurrence in the long history of America's cultural, political, and economic ties to Asia. Vietnam's supposedly minor place in U.S. foreign affairs prior to the Vietnam War finds its counterpart in American literary history, for which Vietnam largely does not exist until the ground conflict got under way in the 1960s.

America's Vietnam challenges the prevailing genealogy of Vietnam's emergence in the American imagination, one that presupposes the Vietnam War as the starting point of meaningful Vietnamese-U.S. political and cultural involvements. Engaging diverse authors and genres from as early as the 1820s, this interdisciplinary project stages a conversation among American,

Vietnamese, and Vietnamese American texts written in English and Vietnamese. My formalist and historicist analyses demonstrate how Vietnam's transitions from an emergent nation in the nineteenth century to a French colony to a Vietnamese-American war zone have shaped literatures of Southeast Asian–American relations. Through readings of five genres that I argue have been key to literary constructions of "Vietnam"—melodrama, cookbooks, journalistic memoir, epistolary forms, and literary magazines—I show that genre has significantly shaped American portrayals of transnational encounter as they have evolved through the space and idea of Southeast Asia and across a longer history. If analyzing genre offers insight into how literary form shapes perceptions of war, race, and empire, a longer, transnational history shows how those forces shape-shift over time.

America's Vietnam explores canonical, noncanonical, and new archival materials that, read together, tell a mostly unexamined story of Southeast Asia's long and varied influence on U.S. political projects and aesthetic concerns. If Vietnam has become known as the war that never ends—a post-1960s benchmark for how we talk about, enact, and remember war—I take Vietnam out of its conventional late twentieth-century, Cold War brackets. I analyze more familiar authors, such as Alice B. Toklas, Michael Herr, and Monique Truong, alongside less studied works, including a nineteenth-century U.S. sea story, Harry Hervey's melodramas of French Indochina of the 1920s–1930s, Võ Phiến's refugee nonfiction of the late 1970s, and South Vietnamese literary criticism of the 1960s and 1970s. This cross-cultural lens spans Paris, Saigon, New York, and multiple oceans, and it reveals rich cross-period connections. For instance, U.S. modernism as depicted by American and Vietnamese American authors acquires a Southeast Asian frame; portrayals of war objects and bodies in different texts foreground overlapping imperialisms and anti-imperialisms in Southeast Asia; varied depictions of Southeast Asian landscapes point to changing ideas about race and revolution. Together, the chapters map the development of American empire and American imperial culture, and they demonstrate how authors represent Vietnam as deeply entwined with the shifting role of the United States in the world while illuminating broader relationships between form and history. My comparative, reconnective, and long historical method offers new configurations to consider as we chart the scope and significance of transnational Asian American and American literature.

America's Vietnam across the *Longue Durée*

As a shared term in the American and global imagination, "Vietnam" has structured enduring forms of collective identity and memory after a devastating conflict.[2] Its circulation tends to mark a range of watershed moments in multiple disciplines—for instance, an era of unprecedented activism and academic emergence for Asian American studies and of decolonizing politics and postmodern innovation for American cultural studies. I identify two problems with these prevailing critical approaches. First, because Vietnam's prewar presence has been largely muted, even erased, in much of the historical trajectory that "Vietnam" has come to define, one of my goals is to undo this truncated temporality. In public discourse, "Vietnam" and the "Vietnam War" are stereotypically conflated, resulting in a willful neglect of pre-conflict contexts that must inform our comprehension of the war's enduring effects in the present.[3] Such severe historical unevenness disconnects the actual overlap of European, American, and Asian imperialisms in Southeast Asia, subordinates the region's own shaping of those contexts, and occludes how the United States and Vietnam have inflected each other's geopolitical imaginaries outside the 1960s–1970s milieu of war. In turn, these critical exclusions sustain literary-historical practices that are premised on Euro-American chronologies and events, smoothing over the heterogeneity of geographies and histories that constitute American literature and literary history.

Advancing more carefully historicized approaches, scholars have begun to take Southeast Asia out of this cultural, ideological, and historical confinement. They account for the region's specificity as the site of multiple, overlapping empires to decenter dominant narratives that stage "Vietnam" as "a US tragedy featuring US heroes and antiheroes, a blockbuster in which Southeast Asians play the supporting cast."[4] Field-defining work by Lan Duong, Yen Le Espiritu, Jodi Kim, Mimi Thi Nguyen, Viet Thanh Nguyen, Isabelle Thuy Pelaud, and Cathy Schlund-Vials rereads Asian American literature as a corpus born of war and not solely of immigration. These scholars remind us that the very category "Southeast Asia" is a geopolitical designation that stems from post–World War II political agendas and rubrics of knowledge.[5] Moreover, several of these critics incorporate Vietnamese-language materials to reconstitute what Aamir R. Mufti describes as a terrain of world literature still dominated by works in English.[6] Calls to interrogate Southeast Asia as a Cold War "epistemic formation" build on other critics' efforts to remap or re-periodize Asian American literature[7]—as in the work of Denise Cruz, Hua Hsu, Yunte Huang, Lisa Lowe, Colleen Lye, Martin Joseph Ponce, and Min Hyoung Song—and offer new geographies and temporalities of Asian American literature that closely link geopolitical context with literary craft.[8]

America's Vietnam affiliates with these scholars' reassessment of the unfolding of the twentieth to twenty-first centuries through Asian American cultures and politics. I also commit to re-constellating canons, histories, and periodizations, and I find specific resonance with the above scholars' interest in the relationships among American empire, literary form, and literary history. However, existing scholarship on Vietnamese-American entanglements remain rooted in Vietnam War and Cold War frames, and I argue that it is requisite to move beyond them to break their historical and ideological constraints. Those emphases can take post–World War II U.S. global power as a given, limiting the extent to which we can depart from the vocabulary and epistemes of U.S. hegemony to further a genealogy of America's Vietnam that is less exceptionalizing and more relational. I fuse the strengths of the critical paradigms outlined above by combining a Southeast Asian Americanist approach specifically focused on Vietnam with a long historical lens. In turn, I direct attention to how U.S. power evolves and revises itself over stretches of time, developing new logics and rhetoric in relation to shifting *inter-imperial* and *anti-imperial* dynamics.

In this way, I find a *longue durée* approach a valuable and practical tool for advancing Southeast Asian Americanist approaches to literary history. There is nothing self-evident about periodizing Vietnamese-American encounters in Vietnam War or Cold War terms; memory and history are geopolitical fabrications. In 1958, Fernand Braudel identified and criticized the prominent turn to short-term conceptions of history—a tendency on the part of social scientists to privilege the event and "the instantaneous," imbuing such episodes with an aura of "newness" that explodes in public consciousness and then quickly fades away.[9] One of the "events" that Braudel had in mind was France's defeat by North Vietnam at Điện Biên Phủ in 1954, a loss that precipitated the end of French rule in Indochina. For Braudel, this flashpoint became an easy substitute for historical understanding, and what lay in its shadows became relegated to "unconscious history": "History was under the illusion that it could derive everything from events. More than one of our contemporaries would be happy to believe that everything is the result of the agreements at Yalta or Potsdam, the incidents at Dien Bien Phu."[10] Braudel advocated a *longue durée* model of critical inquiry that integrates the long term, the short term, and the conjunctural: "The time of today is composed simultaneously of the time of yesterday, of the day before yesterday, and of bygone days."[11] This dialecticizing of different temporalities encourages relating, rather than isolating and extracting, historical moments to avoid facile and perhaps false historical substitutions and causalities.

If Braudel's *longue durée* paradigm invests in long temporal arcs to determine historical causality and totality, I am equally interested in how a text envisions and maps what constitutes history and how these strategies overlap with or diverge from a work's historical reference points. This project draws from recent scholarship in Vietnam studies, whose examinations of under-examined or newly released archives reveal complex landscapes of geopolitical struggle that transform our understanding of Southeast Asia. But I differ in my focus on the formal strategies by which we configure and reconfigure the past, present, and future. The radical potential of a *longue durée* outlook lies in its recognition of both historical continuity and rupture and its openness to cross-spatial and cross-temporal dialogues. Literary critiques that take extended temporal forms can productively loosen sedimented critical habits.[12]

In sum, the *longue durée* impetus that undergirds *America's Vietnam* goes farther back in time and history at the same time that it looks ahead. In this book, "Vietnam" is very much linked to the Vietnam War but also extends beyond it, setting into relief works and lineages that have not been considered by literary history. By situating American imperial desire relative to Southeast Asia in an expanded temporal line, we can begin to account for the close entwinement of the two regions that began even before America's earliest days as a republic. For instance, in the late eighteenth century, Vietnam was a topic of interest in American newspapers, as the emerging nation kept an eye on imperial rivalries in Southeast Asia. Cochinchina, or present-day southern Vietnam, appeared in the letters of Benjamin Franklin and Thomas Jefferson, who both considered the potential benefits of importing and planting Vietnamese rice in the U.S. South. These examples suggest that there is much to learn by de-exceptionalizing "Vietnam" and detaching it from its automatic associations with the Vietnam War and American trauma, instead highlighting a multi-perspectival, centuries-long view that helps us grasp American, Vietnamese, and Vietnamese American literary production and political thought as overlapping and mutually transforming.[13]

Genre and Literary Constructions of "Vietnam"

My second motivation for writing *America's Vietnam* is the under-explored issue of how genres structure the narratives of Vietnam we inherit and continue to produce. In analyses of American literature about Vietnam, questions of form are typically subordinated to those of content. As Fredric Jameson puts it, the historical circumstances of "this terrible first postmodern war cannot be told in any of the traditional paradigms."[14] This formulation that the Vietnam War caused profound aesthetic crises suggests that formal choices follow from unprecedented conditions of history. Taking an approach more akin to Jameson's earlier modeling of form *as* content outlined in works such as *The Political Unconscious* (1981),[15] this study pursues a dialectical understanding of the mutual interaction of literary form and history. I demonstrate how genre significantly shapes the narratives of Vietnam I study and their aesthetic and political effects, as well as how history produces the existence of and need for particular genres.

An anecdote a friend once told me concerning the way that genre permeates our everyday lives helps clarify what I view as genre's force in shaping the literary Vietnams I investigate. As a young boy in Louisville, Kentucky, he, along with young friends, regularly—and raucously—ran around the neighborhood playing seemingly harmless childhood games. One in particular was a recurring favorite; in the shadow of the Veterans Administration hospital, the boys would play a war game, shooting at one another with toy guns, just like in the Hollywood westerns they watched. All the while they revised the lyrics to the song they always sang during these escapades—"Marching to Pretoria"—by substituting "Vietnam" or "Cambodia" for the Dutch colonial city, depending on their moods on the given day. "I didn't know it then, but I had been *genred*," he said, forty years after the fact, as he recalled the peculiarity of reenacting gendered and racialized imperial adventure and violence next to the towering building that housed returning casualties of war.

As this example shows, genres can operate in rigid as well as flexible ways. Here, the American western "adventure," evocative of Richard Slotkin's thesis that America and its ideologies of freedom "regenerate" and rationalize themselves through violence, exposes its power by transposing onto a new war—the Vietnam War—an old story: the global story of colonial conquest. The portability of "cowboys and Indians" demonstrates how genres are keyed to certain tropes and narrative arcs while also remaining open to revision, or what Wai Chee Dimock calls "regenreing."[16] Genres are both irreducible and portable, sometimes strictly applied and conceived but also elastic categories through which authors create literary worlds. By enabling scalar crossover between geopolitical contexts and everyday life, they act as a window into the dynamic relationship between form and history.

While genre is not always an apparent orienting term in Asian American literary studies, the field's evident focus on immigrant autobiography, the realist novel, avant-garde poetics, and, more recently, science fiction and graphic narrative exhibits the organizing logic of genre in the field. Genre might be situated as one thread within a broader discussion of Asian American aesthetics, which has recently emerged most prominently as a question of the relationship between Asian American literary form and history. As Betsy Huang puts it, genre serves as a useful frame through which to comprehend how Asian American authors' generic experiments relate to societal expectations of assimilation and conciliation that correspond with American national imperatives of immigration and identity.[17] In a related but slightly different argument, Truong prescribes literary analyses based on "genres and narrative themes unbounded" by time periods and ethnicities for fuller, more comprehensive Asian Americanist critique.[18] If existing debates revolve around the question of how to give the social content and literary forms of Asian American culture adequate and equal critical attention, my view is that genre is an optimal analytic for parsing this relationship because it arises out of particular material circumstances yet, as the above anecdote shows, undergoes constant renewal.[19] Genres formalize the ways in which literature and history interact,[20] yet their dehiscent contours and recyclability also redraw the boundaries of literary-historical representation. Their contingency means that there is no "pure" genre—it is not an ideal form that travels transhistorically and unchanged.[21] We might think of genre as a gathering of, in Raymond Williams's words, "different levels of the social material process,"[22] of which the structural logic of a genre is just one part and functions in conjunction with myriad sociohistorical currents, whether cultural, economic, or political.[23]

For instance, melodrama, which I discuss in the first chapter, emerges in eighteenth-century France to express collective unrest about class injustice and calls for structural change. In the American context, however, the collectivity of class grievance gives way to an American individualism whereby the person rises above an unjust situation in ways that tend to align with, rather than oppose, U.S. hegemony. This divergent approach to melodramatic conflict manifests in the noticeable hyper-individualism of American melodramas' characters, who are typically tasked with combating injustice on their own. Melodrama's differing practices in the French and American traditions illustrate genre's formal and historical contingency. In their transmission and transformation over time and space, genres reflect and shape our cultural inheritance at the same time that they shift according to changing sociohistorical circumstances.

Genre also allows for capacious, relational analysis of how texts work. It is an expansive yet circumscribed category that allows us to observe the interlocked workings of a text's multiple moving parts. My genre-based analyses attend to literary objects and landscapes in addition to characters.[24] In this light, literary interpretation is based on not only a text's "character-system," as Alex Woloch phrases it, but also its object and landscape systems, among many other possibilities.[25] The linkages within and across these milieus index genre's management, partial management, or failed management of different historical reference points. It is through this very "genreness"— those moments when a work draws attention to its generic boundaries by rupturing them—that literature's enmeshment with the social and political emerges.[26] The collisions therein often erupt as formal tensions that generate multiple and potentially contradictory readings of a work.

Analyzing the multilayered thickness of literary worlds results in a rhizomatic contour for *America's Vietnam*. In *A Thousand Plateaus* (1987), Gilles Deleuze and Félix Guattari posit that a rhizomatic network—formed by diverse "plateaus" of condensed activity that relate to one another in inexhaustible ways—deregulates knowledge by remaining open to different associations rather than imposing restrictive organizations that constrain variation.[27] As provisional condensations to consider, plateaus persistently branch off into new connections and lines of flight. This book likewise suggests that Southeast Asian–American literary encounters continually evolve and are not somehow fatefully fixed, as various narratives of the "Vietnam syndrome" would suggest. Through its attention to the longer history and to multiple genres, the archive-in-progress I collate asserts the fundamental co-constitution of form, literary history, and geopolitics and offers a range of entry points into representations that unhinge "Vietnam" from its Americanist, Cold War patrimony to show that no two literary Vietnams are wholly alike.

Let us now explore what a genre-based reading can illuminate about the long history of America's Vietnam. Below, I provide a reading of John White's *History of a Voyage to the China Sea* (1823), a sea story in which White chronicles a commercial venture to southern Vietnam that took place between 1819 and 1820. While this book concentrates on the period from the early twentieth century onward, I include White's early nineteenth-century text here because the era marks the first time in Vietnam's history that the country is ruled as a united "Viet Nam," and to indicate the provocative depth of the archive we need to recover. We might say that it is during this time period that America first sets its economic-imperialist gaze on "Vietnam" as such. I demonstrate how a genre-based reading of White's narrative unveils how the formal qualities of the American sea story both enable and restrict White's striking depictions of a southern Vietnam negotiating its strategic position as a hot spot of bustling maritime trade at the same time that the country is recovering in the aftermath of civil war. Race, conflict, and competing empires converge on and across Southeast Asian waters in this little studied maritime travel narrative of early Vietnamese-American encounter.

Vietnamese-American Encounter in 1819: Maritime Modernities and the Sea Story

The year 1819 was eventful for maritime America and American literature. The *SS Savannah* became the first steamship to cross the Atlantic Ocean; Congress passed an anti-piracy law "to protect the commerce of the United

States" on the high seas;[28] and the famous *Essex* left Nantucket, undertaking a tormented whaling expedition that would later inspire Herman Melville's *Moby-Dick* (1851). The year 1819 was also when John White, a U.S. Navy lieutenant on furlough, set sail from Salem in a 251-ton brig called the *Franklin*, owned by his brother Stephen. The White brothers were nephews of Captain Joseph White, a wealthy former slave trader and shipmaster who was notoriously murdered in Salem by another established New Englander, Richard Crowninshield.[29] This network of money, maritime trade, and American literature did not stop at the borders of the Northeast. The *Franklin*'s mission, as White framed it in *History of a Voyage to the China Sea* (1823), was to secure a commercial treaty with Cochin China, or present-day southern Vietnam, and become one of "the first American ships that . . . displayed the stars and stripes before the city of Saigon."[30]

White's eighteen-month voyage took place between January 2, 1819, and August 31, 1820, and included stops at Bahia, various ports in Indonesia, and a detour through Manila.[31] Twenty-one chapters encompass the narrative, followed by an Appendix displaying the Romanized Vietnamese alphabet, the *Franklin*'s meteorological diary, and comments on innovations in maritime travel.[32] True to the adventure tales of the era, White documents the ethnocentric suspense of encountering the unknown—replete with pirate attacks, dangerous gales, impassable swamps, and perceived uncouth natives. *History of a Voyage* is one of the earliest attempts to provide an authoritative American account of the region, but the twists and turns of White's Vietnam indicate the difficulty of navigating its waters and the tenuous task of establishing American commercial presence in an area where Dutch, British, French, Spanish, Portuguese, and Vietnamese maritime prowess intersect. At the same time, some of the nautical themes characteristic of a sea story oblige White to recognize Vietnamese sophistication on water, resulting in surprising moments of expressed wonderment at the possibility of multiple, coexisting forms of seafaring modernity.

The 17-inch by 23-inch fold-out map included as the frontispiece to *History of a Voyage* affirms the popular notion, at the time, of Cochinchina as an ultimately inhospitable place—a confounding "maze of perplexity."[33] The map evidences Vietnam's desirability as a commercial partner, outlining the country's long, continuous coastline that directly accesses the expansive South China Sea. It also follows cartographic protocols of knowledge transfer, duly recording latitude and longitude, depth of water, and safe and hazardous areas. Yet the aerial view suggests geographic impenetrability. Rivers and channels wind about the page, and while they eventually lead to the city center of Saigon—at the time, part of the Saigon–Gia Dinh administrative area—their serpentine patterns frustrate clear points of departure and des-

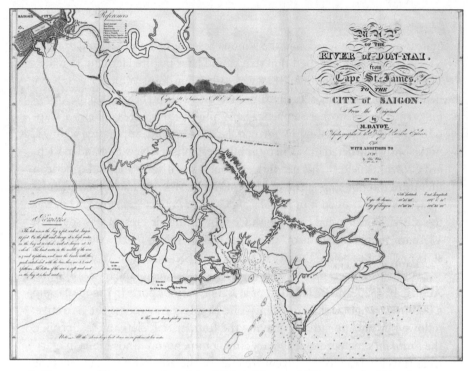

Foldout map of Saigon area from John White's *History of a Voyage to the China Sea* (Boston: Wells and Lilly, 1823). (Map courtesy of Barry Lawrence Ruderman Antique Maps, www.RareMaps.com.)

tination. Saigon itself occupies a tiny, dense corner on the upper left-hand side, its citadel, concentration of pagodas, and king's residence portrayed in miniature.

However, lest we attribute the portrayal of Southeast Asian disproportion and impenetrability to American hands alone, it bears noting that the map, and the book as a whole, is a fundamentally transnational, long historical product. Even though White situates *History of a Voyage* as a corrective to the world's general ignorance about the region—"few correct accounts of it have been published" (vi)—he depends heavily on prior accounts that the book also dismisses. The map borrows from an earlier French map that is itself derived from yet another map, while throughout *History of a Voyage* White excerpts significantly from French and British writings to buttress his claims about Vietnamese barbarity and backwardness. White's mariner text operates as pastiche, as Margaret Cohen might argue, demonstrating how American nationalist themes echo a mixture of rival powers' imperial literary voices.[34]

The visual dominance of winding waterways is appropriate for a sea story's map. But as the narrative's frontispiece, the map's snaking routes anticipate the problems that White and his crew will encounter as they begin to set their sights on land. Exhibiting maritime authors' impulse of "performing description"—or what Cohen describes as providing material information that enlivens and moves the sea story-world forward—White meticulously replays the trials he and his crew face in their initial encounters with Vietnam.[35] As the *Franklin* reaches Vietnam's southern tip, it drifts off path into shoal water and is unable to "stay the course," forced to take a series of detours (15). Upon seeing the first identifiable landmarks in Vietnam, they encounter a strong change in current, which again diverts the ship and slows them down, "[rendering] the time tedious and irksome" (29). When the *Franklin* finally reaches the Vietnamese island of Poulo Condore, White is disappointed, asserting that, despite its good harbor, "the island is very unhealthy and unproductive, abounding in noxious reptiles, and affording no good fresh water.... There are a few miserable inhabitants on the island" (30). Southeast Asian waters hit White and his crew with all kinds of obstacles, resulting in delay after delay for the *Franklin*.

In addition to navigational hurdles that obstruct the narrative's progressive thrust, other diplomatic vexations frustrate the tale of White's journey to Saigon. During the first meeting between the Americans and Vietnamese, Vietnamese officials regale White's dispatched representative with tea, Vietnamese delicacies, and honorific trumpeters. But the challenges of communication in an international maritime era soon become apparent. Lacking local knowledge, the *Franklin*'s crew requests a Vietnamese pilot to guide them upriver, but lack of a shared language makes it difficult even to make the request, highlighting America's benighted foreignness; White's officer cannot relay "of what nation we were, or what language we spoke" (34). Furthermore, the Vietnamese claim that they use Spanish dollars as their currency, which the Americans do not have, and request copies of certain documents, which White's crew also lacks. In turn, Vietnamese officials repeatedly stall trade talks, expressing their displeasure that the Americans have come in ignorance of Vietnamese diplomatic customs. When White wants to bypass Vietnamese procedures in order to proceed, he rapidly learns that the risk of continuing his journey without proper documentation is decapitation (40). Perhaps the biggest disappointment of all is that the *Franklin* cannot even go to Saigon without the local governor's permission, and the governor is unavailable. In the early nineteenth century, Vietnam rebuffs a young and impudent America's diplomatic and economic agenda.[36] White's key goal—securing trade rights with Vietnam—is never achieved.

White insists that Vietnamese political and economic practices are inefficient, taxed by empty formalities, needless hierarchies, and bureaucratic excesses. The "view from the masthead" in *History of a Voyage*—to borrow

Hester Blum's phrase that describes the analytical and imaginative work of antebellum sea narratives[37]—is that the Vietnamese are "but little removed from a state of deplorable barbarism," and Vietnam is a country that is isolationist and undemocratic at its core (36). The *Franklin's* interruptions and ultimate commercial failure not only put White behind schedule and trouble hopes for literal "smooth sailing"; they also thwart desires for diplomatic and economic alliance and divert the flow of American capital. "In the present state of the kingdom," White concludes, "no commercial operations can be expected to result in a manner to warrant further trials" (31). He blames "the tyrannical nature of the government" for having "interdicted all direct commerce between foreigners and that country" (261). Vietnam is a "court of Pandemonium," an impediment to America's vision of free and open trade in Southeast Asia (47).

White's nationalist, capitalist account of Vietnam's uncompromising routes, peoples, and government minimizes how Vietnam and other Asias determine the *Franklin's* fate, and it justifies his conclusion that Vietnam is geographically secluded and enforces its own political and economic isolation. However, if a nation-based approach to *History of a Voyage* might rest with this reading, a transnational and interdisciplinary take attends to the rich but muted subtexts of White's account. Historically, southern Vietnam was part of what the Asia historian Tana Li calls a dynamic "water frontier,"[38] or what the China and Vietnam historian Alexander Woodside terms "a crossroad of the Southeast Asia crossroad."[39] This region, which stretched from the Mekong Delta of present-day southern Vietnam to the Gulf of Thailand and Malay Peninsula, was tied together for centuries as an interconnected "ensemble."[40] For example, the commercial network along the water frontier was multinational and multiethnic. "Vietnamese" identity might actually have referenced one of many Vietnamese or Khmer ethnicities,[41] while "Chinese" also referred to many ethnicities and dialects.[42] In the late eighteenth century, Saigon and Bangkok were central sites of political and economic activity in Southeast Asia,[43] and by the nineteenth century the water frontier had become a vital region of extensive trade and state formation.[44] The establishment of Singapore in 1819—the same year that White departed Salem—was a game changer, competing directly with the Dutch East India Company to mark the apex of free trade and fortune.[45] Traders from independent Southeast Asia dominated commercial exchanges at British colonial territories during the time of White's voyage, not traders from other European territories.[46] Parts of Vietnam had long been an integral part of these vast networks of trade, its ports dotting the world's busiest shipping routes.[47]

White's *History of a Voyage* gives short shrift to Southeast Asia's internationalism to mobilize an American national identity that is at stake in the nineteenth-century sea narrative. Relatedly, it diminishes Vietnam's domestic historical complexities. White's arrival coincided with Gia Long's rule (1802–1820) over a Vietnam deep in post—civil war recovery.[48] For thirty years before his ascendance, the rebel Tây Sơn brothers had waged and won a bloody war against Vietnam's existing regimes, which since 1627 had ruled a country that was effectively divided. The Trịnh dynasty had reigned in the north while the Nguyễn dynasty governed the south—a division situated at almost exactly the same line that would divide North Vietnam and South Vietnam in 1954. As Christopher Goscha notes, there is "nothing necessarily aberrant about the existence of 'two Vietnams' during the second half of the twentieth century."[49] As they took the country from north to south, the Tây Sơn brothers mobilized widespread popular unrest over taxation, corruption, and Nguyễn imperial expansion into Cambodia and Champa.[50] Their victory would forever transform Vietnamese geography and politics, tenuously uniting the country of Đại Việt (Great Viet) from 1788 to 1802 and helping to carve the S-shaped Vietnam of today.[51] When Gia Long defeated the Tây Sơn leaders and ascended the throne, he declared "Việt Nam" the official name of the country in 1804 and began the difficult process of connecting a space that had not been united as such before his reign. He oversaw the development of infrastructure, including establishing a postal system, modifying laws, and strengthening local and international networks. His court was populated by officials from China, Spain, France, Portugal, Italy, Cambodia, Thailand, Ireland, Siam, and Java.

Yet the emperor is an elusive figure in *History of a Voyage*, relatively disconnected from the Vietnamese military, political, and economic developments he spearheaded. America would soon face the challenges of its own civil war, but here White suggests that Vietnam's clannish internal feuds have undercut Vietnam's modern potential, racializing Vietnamese space, time, and money to foreclose possibilities of Asiatic modernity and expunging foundational material contexts.[52] By contrast, Lê Quang Định, a trusted member of Gia Long's court, described Vietnam's geographically and politically expansive outlook in 1806: "Now, after more than two hundred years, those [Vietnam's] borders and edges have all been brought together, ... unified as one, all becoming units of imperial cultural enlightenment."[53] His remarks reveal the critical role of the emergent genre of the imperial gazette in Vietnam, which supplied information about the country's disparate locales by recording stories specific to each region while also generating a cohesive narrative of Vietnam.[54] In the nineteenth century, the Nguyen dynasty prioritized cultural and historical record keeping, as evident in the rise of gazettes, to produce an impressive output of literary documentation about the region. Although Vietnam would be embroiled in struggles against the

French just a few decades later, at this point in time, writings expressed sanguinity about Vietnam's future and resonated with the energy found at the water frontier—a space where "different flows of energy came in, mixed, and blended with various indigenous elements . . . and reemerged in different local forms."[55]

Intersecting with Vietnam's terrestrial and aqueous energies at the time, a striking example emerges in *History of a Voyage* that momentarily creates an 1819–1820 story world in which Vietnam and America are coeval and overlapping rather than inherently divided by reifications of geography, race, and politico-economic difference. It is oriented around White's observation of Vietnamese sailing culture and shipbuilding. As the *Franklin* navigates various hurdles, signs of promise emerge out of these entangled scenes in animated snapshots of Southeast Asian nautical achievement. Observing small trading boats "as far as the eye could extend," bustling in "piscatory excursions" (54), White discerns not only commercial possibility but also sailing ingenuity, expressing simultaneous befuddlement by and admiration for the proportions and methods of Vietnamese marine engineering. He is worth quoting at length to give a sense of the entwined quantitative and qualitative richness of sea stories—how their depiction of material details relates mariners' experience or how the text's object-system interacts with its character-system:

> They are of great length, sharp at both ends, projecting far out above, giving their decks about one-third part greater length than their keels, which are not deep; and it may be a subject of curiosity with nautical readers for me to state further, that the *rebate* which receives the *garboard strake*, being near the bottom of it, gives it but a very slight degree of elevation from the plank; this latter circumstance would not perform well in working to windward; but this is not the case, *for it is presumed that these vessels are equal, if not superior, to any in the world in this respect.* Should it be asked, wherein this superiority consists, a satisfactory answer may be difficult to be found; our conclusions, however, were that it might be discovered in their great depth, which, according to our ideas of naval architecture, is somewhat disproportionate to the breadth below. . . . Their frames are much farther apart than those of our vessels, and they have no ceilings; they are secured together with iron nails, the heads of which are made in a peculiar form. (55–56, emphasis added)

This is a rare occasion when White's ethnocentric, universalist assumptions about naval construction cede to the promise of maritime difference. Perceived incongruity and disproportion are shown to be nautically effective, even "superior to any in the world," upending White's expectations about naval measurement and architecture and destabilizing his literary constructions of American modernity and Vietnamese unmodernity. Images of Vietnamese vessels included in *History of a Voyage* visualize the Vietnamese maritime sophistication that White confronts and describes at length.

The image of the junk has clean, smooth lines, drawn to convey its functionality of purpose and scale, while the state vessel emanates grandeur through its ornate engravings that befit the occasion portrayed—the arrival of Saigon's viceroy (see the "Trader" and "State Galley" images). Its defined geometry communicates discipline and tasteful majesty, quite unlike the depictions of barbarous natives and immoderate cultural and political customs White perceives on land. That the vessels—which we must recognize as potentially crafted by multiethnic Asians living in the region—are depicted as "superior" to any other on the globe runs counter to the idea of a cartographically and politically opaque Vietnam. In these nautical scenes of Vietnamese-American encounter, White offers a more open account of what Kale Fajardo calls "crosscurrents"—the long historical abundance of "maritime routes and maritime trade" in the Pacific and Oceania.[56] White is utterly struck by nautical craftsmanship on the water frontier, admitting multiple maritime modernities across early nineteenth-century New England and Southeast Asia.

A second example that appears toward the end of *History of a Voyage* punctuates the ways in which Vietnam's historical and political depth undercuts White's consolidation of U.S. nationalist chronology. When White is finally able to meet with the governor of Saigon, likely the figure Nguyễn Văn Nhơn, he presents an array of gifts, having accepted the protocols of Vietnamese diplomacy.[57] Among the gifts is a kaleidoscope, which White describes as a brand-new innovation: "The kaleidoscope, being of superior workmanship, and handsomely ornamented, was particularly admired. I directed the linguists to inform the viceroy, that this was a new invention, and had excited much admiration in Europe, and then proceeded to explain its uses and mode of application" (307). This translated conversation suggests the possibility of productive interlingual and intercultural transference between Americans and Vietnamese and relates White's desire to demonstrate to Saigon's governor the benefits of Western modernity and innovation.

An object that brought random pieces of materials together to create a spectacle of color and unpredictable patterns, the kaleidoscope was a modern European sensation. In *A Treatise on the Kaleidoscope* (1819), David Brewster, who invented the instrument, recounts, "The idea occurred to me *of giving motion to objects, such as pieces of coloured glass, &c., which were either fixed or placed loosely in a cell at the end of the instrument.* When

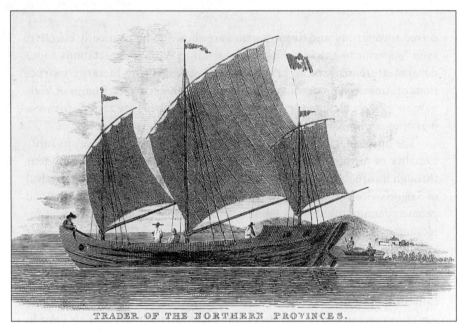

TRADER OF THE NORTHERN PROVINCES.

"Trader of the Northern Provinces" illustration from John White's *History of a Voyage to the China Sea* (Boston: Wells and Lilly, 1823).

"State Galley of the Viceroy of Don-nai" illustration from John White's *History of a Voyage to the China Sea* (Boston: Wells and Lilly, 1823).

State Galley of the Viceroy of Don-nai

this idea was carried into execution, and the reflectors placed in a tube, and fitted up on the preceding principles, the Kaleidoscope, in its *simple form*, was completed."[58] A product of serious scientific and mathematical deliberation,[59] the kaleidoscope took what might otherwise be discarded materials— shards of colored glass—and brought them together to produce a seemingly endless array of symmetrical, colorful, and optically interesting combinations. Brewster predicted that the results would be universally appealing: "The succession of splendid colours formed a phenomenon which I had no doubt would be considered, by every person who saw it to advantage, as one of the most beautiful in optics."[60] The kaleidoscope encapsulated modern and innovative ways of seeing in the early nineteenth century and, in an age of global sail and exploration, marked a time when the world opened up to "different cultural sensations" that could be personally experienced with the simple turning of one's hand.[61]

True enough, the governor takes note of the kaleidoscope and even "particularly [admires]" it (307). But to White's utter astonishment, the governor remarks that the kaleidoscope is old news in Vietnam:

> No sooner, however, had he looked through it, than he took it from his eye, and addressed a few words to the linguist, who repeated to me from his excellency, that the instrument might be new in Europe, but was by no means rare with them. He then directed a few words to an officer in attendance, who returned in a few minutes with several kaleidoscopes, covered with red embossed paper: they were, it is true, of inferior workmanship, but in principle did not differ in the least from that of Dr. Brewster. We were, however, greatly surprised, that an invention of such recent origin in Europe should be found in this secluded part of the world, especially as those we saw were evidently of Chinese manufacture. And if it was not a Chinese invention also, but had been brought from Europe by the way of China, it was not a little remarkable, because the trade between China and Saigon was . . . remote from scenes of European intercourse. (307–308)

Corresponding with its effect of multiplying colorful patterns, the kaleidoscope refracts White's ethnocentrism into new ways of seeing, confronting him with unexpected circuits and velocities of trade, production, and consumption. A device that achieves its spectrum of effects through tactile viewing, it forces White to admit Vietnamese commercial modernity up close and face-to-face in this momentary re-vision of early nineteenth-century Vietnamese-American relations. A striking device with which White begins to draw *History of a Voyage* to a close, the decorative object is an apt metaphor for the instability of the text's misreading of Vietnam as "anti-commercial," "secluded," and "remote"—a logic that allows White to assert that the rejection of U.S. economic "friendship" is no real loss. The kaleidoscope-as-trope disrupts the knowledge and confidence of the mariner-author himself, upending White's "epistemology of the sea."

A historicized, genre-based reading of White's practice of the sea story adventure draws critical attention to this overlooked archive and history of Vietnamese-American encounter and illustrates a dynamic central to this book: how authors transform unfamiliar historical materials into familiar forms and unfamiliar forms into recognizable historical narratives. It is the seaman-author's respect for maritime craft and life on water that compels White's recognition of Vietnamese maritime modernity in his sea story. Yet it is also the genre's historical potential to subordinate non-American nautical advancements to a U.S. nationalism that ultimately places Vietnam's political system and economy on the edge of White's perception. White is, in sum, *genred*. The fleeting moments of maritime kinship in *History of a Voyage* that exceed national difference cede to an imperialist racialization that casts Vietnam as backward and unmodern in the face of American trade and capital, despite the commercial and cross-cultural dynamism of the water frontier. Toni Morrison states in *Playing in the Dark* (1992) that early American literature insistently "[presses] toward a future of freedom, a kind of human dignity believed unprecedented in the world."[62] This liberation has everything to do with capital, and what impedes that flow becomes an obstruction to American freedom and modernity. *History of a Voyage* thereby works through a doubled logic in which Vietnamese waters are both a site of "pandemonium" and an aquatic frontier of mercantile possibility. But the latter is dominated by White's repeated Hegelian configurations of Vietnamese non-history at a time when "the whole navigation of the world was in motion" (1). The overarching theme of Vietnamese ahistoricity results in a stunted quality to White's own narrative, which is threaded with extended periods of "doing nothing" and "nothing remarkable" (352) in an adventure sea genre that, in Cohen's terms, depends on the "remarkable."[63]

Thus, despite being utterly struck by Vietnamese nautical craftsmanship, as the mariner-author White generically manages the tensions of Euro-American imperial competition on the water frontier, an international cast of Southeast Asian characters, and diverted American imperialist aims. He reasserts "the superiority of our [American] sailing" and trade (1). Recalling Williams's observation that genre serves as a site in which "different levels of the social material process" interact,[64] we can read White's *History of a Voyage* as an example of how the genre of the American sea story episodically fuses but more consistently hierarchizes interlinked cultural and social forces. In

White's hands, the maritime tale reaffirms American ability on the high seas and negates Vietnam's domestic and international complexity, even as the *Franklin* returns to its home port empty-handed, revealing how the sea story can enact literary hegemony and operate as a genre of evolving American empire. However, I would not position the Vietnamese perspectives and histories I have highlighted as mere counter-archives to White's text. Rather, I suggest that they both are at odds and intersect. Vietnamese writings of the period have their own, imperialist inflections. The wealth of literary production under the Nguyễn dynasty in the nineteenth century bespeaks the emergent country's efforts at self-legitimation—not unlike a young America's attempts to do the same through its own literary efforts.

The transnational network of trade in southern Vietnam is lost not only to White, but also to us, the contemporary audience, and to American literary history.[65] Time and time again, American literature has depicted Vietnam as a novelty, despite Americans' recurrent interfaces with it. As I have shown, Vietnamese-American encounters have been long in the making and oblige an analytical approach that does not render "Vietnam" passive but, rather, attends to the contingencies and varied, often conflicting desires that constitute a work's story world. In addition to Franklin's and Jefferson's interest in the potential benefits of Vietnamese rice for American agriculture and economy as early as the 1770s, White's own journey crossed paths with at least three other American ships traveling to or through Vietnam (157, 172). American commercial missions were reportedly dispatched to Vietnam in 1803, 1832, 1836, 1845, and 1850, but they also all failed in their efforts.[66] Attention to these narratives and their generic contours is valuable in researching and developing a more comprehensive literary history of Vietnamese-American encounters.

Overview

The book's title, *America's Vietnam*, invokes the possessive to diffuse and ironize it. Colleen Lye's *America's Asia* has informed my study in its concern with the fluctuating formal and historical dynamics of Asiatic character in U.S. literature.[67] Similarly, the "America" in this project does not presuppose nationalist ownership but is, rather, heterogeneous and a changing configuration, and its inclusion of Vietnamese and Vietnamese American considerations further demonstrates the term's instability. Consequently, rather than deliver a comprehensive genealogy of Vietnamese-American literary exchanges or an authoritative, singular reading of what "Vietnam" means, this book undoes some prevailing conventions of American Vietnam War discourses to make more room for Southeast Asian Americanist approaches to literary history.[68] In addition, because I locate *America's Vietnam* primarily in my area of training, Asian American literary studies, the links I forge to Southeast Asia studies do not aim for ideal comparative balance. Instead, they help set into relief the kinds of dialogues that an ongoing, vigorous project of collaborative and interdisciplinary transnationalism in American literature requires.[69]

The chapters' organization results in a seeming chronology of Vietnamese-American contact, but this chronology is provisional and means to give readers some sense of the historical transitions and accompanying literary logics that connect the chapters. The object is for the longer overall history I track to facilitate readings within and across periods. While each chapter treats a genre that has been formative in the construction and consumption of "Vietnam," in dialogue the chapters demonstrate how authors negotiate multiple narrative threads through generic means and in specific historical conditions. Most chapters focus on a single genre to illustrate its complexity, but they invite, rather than foreclose, analysis of other genres that may be operating in the works. Overall, the texts I study are bilingual and multisited, incorporating widely read works printed by major publishing houses as well as manuscripts in major and minor archives. Some materials, such as Võ Phiến's writings in Chapter 4, were found on my parents' bookshelves—their bindings taped and pages yellowed—and illustrate how the field of Southeast Asian American literary studies comprises official and unofficial archives. By considering new literary constructions of Vietnam, I help lay a foundation for future scholarship, work that will, among other things, deepen as well as expand Asian American studies' refiguring of the literary canon and the conventions of reading associated with it.

Chapter 1, "Melodrama, Miscegenation, and Americanized Empire in French Indochina," introduces Harry Hervey's popular melodramas of the region that circulated in prose (1927), on Broadway (1928–1929), and as a censored Hollywood screenplay (1931). Focusing mainly on the novel, I analyze how Hervey traces the life of a mixed-race figure to interrogate overlapping French and U.S. imperialisms in Southeast Asia. More specifically, I concentrate on the politics of the sartorial—how imperial France clothes the biracial protagonist literally, socially, and legalistically, and how these dynamics constitute a logic against which America crafts a "softer" racialized and gendered rhetoric of empire. A vital genre of imperialism, melodrama positions America as a heroic savior of the world's dispossessed, setting in place the enduring contradiction between U.S. anticolonial rhetoric and colonial acts that undergird the texts I examine in subsequent chapters. However, my reading of Hervey's works also draws attention to melodrama's instabilities, which manifest most strongly in the queer threads of his writings, to consider the question of intersectional representation as a narrative problem.

Having demonstrated how American melodrama cloaks colonial in-equality in a language of salvation, Chapter 1 is followed by a discussion that centers on two queer texts to probe intersecting racialized and gendered mechanisms of American imperial expansion. Chapter 2, "Who Served Up Modernism? Vietnamese Labor and Anticolonialism in Modernist Paris," considers Alice B. Toklas's *The Alice B. Toklas Cook Book* (1954) and Monique Truong's reimagining of the conditions under which that text was produced, *The Book of Salt* (2003). While Toklas and Gertrude Stein delight in the cu-linary skills of the Vietnamese servants they employ and claim to nurture in their Parisian home, Truong queers the Vietnamese cooks to consider the limits of Toklas and Stein's bourgeois, proto-multicultural queer politics, foregrounding networks of Southeast Asian labor that help to sustain mod-ernist Paris. My comparative analysis demonstrates that cookbooks consti-tute an important genre for mapping imperial webs of food and labor exploi-tation that implicate literary modernism in colonialism in Southeast Asia. At the same time, while Truong's novelization of Toklas's text fuses queer with decolonizing critique, it also occludes the history of Vietnamese revolution-ary networks in Paris, marking the formal and ideological boundaries of the novel's depiction of colonial and decolonizing dynamics in Vietnam within the contemporary literary marketplace.

Chapter 3, "Vietnam War Exceptionalism: Dismembering and Disremem-bering Vietnam," extends the previous chapter's critique of Americanized in-gestion of Vietnamese food, labor, and sexuality by examining how Michael Herr, a celebrated architect of Vietnam War culture, takes the literary com-modification and consumption of Vietnamese bodies to the extreme. Chapter 3 focuses on *Dispatches* (1977) to analyze how Herr's memoirist, gothic ap-proach to journalism foregrounds American soldiers' experiences of war to critique U.S. state meta-narratives of the conflict. However, Herr predicates his poetics on a logic and practice of corporeal and formal fragmentation that sensationalizes, more than historicizes, the conflict. Juxtaposing my reading of Herr's text with a range of Vietnamese perspectives on empire and postco-loniality—including writings by Trần Đức Thảo (a Vietnamese philosopher and student of Maurice Merleau-Ponty) and Ocean Vuong (a contemporary Vietnamese American poet)—I argue that the model of journalism in *Dis-patches*, a work viewed as one of the most important on the Vietnam War, exceptionalizes Vietnamese mutilation and, consequently, disconnects from a long history of colonial violence in Southeast Asia.

Chapter 4, "Critical Refugee Studies and the Emergence of Vietnamese American Letters," de-exceptionalizes and re-historicizes "Vietnam" by ex-amining the layered histories embedded in Võ Phiến's Vietnamese-language epistolary works (1976, 1979), which are some of the earliest conceptions of

Vietnamese American subjectivity and literature. Taking the form of letters addressed to an emerging Vietnamese diaspora, these texts are marked by uncertainty and ambivalence about Vietnamese American futures. They offer a refugee aesthetic whereby refugees—putatively "saved" by their host countries—must rewrite layered pasts in a public language of indebtedness while privately grappling with the ongoing imperial destruction sketched in the previous chapters. Placing Võ Phiến's letters in conversation with "missing persons" ads that refugees wrote to connect with the diaspora after forced migration, I argue that the animating, historicizing possibilities of the epistolary form have been integral to Southeast Asian diasporic formation and Southeast Asian American literature.

The Conclusion, "Vietnam's America in a Time of Smoke and Fire," examines the genre of the literary magazine from the vibrant and under-studied South Vietnamese literary scene of the 1960s–1970s. In these texts, Vietnamese critics look to a range of twentieth-century American writers and contexts—from William Faulkner and Carson McCullers to black struggles—to reflect on literary and national reconstruction after the division of Vietnam in 1954. I position this conversation as constitutive of Vietnamese American studies and suggest two potential critical directions: (1) exploring U.S. state-sponsored projects of cultural dissemination to Asia (e.g., the activities of the Congress for Cultural Freedom) as a vital component of Southeast Asian American literary studies; and (2) investigating the literary magazine as a site of political critique and complicity in South Vietnam. These archives reveal under-explored conversations about literature, race, and empire and open up new ways to analyze American and Asian American literary history in a long historical, transnational frame.

America's Vietnam reexamines the history of Vietnam and America and the literature about this relationship. The picture that emerges in this study involves long histories of regional and international conflict and division, alternating alliances and antagonisms among Euro-American and Asian colonial regimes and regional Vietnamese polities, and multiple Vietnamese and Vietnamese diasporic visions of empire and decolonization that variously clash and coincide. Genre comes into play to formalize various aesthetic-political projects within this history—a means of legitimation, persuasion, and investigation. *America's Vietnam* thus has an open and invitational spirit, provoking further inquiry into the many possible configurations of Southeast Asian and American cultural involvements across the *longue durée*.

1

MELODRAMA, MISCEGENATION, AND AMERICANIZED EMPIRE IN FRENCH INDOCHINA

In 1927, the boxing manager turned Broadway producer Sam H. Harris decided to stage a play called *Congaï*, based on a novel about a half-Vietnamese, half-French woman named Thi-Linh set in World War I–era French Indochina.[1] The melodrama tells the story of Thi-Linh's suffering in a series of colonial interracial relationships and, while setting up the expectation for her rescue, ends with Thi-Linh bound by a structure of imperial power in which she is passed between men.[2] *Congaï* was adapted for the theater by Harry Hervey, a writer from Texas, and his fellow southerner, lifelong partner, and collaborator, Carleton Hildreth, from Hervey's novel of the same title that had been published earlier that year. The play premiered near the peak of Broadway's high season at the Sam H. Harris Theater in New York, on November 27, 1928, and ran for 135 performances.[3] Its run marked the first time that a sustained treatment of French Indochina had been performed before the American public on stage.

Congaï's tenure on Broadway, in addition to productions in Philadelphia, Brooklyn, Chicago, and Washington, DC, took place during a 1928–1929 season in which only a few shows were chosen for continued production. Hervey would eventually write more than a dozen novels about the colonized world that would be translated into several languages. He was also hired by Hollywood studios throughout the 1930s and 1940s for his storylines about Asia; among his credits are *Road to Singapore* (1940) and *Shanghai Express* (1932), which starred the pioneering Asian American actress Anna May Wong. Despite *Congaï*'s popularity and the lively discussions it generated in U.S. newspapers, it would not endure in public consciousness as a period-defining text in American culture. Hervey today is relatively unheard of, identified as a southern pulp fiction writer of only limited renown, if he is recalled at all.

Placing Hervey's fiction in conversation with various archival materials related to Hervey and *Congaï*'s historical context, this chapter examines how melodrama and miscegenation in French Indochina shaped discourses of America's early twentieth-century Asia. *Congaï* may be unknown to us today, but its subject of Indochina—France's "pearl of the Orient"—captured the attention of American readers and theatergoers at a time when, according to current scholarship, Vietnam barely registered on America's cultural radar.[4] Focusing on the novel version, this chapter posits that much of *Congaï*'s popularity was due to the melodramatic conventions that Hervey used to bring French Indochina to the American public in an era of U.S. imperial ascendance. As a genre with mass appeal, melodrama enlists binaries of good and evil and vivid depictions of deep feelings to establish a central conflict and bring it to a resolution. In turn, a melodrama can make powerful claims about what constitutes justice and morality. However, I suggest that objects rather than feelings perform much of *Congaï*'s melodramatic work, functioning to concretize Euro-American colonial injustice as the key grievance at play in Hervey's story. In particular, sartorial objects circulate as seemingly inconsequential items, yet they are crucial in helping empires scale down grand imperial claims to the level of everyday life. Clothes and accoutrements help hegemonies differentiate colonizer from colonized, and in *Congaï* it is not until sartorial materials are cast as products of colonial labor, rather than as evidence of good and bad taste, that overturning colonial apparatuses becomes feasible and anticolonial feelings emerge.

Congaï's materialist core gives rise to anticolonial thought as the authentic form of melodramatic salvation, yet this desired outcome does not constitute the narrative's ostensible ending. Rather, the novel concludes in a return to the colonial social hierarchies and moral simplifications with which it begins, a denouement sharply undercut by a host of unsettled scores. Consequently, rather than approach melodrama as culminating in rescue and resolution, I interpret it as an unstable genre whose characteristic polarities contain more complex political landscapes. *Congaï*'s unresolved treatments of the relationship among race, class, sexuality, and geopolitics become even more apparent when we attend to the novel's subtext of queer desire, which attempts to reimagine norms of family and belonging that undergird colonial melodramas, and a latent Orientalism that threads Hervey's works, whereby his own, ornamentalist fascination with Asia conflicts with his portrayal of anticolonial themes. The resulting tensions suggest the contradictory nature of representing intersectional social relations through the melodramatic form.

More broadly, my interpretation of *Congaï* suggests that French Indochina is an unacknowledged undercurrent in early twentieth-century American culture and a space of interimperial rivalry *against* which the United States defines its own, emerging imperial vision. Through its streamlined staging of conflict, melodrama narrates American political objectives through an exceptionalist story of saving the world's dispossessed, shrouding the disparity between U.S. anticolonial rhetoric and colonial acts. In addition, melodrama in the American vein tends to script individualistic solutions, avoiding portrayal of structural problems that must be considered when representing not only anti-imperialism but also its necessary counterpart, decolonization. *Congaï* critiques both French and American melodramatic theatrics but also demonstrates how the form's repackaging of geopolitical tensions into consumable cultural narratives has made melodrama an effective and enduring genre of empire. Toward the end of the chapter, I consider the popularity of melodrama in terms of institutional politics by examining the theater production and screenplay of *Congaï*, which was scheduled for production by Paramount Pictures but ultimately censored for its combined miscegenous and anticolonial content. I suggest that the longer history of America's Vietnam I trace remains relatively unrecognized in part because it was culturally censored.[5] By analyzing *Congaï*'s textual and paratextual dimensions, the chapter understands the evolution of American portrayals of Asia across the twentieth century as a product of thematic, formal, and institutional contingencies.

Congaï: An Introduction

Hervey was born in 1900, in Beaumont, Texas, and came from a family of hoteliers with properties across the U.S. South. His father abandoned the family when Hervey was young, leaving Hervey to come of age in hotels, where his encounters with travelers reportedly fed dreams of exotic peoples and places. Hervey was sent to the Georgia Military Academy in Atlanta and, an avid reader and writer, sold his first story to H. L. Mencken at sixteen.[6] He subsequently contributed pieces to a variety of publications, including *Black Mask* and *The Nation*.[7] Early desires to travel to Angkor Wat in present-day Cambodia sparked Hervey's interest in French Indochina, and he convinced *McCall's* magazine to fund a trip to the region. He and a young Hildreth traveled to Southeast Asia in 1925, a trip that informed Hervey's works for many years to come and helped secure his status in Hollywood as, in the words of the motion picture producer Samuel Goldwyn, a writer with "'high academic standing as an Orientalist.'"[8] After his Hollywood career, Hervey moved to Savannah, Georgia, where he continued to write and moved more strongly toward political themes; he explicitly stated later in life that one of his goals as an author was to bring attention to worldwide injustices. He died in New York City in 1951.

Published in 1927, *Congaï* demonstrates how melodrama's formal characteristics both facilitate and limit Hervey's anticolonial message. A brief overview of key plot elements helps to lay a foundation for understanding these narrative dynamics. The story follows Thi-Linh as she evolves from a love-struck teenager to a woman indefinitely bound by *métissage*, a form of miscegenation characterized by longer-term, non- or semi-conjugal interracial relationships. "Con gái" translates as "girl" or "young girl," but Hervey follows literary precedent and sexualizes the term; in most French and American translations of the time, it was associated with sex, and while a range of relationships defined *métissage*, Hervey is interested in it as a form of sex work.[9] When the novel begins in 1912, Thi-Linh is fifteen years old, interested in French culture, and in love with the charismatic Kim Khouan, an upperclass boy from Stung Treng, Cambodia, who is also biracial. (Annam was the central part of the Vietnamese section of French Indochina.)[10] Rather than half Vietnamese and half French, he is half Vietnamese and half Laotian. Despite Kim Khouan's professions of love and repeated promises that he will marry Thi-Linh, his father rejects the relationship because of her mixed race and instead weds his son to a "pure Annamite" (17). Shunned by Kim Khouan and the racialized, gendered, and classed notion of Indochinese identity he represents, Thi-Linh understands the social ostracism that attends her racial hybridity: "I know—my blood" (30). She then resigns herself to a life similar to the one her mother, Thi-Bao, once led as a "congaï."

The bulk of the novel traces Thi-Linh's relationships with four French "husbands," whose varied occupations span the cultural, military, economic, and political domains of French colonial rule. This chapter touches on only two of these colonists—Justin Batteur, a writer, and Urbain Chauvet, director of the Banque de l'Indochine—whose appearances most prominently flag Thi-Linh's changing political consciousness. Throughout *Congaï*, Thi-Linh suffers a number of trials and tribulations, including bearing Kim Khouan's illegitimate son, Justin, who is raised by Mama Thi-Bao (I refer to this character as Justin Jr. to avoid confusion with Justin Batteur); taking a temporary hiatus from sex work to find employment in a sewing shop that reveals a network of exploited colonized labor; falling in and out of love with an American seaman who initially appears to be the novel's hero but is ultimately excised from the story; and witnessing Justin Jr.'s accidental killing of Chauvet, which leads her back to *métissage* at the moment of her seeming liberation, in trade for her son's immunity. When the novel concludes, Thi-Linh has veered significantly from her initial enthrallment with French culture to a "pity" for "white men" and a strengthened belief in a future anticolonial movement to be led by mixed-race subjects (143).

Thi-Linh's suffering and staged need for rescue illustrate the genre of melodrama at work. Understanding how scholars have defined the form and how *Congaï* exemplifies and departs from this cultural history helps to situate my reading of melodrama. According to Peter Brooks's paradigmatic study *The Melodramatic Imagination* (1976), melodrama is a mode of excess—a quintessentially modern form that enlists symbolic signs, dramatic gestures, and heightened emotions to restore moral legibility in an unstable, constantly changing world. In an era made post-sacred by the tragedies of the French Revolution, melodrama initially concerns class exploitation, presenting morally muddied scenarios to dramatize the loss of what were once clear-cut "ethical imperatives."[11] In the process of reestablishing justice, characters personify French liberal philosophy's conviction that individuals can act against wrongdoing[12]—hence, the form's Manichean structure of good and evil that begins with a demarcated space of virtue into which "a villain," or "force of evil," intrudes.[13] This violation of morality launches melodrama's teleological cycle of conflict, recognition of virtue, and return to justice, typically achieved through the rescue of a suffering victim carried out in temporalized terms—in the words of Linda Williams, a salvation executed "in the nick of time."[14]

For Brooks, the force of melodrama rests largely on feeling as an organizing mechanism, whose expression in concentrated, histrionic scenes articulates a central grievance and advances the narrative's progressive return to justice and moral legibility. As Brooks puts it, "Characters stand on stage and utter the unspeakable, give voice to their *deepest* feelings, dramatized through their heightened and polarized words and gestures the whole lesson of their relationship."[15] Elisabeth R. Anker provocatively calls these occasions of packed emotion "orgies of feeling."[16] However, many scholars have critiqued melodrama for the very emotional registers that define it; it is precisely these aspects that can turn melodramas toward conservative ends, keeping unjust plots and structures in place. For Laura Wexler, melodrama historically has been a form that uses marginalized subjects as "human scenery" for bourgeois contemplation,[17] while Lauren Berlant charges melodrama with placing a premium on excesses of feeling and drama at the expense of attending to that which is less visibly emotional and theatrical.[18] From these critical perspectives, the grievances and feelings of marginalized subjects fall through the cracks. Melodrama's sympathy-driven structure thus fails at radical critique because it substitutes sentiment—sentiment that typically entrenches white heteropatriarchy—for effective political action.[19]

Melodrama, then, is not only a project of moral legibility; it is also always a project of racial and political legibility.[20]

The potential for melodrama to substitute emotion for trenchant political commentary suggests that a more critical interpretation of melodramatic feeling is needed. To undertake an effective analysis of *Congaï* as a melodrama, it is necessary to combine a reading of the genre's affects with one that attends to its objects. Much attention has been paid to the visual registers of theatrical and cinematic melodramas, such as decorative details, clothing, and set design.[21] Yet visual iconography also plays an important, somewhat overlooked role in prose melodramas. If, as Joseph Jonghyun Jeon argues, "racial things" are intimately connected to racial persons,[22] then objects carry substantial weight in delineating the terms of Thi-Linh's rescue in *Congaï*. Rather than focus solely on feeling, then, shifting attention to objects reveals their vital role in expressing the heightened sensations, dramatic gestures, and symbolic systems that populate melodramatic story worlds; objects help to concretize the injustices that require correction.[23]

In *Congaï*, sartorial materials in particular most vividly express Thi-Linh's shifting desires and index how systems of meaning and power are made. Thi-Linh laments her "rusty black [tunic], frayed and soiled at the cuffs" when compared with the rich colors and textures of French garments. Enthralled by the glossy images found in French fashion journals imported from the metropole, she "[purloins] the Parisian fashion sheets" and "[yearns] for the extravagant feel of a French gown" (16). A visit to a fabric shop is described as a sensuous experience of vibrant textiles: "Smoke of black tissue and smoldering cerise; dragon-green and stiff purple" (48). Sartorial objects drive Thi-Linh's ecstatic feelings as she experiences sheer pleasure at the sight and touch of luxurious materials and the tactile, optical workings of sartorial layering and light.

However, such sensory activation and yearning exist within a complex political matrix. On the one hand, Thi-Linh's faith in self-cladding becomes a way to counter idealized notions of Indochinese identity. As she agonizes over the loss of Kim Khouan, Thi-Linh takes pleasure in dreaming of a better wardrobe: "Oh yes, she would rise! She could see herself in a French gown, with her hair done in the European manner" (49). Positioned as Thi-Linh is within a socially symbolic system that reads her mixed raced as evidence of sexual and racial transgression, ornamentation allows her to mediate the imperial gaze in ways that, as Anne Anlin Cheng might suggest, reconfigure colonial space.[24] Yet Thi-Linh's desires also show how clothing functions in the colony as long-distance ideology—what Minh-Ha T. Pham calls a fashion-based "virtual technology" of nationalism and race.[25] French taste as circulated in magazines and in the streets manifests supposed French exclusivity, prestige, and modernity, in contrast with the putative backwardness of the Indochinese. Such differentiations contribute to imperial hierarchies by making otherness seem concrete and self-evident, thereby cloaking actual social and legal disparities. Indeed, compulsory negotiation of colonial constructions of race emerges in Thi-Linh's first meeting with Justin Batteur, her first French "husband," as she capitalizes on her perceived difference to maximize chances of entering the network of *métissage*: "Her eyes gave an illusion of sultry brooding together with a quality of exquisite frailty" (39–40). Combining chromatic vividness with expressed need, Thi-Linh enacts a pleasing mixture of sexuality and submission to obtain social and financial means. Her sartorial performances do not simply evidence internalized French cultural ideology; they are also a form of sustenance and survival.

By delineating asymmetrical social relations in French Indochina, sartorial object worlds in Hervey's melodrama expose how a central unit of French ideologies of social order—that of the legitimate family—is undermined by circuits of *métissage*. Camille Robcis suggests that "French familialism" has long defined the proper family in terms of permanent, heterosexual relationships with identifiable chains of ancestry and descent. This form of kinship, in turn, becomes the foundation of the French nation.[26] Yet *métissage* undercuts purist notions of the French individual and national family and illustrates how colonial erotics of race merge political and sexual desire in the name of French nationalism overseas. Consider what a French character named Malardier claims about the necessity of finding a "congaï" in Hervey's novel: "If you come to Indo-China to know it, then become intoxicated with it— and the surest draught is a woman. . . . [T]he congaï, she is our symbol—the symbol of the ability of the Frenchman to mingle with the natives, whereas the Englishman only conquers them" (14). Miscegenation in Indochina not only advances the rationale of colonial salvation but also cultivates homosocial bonding. Masculinist ties work to strengthen the paternal authority that structures French familialism and, as Malardier implies, to distinguish the romance of French empire from the violence of British imperial conquest.

Congaï's depiction of *métissage* as playing a formative role in French imperial ideology conveys how Indochinese women who are implicated in these networks occupy a liminal space that straddles incorporation and possible abandonment. On one level, a strategic approach to self-ornamentation, as I have discussed, allows Thi-Linh access to social and financial means, and being able to enter circuits of *métissage* is one way to secure long-term sustenance. Thi-Linh discerns how *métissage* can function as a socioeconomic solution, as her friendship with a Vietnamese character named Nanette, who is also a professional mistress, reveals how the ability to attract a steady stream of French partners of increasingly higher ranks provides financial comfort that is evident in a glamorous, magnetic appearance: "Reclining there in her soft tunic, with the faintest hint of diamonds at her ears, and gazing at Thi-Linh through a drift of smoke, she had something undeniably French about her. It was an air that Thi-Linh admired" (79). Thi-Linh's praise not only concerns the allure, elegance, and means that *métissage* enables for Nanette; in referencing the ability to pass as "undeniably French," it also suggests Thi-Linh's unspoken longing for admission to some form of French familialism and society.

Thi-Linh's own biography, however, implies a continual exclusion from any kind of family at all. She must separate from her own family, is rejected by Kim Khouan and his father, and reproduces familial disconnect by leaving Justin Jr. to Mama Thi-Bao's care. This cycle of abandonment intimates that women who participate in *métissage* cannot be a part of normative familial structures and constantly face the threat of being excised from various colonial social networks. The awareness that most interracial liaisons will end establishes a perpetual sense of uncertainty that, in *Congaï*, is symbolically portrayed as an undesirable return to sartorial dispossession—garments of "ashy" quality (39) or, as previously cited, "rusty . . . frayed and soiled" (47). As Nanette expresses, once she perceives that a relationship may terminate, she must investigate other opportunities to "'continue [her] profession of acquiring husbands'" (80). Miscegenous circuits create transient social structures and knotty webs of ancestry that expose the fiction of French and Indochinese standards of familial stability and lines of descent. Indochinese women carry the dual weight of ideals of national purity and the possibility of their contamination, and their dress marks the precariousness of their unpredictable financial fortunes.

In the next section, I consider further the political implications of familial-sartorial vocabularies of miscegenation in French Indochina by examining the melodramatic language of French discourses concerning mixed-race subjects alongside a Vietnamese critique of colonial notions of rescue by the early twentieth-century writer Vũ Trọng Phụng. Interpreted together, these documents elaborate how imperial France joined ideals of sartorial "taste" with those of morality to position mixed-race contexts as perverse manifestations of family. Hybrid subjects' externality to French social and legal belonging constituted a logic through which to justify endless cycles of colonial exploitation framed within melodramas of imperial uplift.

The Old Empire's Clothes

As France formalized its hold in Southeast Asia in the late nineteenth century, capturing Saigon in 1861 and establishing the Indochinese Union in 1883

(Cambodia, Laos, Tonkin, Annam, and Cochinchina), it established a plural legal system consisting of one set of policies for French citizens and another for "Indochinese," a newly created identity category.[27] However, the proliferation of *métissage* blurred social and legal categories and hierarchies, and by the turn of the twentieth century domestic arrangements of *métissage* had become a trope for social transgression at large.[28] Charity workers worried that miscegenous arrangements would cause European physical and moral decline, consequently, they cast *métis*, or mixed-race subjects born outside of marriage, as embodiments of vice. Their supposed immoral behavior would carry across generations and threaten the essential virtues of French identity, requiring the beneficent uplift of the empire.[29]

French discourses of miscegenation not only drew from melodrama's telos of redemption and return to morality to argue for the salvation of mixed-race progeny from the degenerate and transgressive potential of their non-French blood; these conversations also took on a sartorial logic. "Natives" were banned from wearing European styles in areas where colonials wanted clear, unmixed social distinctions, and philanthropists working with biracial orphans made it a point to provide them with European clothing.[30] Officials warned that mothers of mixed-race children would transmit inappropriate sartorial tastes, suggesting that excessive bodily cladding would lead to immoral bodily excesses. A report noted, "[They] adorn them with *bracelets* and *necklaces* and maintain in them a love of *luxury* innate in the Annamites."[31] These comments presume that overly decorated—overly coded— Asian mothers will result in intergenerations of *métis* with similar vulgar dress and morals, an improper "love of luxury" that would counteract the exclusivity and gentility of French prestige. Cheng and Lisa Lowe have argued that Euro-American culture historically has linked decadence and barbarism to Oriental garments. Here, miscegenous mothers' perceived stylistic excesses fatefully engender a lack of immorality and modernity.[32] A *métisse* becomes an exemplary case, seemingly destined for prostitution: "She fatally returns to the vice from which she came."[33] Decorative extravagances enforce a temporal repetition that loops *métis* back to some inescapable and transhistorical moral-sexual evil.

The sartorial logic of cultural debates about miscegenation were matched in the courts, where juridical attempts to uphold myths of French virtue and prestige turned to more flexible tropes of cladding. A landmark decree passed in 1928 declared that an abandoned *métis* could acquire French citizenship if the courts could confirm that the individual was sufficiently "French." This policy marks Indochina's broader significance in the global history of race because it contains the first mention of race in French jurisprudence,[34] and French laws concerning miscegenation and mixed-race subjects were first tested in Indochina and then applied elsewhere in the empire.[35] In court cases held to determine the citizenship status of *métis* individuals according to the 1928 law, jurists considered "the name of the child, the fact that he or she has received a French education, upbringing, and culture, and the child's situation in society." Jurists also looked for "prestige" and "possession of status"—abstract standards of French "dress," as we might call it, by which to ascertain Frenchness.[36] Unrefined style and bearing canceled out the prospect of French kinship and negated the possibility of becoming a legal member of France's international family.

In practice, what legally constituted Frenchness in *métis* could be "established by *any means whatsoever*,"[37] as the decree astonishingly stated, and very few multiracial individuals successfully petitioned for French citizenship. These realities expose the myth of the mixed-race subject, who is conjured as an ontological body to buttress imperial law but is a product of the racialized bodily management that it purportedly causes.[38] Social and legal debates would return time and time again to the terms and frames of melodrama to differentiate colonist from colonized and give the muddled *métis* question seeming clarity. Cycles of moral conflict, redemption, and rescue threaded these conversations and enlisted melodrama's sartorial turns to concretize the privilege of French identity, family, and citizenship and ensure the justness of French imperial law.

For many Vietnamese, French melodramas of interracial relations were topics of deep social and political concern. In *Kỹ Nghệ Lấy Tây* (*The Industry of Marrying Europeans*, 1934), Vũ Trọng Phụng, a writer who died in 1939 at twenty-seven but whose remarkable corpus stands as a hallmark of modern Vietnamese literature, contrasts colonial melodramas of *métissage* with realities of its racialized and gendered harm.[39] While Hervey enlists melodrama to scrutinize French empire's melodramatic proclamations, Vũ Trọng Phụng couples the documentary possibilities of *phóng sự*, a genre of first-person reportage emerging in Vietnam at the time,[40] with satire to question Europeans' moral and emotional rationales for *métissage*. He asks, "Are the relations that many of our women have with Westerners worth thinking about as matters of marital affection only?"[41] Vũ Trọng Phụng discovers that, for Foreign Legionnaires (foreign nationals serving in the French military) interviewed in Thị Cầu, Bắc Ninh Province, miscegenation is merely another opportunity to enact familiar narratives of the West's rescue of the East, or, to return to Malardier's words, a chance to demonstrate the continent's virility and unique capacity to "associate" with, rather than violently conquer, the colonized. Attributing disease and moral laxity to Vietnamese women involved in interracial liaisons,[42] European expatriates rehearse melodramas of crossracial desire in which white men save impoverished damsels from degradation. Scripts of European male uplift and affection—a rhetoric that helps to shape what Matt Matsuda describes as France's "empire of love"[43]—expose the biopolitical value of *métissage*, as masculinist assertions of chivalry, romance, and salvation circulate as valuable contributions to the moral and biological health of the colonies.

Yet Vũ Trọng Phụng debunks melodramatic myths of miscegenation and reframes *métissage* as an "industry" that exploits poor families. Implicated women recognize their exchangeability within colonial society, fully aware that European men "marry" Indochinese wives as if the entire affair is merely a "business transaction."[44] The women have their own economies of miscegenation, like Nanette, crossing off "husbands" as if going through a checklist—one of few options in an economy in which French conglomerates hold a monopoly on the colony's main industries.[45] One woman states, "'We marry them for money, that's all!'" while another elaborates that interracial relations should be seen not as socially taboo but as efforts to provide for families in a space where local and colonial structures require deft maneuvering.[46] As one interviewee puts it, "'One woman marries a European, everybody in her family benefits.'"[47] In a reversal of the modern flow from country to city, Indochinese women flock to rural villages to make an "occupation" out of marrying foreigners who are stationed in these areas. The marriage market has become so common in many of these villages that Vũ Trọng Phụng reluctantly comes to the conclusion that miscegenation is just another form of exchange in a modern capitalist economy: "It's just a buying and selling world, and it all has to do with the right price."[48]

Equally important, however, Vũ Trọng Phụng observes that a logical conundrum characterizes colonial economies of morality wherein exploited Indochinese women are preempted from the realm of the good and virtuous. One woman believes that, fundamentally, "women of our class are of the class that gets written off; society does not need to think of us."[49] Another interviewee notes, "'The notion of virtue is something that should never be bestowed onto someone who has married a Westerner.'"[50] Indochinese women passed between men are denied a moral being and thus end up becoming the very rationale for their perpetual rescue. Vũ Trọng Phụng exposes how the rhetoric of morality cloaks miscegenation's instrumentality in establishing European male power. He scrutinizes the structure of "fraternal friendship" that European men establish through their hypersexualization of Indochinese women—similar to the way in which Malardier encourages Justin to embrace *métissage* as a means not only of garnering pleasure but also of strengthening French male bonds and nationhood. It becomes apparent that homosocial bonding entails routine violence that occurs in spaces where *métissage* is brokered. A Russian named Dimitov openly acknowledges that he raped one of his wives because she behaved "like a whore."[51] In another scene, Vũ Trọng Phụng witnesses a Vietnamese "madam" flogging one of her prostitutes to "educate" the victim, who turns out to be her daughter.[52] Vietnamese complicity colludes with European male power to entangle sex laborers in regimes of violent masculinity and miscegenation.

Perhaps the figure who expresses *métissage*'s most damaging effects is Suzanne, who evokes Thi-Linh's character as a suffering biracial figure. Vũ Trọng Phụng's talks with Suzanne reveal the feeling of total social dispossession that accompanies being a *métisse*: "To be mixed-race is to suffer. The Europeans don't entirely respect us, and the Annamese don't fully love us. . . . Oh! That means I don't have a country!"[53] Similar to Thi-Linh's plight of signifying both sexual desirability and contamination, overlapping and impossibly purist ideologies of Indochinese and French identity and morality traffic through her body. Even Vũ Trọng Phụng finds himself seduced by melodrama's requisite of rescue, accompanying Suzanne for several days and finding himself wanting to save her from the moral, social, and political dilemmas of being mixed-race.

The multiple perspectives that Vũ Trọng Phụng takes into account—European men, French legionnaires, Vietnamese madams, sex workers from the city and the country, *métis* children—expose the contradictory narrative layers of miscegenation in French Indochina. By trying to understand colonial power as practiced through economies of miscegenation framed in melodramatic terms, Vũ Trọng Phụng moves beyond positioning women as emblems of absolutist social and political claims and dissects seemingly fixed, reductive categories of colonial virtue, identity, and family. Through the emergent genre of *phóng sự*, he deflates colonial melodramas' hyperbolic claims of *métissage*'s moral and social benefits to home in on the industry's undergirding capitalist logic. Taking stock of what he has seen, Vũ Trọng Phụng considers how melodramas of *métissage* can be deconstructed and overcome in future time.

Sartorialism as Labor

Analyzing *Congaï* in relation to French colonial discourse and Vũ Trọng Phụng's reportage reveals French imperial melodrama's negotiation of webs of colonial contradictions—its function as a form of political persuasion that covers circumstances of abuse and inequity, with the *métisse* serving as a limit case for ideals of the French social contract.[54] *Congaï* engages the question that Vũ Trọng Phụng raises concerning how to disrupt the force of such narratives—in particular, their power to condition understandings of the material world and of sentient, emotional life. The novel suggests that recognizing socially symbolic systems as, literally, products of labor marks an important step in shifting phenomenologies of colonized existence.

In a crucial plot turn, *Congaï* destabilizes entwined sartorial, familial, and moral ideologies of French imperial melodrama by delving into colonial capitalism's conditions of labor. Unhinging the telos of French modernity as moral and just, this narrative episode begins to turn the novel in an intriguing anti-imperial direction while also opening the door for potential American correction of European wrongs. About halfway through the novel, Thi-Linh briefly leaves the circuit of *métissage* and finds employment as a seamstress in Saigon, confronting sartorialism as not merely a source of pleasure but also a material economy that reveals how empire literally dresses various segments of colonial populations differently. Her relationship to garments shifts from one that assumes their socially symbolic significance to one that despairs over the conditions in which they are made. In the bustling colonial city of Saigon of the 1910s, the Southeast Asian commodities that John White dreamed of accessing in the prior century, as discussed in the Introduction, saturate the streets of *Congaï*—"perfumes and powders and imported wines," Tonkinese embroidery and brass gods, "silks from China and India" (97). But behind these seductive displays, Thi-Linh works in poor conditions in a sewing shop owned by South Asian merchants and run by a French dress-maker named Madame Dessard. As part of a transnational group of invisible laborers, Thi-Linh repetitively cuts, sews, and stitches: "needles and thread; cloth and scissors; and Madame Dessard fuming about with a mouthful of pins. Dull days, opaque" (101). Compounding the monotony of her work, she observes the apparently insurmountable socioeconomic difference between her unseen labor and the shop's finely clothed customers—"suave and cool-looking" Frenchwomen who saunter in and out of the shop wearing their "prestige" (94).

Congaï's portrayal of labor behind sartorial doors reveals that miscegenation is not prohibited at all but a cross-class, cross-racial reality. Not only are Frenchmen having affairs with Vietnamese women; French women are having affairs with Vietnamese men, and Vietnamese across genders and classes are involved.[55] "Immorality" is being committed by those who define it, and, while she has long accepted her lower social status as a mixed-race subject, Thi-Linh sees daily that broad swaths of the population are implicated in miscegenation. Her recognition of colonialism's wrongful devaluation of her classed, biracial body is accompanied by a widening vision through which the narration connects her labor as a seamstress and professional consort to a vast network of colonized workers: "In the road a low fog of dust was raised under the cumbersome wheels of ox-drawn carts and rickshaws; cool-ies went soundlessly by, pale-flanked with that same dust, and bent under great bales or with bamboo carrying-poles swinging to the polished rhythm of their bare shoulders" (96). Visibly weighted down by the commodities they carry, these figures' homogenized motion and evacuation of sensuous, embodied life expose a French colonial society and economy dependent on the toil of colonized bodies. Such networks stretch across geographies, as a group of Tirailleurs Annamites—Indochinese who served France during World War I—also briefly appear in *Congaï*'s story world. Perhaps anticipating Hervey's future cinematic career, *Congaï* jump cuts from one image of labor to another, connecting Thi-Linh's individual sufferings to the heterogeneous Indochinese collectivity that makes French Indochina work.

Although the coolies and Tirailleurs Annamites quickly dissolve into a faceless crowd, their fleeting emergence illuminates how, as a melodrama, *Congaï* flirts with opening its storyline to a multiplicity of potential protagonists who expand Thi-Linh's isolated, private sufferings. The mention of Tirailleurs Annamites in particular takes us out of the novel's diegesis and into the historical-political world, recalling the thousands of Indochinese who served France during the Great War and evoking the increased anticolonial unrest of the period.[56] About 99,000 Indochinese went to Europe in various capacities during World War I,[57] and a total of 1,548 Indochinese died. After the war, those who returned had witnessed poor social conditions in the metropole that exposed the fiction of French prestige, and many Vietnamese were sent to work in unlivable conditions on plantations and mines in Indochina for the recently expanded rubber and coal industries.[58] The 1910s–1920s were a time of organized Vietnamese protests, bombings, and attacks on French military posts in the colony,[59] with thousands incarcerated and executed throughout this period.[60] Albert Sarraut, French Indochina's governor-general in 1911–1914 and 1917–1919, attempted to ameliorate political discontent by employing a melodramatic language of "sentimental imperialism," "idealistic overstatement," and "collaboration" as opposed to the top-down domination of the prior era. But revised melodramatic performances aimed at tempering stern "authority" with "a certain kind of liberalism" rang empty,[61] especially given the sacrifices of the colonized in World War I.

While Hervey mutes the specific political context of his story, the interwar time frame of Thi-Linh's time in the Saigon shop coincides with rising anti-imperial sentiment and French anxiety about the security of their rule—a tension hinted at in the Tirailleurs Annamites' clashing and ominous imagery of "dark tunics," "spiked" headgear, and "soft tread" (96). Corresponding to this historical moment of shifting French colonial rhetoric and Vietnamese anticolonial organization, *Congaï* reframes the unequal dynamics of colonial power from below and positions Thi-Linh on different sides of the sartorial equation—from a desirer of French things to a maker of things that are desired—to link her to labor-based, nonfamilial forms of social connection. Allegorizing possibilities for upending the telos of imperial melodrama, Thi-Linh's production of commodities makes available the somatic desire and conceptual tools needed to unstitch and restitch, unmake and remake her story: "As she cut and sewed daily under Madame Dessard it seemed as if she were taking apart her past and making it into a new model" (100). Having believed French colonial ideology that Indochina is "where all the evil accumulated, surviving time," Thi-Linh flips the imperial script to invert its logic of melodramatic virtue and consider not "Where is evil?" but, rather, "What is evil?" (96). If melodrama repackages structural asymmetries into a romance of Indochinese aspiration with French virtues leading the way, Thi-Linh's moment of self-reflection stemming from her newfound kinship with other laboring Indochinese begins to deconstruct melodrama's foundational terms.

The New Empire's Clothes

The critical lens on notions and narratives of French morality that results from Thi-Linh's structural, collective understanding of labor becomes the melodramatic grounds for rescue and stages a transition from French to U.S. power and a shift in iconographies of empire. The novel's potential rescuer, Richard Garstin, is the only American in *Congaï* and enters as tactically situated between the insecurity of French rule and rising Vietnamese anticolonialism, with America presenting itself as a force more in tune—and on time—with colonial material reality and associated colonized grievance. "Just in time" rescue often occurs to mark the final third of melodramatic narratives, and this is precisely when Garstin arrives. His depiction noticeably contrasts with Hervey's unflattering and caricaturist portraits of Frenchmen, who are satirized for their white pallor, Orientalist attitudes, and pop-psychology impulse to discover the primitive within through interracial sex.[62] Garstin's entry triangulates French-Vietnamese geopolitical relations by personifying American intervention in early twentieth-century Indochina.

While Frenchmen stand out in a variety of sore ways, Garstin is different. His American identity positions him outside French empire's symbolic paradigms of dress. Accordingly, he is depicted not through clothing but through his physiognomy. A character whose physical qualities sparkle and attract, Garstin is what Cheng might call a "body-jewel,"[63] whose "eyes [haunt] with their very luxury of color" (235) and whose muscular physique transmits protection and vitality: "the warmth of his presence spread to her and excited her" (279). In contrast to awkward-looking Frenchmen, Garstin is a "tawny" figure who emits a "dark radiance," causing confusion about his ethnicity and nationality (275). The brownness of his body aligns with the physicality of Vietnamese subjects more so than other white males, drawing a phenotypical match between Garstin and Thi-Linh that corresponds to their spiritual harmony. Exhibiting an interest in adapting to rather than appropriating the foreign, Garstin's own hybridity complements Thi-Linh's rejection of French imperial ideology premised on the prestige, purity, and virtue of family and national blood. The two travel up the coast together, and Garstin declares his love for Thi-Linh and asks her to go with him to America (276).

While *Congaï*'s cultural predecessors typically conclude with Asian women crassly abandoned by opportunistic European and American lovers—as in Pierre Loti's *Madame Chrysanthème* (1887) and John Luther Long's "Madame Butterfly" (1898)[64]—Hervey's novel portrays Garstin and Thi-Linh's desire as mutual and temporally synced. Perhaps most prominent, the bareness of Garstin's body aligns with the seeming transparency of his motives. He emanates goodwill and naïveté, his stuttered expression mirroring the artlessness of his travels: "'I'm—fluid, I guess. . . . I like the sea—going to new places—not knowing what will happen'" (261–262). Garstin's uncloaked corporeality not only conveys to Thi-Linh the natural, visceral desire that arises between them; it also communicates a sincerity of American purpose—a lack of accoutrements signals a lack of political ideology and imperial ambition. Garstin appears to fuse inner virtue and outer attractiveness rather than to possess an external beauty that masks inner imperial vice.

Sartorialism, then, continues to operate in Garstin, but it is of a different kind, organized around the features of his body and morphed to become inscribed on the body itself. In the American context as Hervey presents it, sartorial logic manifests most enigmatically in the trope of the tattoo. When Thi-Linh first sees Garstin, she notices an image of "an anchor delicately stenciled in blue." The tattoo encircles his wrist like a bracelet, accentuating his characterization as a seductive body-jewel (228). Historically, the leitmotif of the tattoo has had a range of associations, straddling the "decorative" and "punitive," as Jane Caplan describes. As a recurring image in Herman Melville's sea stories, for example, it often identifies the body that exists beyond nationalist, mainland frames. A tattooed anchor in particular could indicate both community and marginalization, marking the American seaman as a member of maritime fraternity as well as someone peripheral to the national body politic.[65] The fact that Garstin's tattoo immediately catches Thi-Linh's notice and is the first sign of her attraction to him suggests her interest in his different kind of body, one whose bareness and mobility as encapsulated in the tattoo suggest an openness to racial plurality and fluid identities—a kind of sociality that diverges from France's purist notions of family. Moreover, as a pictorial inscription, the tattoo's iconic form seems to need no narrative or translation; its fusion with organic matter naturalizes symbolic representation. In Garstin's case, the immediate appeal of the tattooed anchor, combined with his seemingly guileless speech, suggests the palpable strength and translucence of American presence in French Indochina.

Yet as we weigh the stakes of Hervey's critique of French colonialism and depiction of U.S. arrival, the question remains: does Hervey do more than what many other Americans were doing in the opening decades of the twentieth century—interrogate the failures of Old World European empire only to create a political vacuum to be filled by New World forms of American power?[66] *Congaï*, through the depiction of Garstin's bare physique and rhetoric, shows how American empire emerges as less baroque, ostensibly "dressed down" compared with France's elaborate, "dressed-up" version of colonial uplift and care. The United States as Garstin embodies it assumes more authenticity in its concern for the colonized, more transparency of political purpose. Nevertheless, his attempt to persuade Thi-Linh of his virtuous intentions fails, resulting in the collapse of Asian-American romance toward which the entire novel has moved. This narrative twist is anticipated by the tattoo's injurious effects on Thi-Linh. Initially expressing Garstin's appeal and sensuality, its signification gradually shifts to become associated with coldness and potential danger: "How cool were those silver veins on his wrists!" (291). The emerging metallic quality of Garstin's body makes Thi-Linh vulnerable to his force: "Involuntarily she touched him. . . . The tattooed anchor seemed to have needled its pattern in fire upon her finger-tips" (271). A form of bodily enhancement for Garstin, the tattoo becomes a source of pain for Thi-Linh, as if branding her by force into an American iconography of power. If French imperial discourse in *Congaï* revolves around *looking* French and basking in the aura of Frenchness, Garstin's tattooed body becomes the vehicle through which an American imperium is made sensate and tactile—meant to be *felt* inside.

Thi-Linh views Garstin as simply reshaping imperialism for the long term, as "a mammoth body—a giant taking life from the bosom of ripe hills" (260), and names the United States as the world's next aggressor, "the death-house of Europe" (287). In this light, Garstin's denial of U.S. imperial ambitions is more an illustration of America's particular brand of empire—one whose anti-imperial veneer is a defining tactic of U.S. extraterritorial politics. While hybrid figures in early twentieth-century American culture were often enlisted to show how immigrant groups within the United States could change over time and mutate into an ideal Anglo-American type,[67] *Congaï*'s transnational focus suggests that outside U.S. borders such assimilation reverses itself: the mixed, diverse American body can "go native." The traveling hybrid epitomizes the modern American colonizer able to navigate the overlapping networks of a world in motion through a dispersed and intractable reach.

By portraying Garstin as a well-intentioned American ready to make good on his promises to his love object, *Congaï* points to a transitional moment in early twentieth-century global history: European decline and U.S. imperial ascendance. Hervey portrays U.S. presence in Indochina as an innovative pluralist modernization of, rather than a break with, European hegemony. Indeed, Garstin's tattooed anchor might be interpreted as a symbol of early twentieth-century U.S. maritime hegemony, as Theodore Roosevelt's Great White Fleet circumnavigated the globe between 1907 and 1909 to showcase U.S. martial strength, and in 1918 President Woodrow Wilson called for "absolute freedom of navigation upon the seas."[68] In the next section, I investigate how the United States imagined a shift from European to American influence by crafting a different melodrama of empire whose final rejection in *Congaï* opens a narrative space for considering alternative configurations of social relations and of melodrama itself.

Americanizing Empire: Pluralist Imperialism

Much scholarship on American empire during the late nineteenth and early twentieth centuries focuses on the territories gained after the Spanish-American War. But French colonialism in Indochina also significantly shaped the Americanization of empire. As the United States aimed to contrive a more durable, multidimensional logic for increased American intervention in world affairs, French Indochina became an object lesson in what could go wrong in colonial rule—an example *against* which to redefine and modernize benevolent empire. U.S. officials consistently noted French economic and political crises in Southeast Asia to suggest the superiority of American geopolitical strategy. For instance, U.S. administrators emphasized that France's post–World War I devastation had resulted in a shortage of resources in the colonies, forcing Indochinese dependence on American goods and services. American officials also charged the French imperial administration with grave ignorance of the concerns of the colonized. Memos recorded "native uprisings" followed by severe French crackdowns and executions, emphasizing Sarraut's hypocrisy in preaching embellished ideals of "Liberty, Equality, and Fraternity" without any intention of granting Indochina independence.[69] In America's logic of imperial rivalry, France's obvious "seeking for empire" and overall "bad policy and mismanagement" would fail to secure the longevity of its imperial authority; powerful countries required "some element of greater permanence."[70] Needing a distinct rationale for American overseas ambitions without undermining its own, mythologized history of republican revolution and democratic self-determination, U.S. imperial discourse, like that of France, turned to melodrama as a political narrative frame.

If France's fault was its purported inability to communicate a convincing vision beyond immediate economic aims, America took melodrama's elements of morality, good versus evil, and rescue and return to justice to the next level, enlisting, as Mae M. Ngai argues, the notion of "duty" to make U.S. imperialism invisible and posit Europe as the culprit of injustice.[71] Americanized empire used melodrama's querying of what is virtue to define American *anti-imperialism* in contrast to European imperial values. In remarks to Congress after the Cuban War of Independence, for example, President William McKinley used a moralizing language of nonaggression to distance American expansion from the ongoing onslaughts of European empire: "I speak not of forcible annexation, for that cannot be thought of. That, by our code of morals would be criminal aggression."[72] McKinley would proceed to squash anticolonial insurgencies in the Philippines, leading to the deaths of hundreds of thousands of Filipinos, while at the same time proclaiming anti-imperialism to be a founding principle of American global politics.

President Woodrow Wilson expanded on McKinley's words a few years later in his Fourteen Points speech outlining post–World War I stability. He coupled anti-imperial rhetoric with a global *pluralist* outlook to anticipate "political independence and territorial integrity to great and small states alike." He further suggested that American anti-imperialism would advance unprecedented global peace and freedom, declaring that the world would "*be made* safe for every peace-loving nation which, like *our* own, wishes to live its own life, . . . be assured of justice and fair dealing . . . as against force and selfish aggression."[73] A passive and collective grammar buried U.S. agendas to reinforce moral rectitude, positioning the nation as an equitable, democratic force that would work side by side with other countries to facilitate their liberation and self-governance. The question for American colonialism, at least on the surface, was not how the immorality or degradation of mixing races contaminated the virtue of American blood or political goals—since the nation was founded on hybrid ethnohistories, a *métis* history of sorts—but whether colonized subjects, regardless of origin, would voluntarily cultivate a sense of shared national identity and duty to match their desires and values with "American" desires and values. As an ideology of equal integration of difference at home and worldwide, pluralism joined anti-imperialism to become a U.S. ethical imperative—a premise of, rather than hindrance to, American expansion and the global freedom that the nation promised to deliver. While Europe's discursive strategy was to claim salvation of the colonized from themselves, the United States claimed to save the colonized from Europe. Imagining itself as a nation not only against colonialism but also able to see beyond this outmoded model, the United States defined itself as a savior in horizontal, postimperial terms.

A significant backdrop to these imaginaries of American redemption of colonized suffering was U.S. capitalist expansion in Asia. Continuing the young American republic's targeting of Southeast Asian markets discussed in the Introduction, U.S. State Department records dating from 1889 regularly noted American export opportunities—in dyes, cheese, cotton, and, a little later, automobiles—as well as Vietnamese resources in rice, spices, rubber, mining, and tourism. Gaston Giraud, the U.S. commercial attaché for French Indochina, expressed delight in 1920 that many Americans were departing from San Francisco for the region "to see for themselves" what rich prospects and opportunities lay ahead. He commended an American steamship company for launching a line connecting San Francisco and Saigon.[74] American Consul Leland L. Smith recalled in 1921 that France had offered Indochina to the United States as payment for wartime debts, adding that it "is said [France] does not appreciate or realize the value of her colony,"[75] which implied that France either underestimated or was ill-equipped to maximize Indochina's profitability. Smith's remark demonstrates how forcing other countries' indebtedness has long been a tactic of U.S. global power and shows how far back French, American, and Indochinese entanglements have stretched. These prior, overlooked inroads outline a long chronology of American involvement in the region that helped pave the way for heightened U.S. presence later in the century.

America's early twentieth-century soft imperial rhetoric aimed to persuade foreign subjects' hearts and minds to promote a common national attitude across geographical boundaries and create a more hospitable, diverse international family free of purist ideology. It asserted that mutual benefit and desire among subjects at home and abroad arose naturally and voluntarily, despite varied ethnohistories (and the realities of war and conflict attached to them). American pluralist empire as characterized by the ideal of reciprocity obtained a rhetorical dressing based on the body itself rather than its coverings and was strikingly nominated, in the words of President William Howard Taft, as a "policy of attraction."[76]

Melodrama and the Problem of Intersectional Representation

Thi-Linh's definitive rejection of Garstin's proposal stages a negative outcome of early twentieth-century Indochinese-American intimacy and its associated Americanist rhetoric of interracial cooperation. Although Garstin personifies Taft's "policy of attraction," with his tattoo mediating America's revision of European colonial ideologies and iconographies, his exit from the novel stems from Thi-Linh's discernment of the imperialist underpinnings of his egalitarian language. *Congaï* suggests that U.S. pluralist ideology is simply another outfit that empire wears; external salvation by an American is a deceptive remedy for colonialism's evils. Thi-Linh and Garstin's separation thus pauses the romance and salvation that melodramas are supposed to achieve—not in a way that reproduces common portrayals of essential East-West difference and U.S. modernity but to suggest, in this case, the fiction of American imperial melodrama and the failure of sex as an alibi for the biopolitical management of "others" overseas. Garstin's departure from *Congaï* locates a formal tension whereby the American hero emerges at precisely the right moment, but the melodramatic rescue promised remains unfulfilled.[77] His presence is out of sync, rendering U.S. melodramatic rescue untimely even if, structurally, it is perfectly timed.

Disparate trajectories of resolution thus emerge in Hervey's novel, as the American myths of colonized salvation that Garstin professes sound similar to but clash with Thi-Linh's evolving anticolonial thinking. While Garstin's desire to rescue Thi-Linh is based in an expressed apolitical, personal feeling of love, her preliminary vision of salvation as it surfaces in the sewing shop encompasses a structural understanding of collective colonized grievances. Moreover, Thi-Linh's truncated affair with Garstin forges a juxtaposition of French colonialism, American presence, and Thi-Linh's phenomenological shift toward a more liberatory vision of Indochinese existence, in turn establishing a multiplicity of competing notions of justice as they circulate in the colony. The particular tension between inauthentic French and U.S. salvation and Thi-Linh's anticolonial feeling carves out a narrative space for reimagining the familial norms and, thus, the social and political expectations that the novel suggests govern imperial melodrama. This nexus of conflicting colonial politics raises the question of if and how the novel might direct Thi-Linh's nascent counter-hegemonic thought toward concrete realization.

Congaï's queer orientations, I suggest, constitute a minor thread next to the novel's central plotline but become essential to how the narrative attempts to imagine decolonization. Queer moments appear episodically in the story as Thi-Linh's seemingly passing resistance to social assumptions concerning love, desire, and affiliation.[78] They have an accretive effect, however, culminating in the novel's final climax, which involves a face-off between Justin Jr. and Chauvet, Thi-Linh's third "husband," and potentially rupturing the structure of *métissage* and the requisites of melodrama itself. In one scene, Thi-Linh walks through the streets of Saigon and luxuriates in observing the animation and inquisitiveness of the urban crowd: "So many people astir. . . . People searching. Like herself" (101). She then eroticizes their energized presence in her description: "Bodies so pliant and eager, yearning to one another. Bodies of sailors. Bodies of soldiers. Bodies of young girls calling to sailors and soldiers. . . . What was life but an immense desire, an immense yearning interpreted through bodies?" (102). Thi-Linh's reclamation of sexual yearning evokes Celine Parreñas Shimizu's argument that we must consider the hypersexualized Asian woman's body not just as a "punitive" site but also as a site of pleasure.[79] Thi-Linh's admiration also crosses gender, as the attraction to bodies she experiences does not submit to a presumed male power: "She loved to watch their forms mold patterns against the night. Not only the men's, but the women's as well. Was it wrong to love bodies?" (101). Whereas desire in *métissage* is fundamentally tainted both socially and legally, here Thi-Linh finds intrinsic virtue and purpose in various forms of corporealized longing, even if, as this scene demonstrates, there is no outlet for it. The racially and sexually anonymous, transgender passion Thi-Linh admits refracts the dominance of *métissage*'s masculinist heteronormativity.

The sexual energy that saturates Thi-Linh's proximity to bodies takes de-eroticized turns when she tries to imagine how the virtues of an embodied existence might acquire longevity. In another scene in which Thi-Linh continues to consider the morality and legitimacy of corporeal desire, she finds herself entranced by Indochinese men performing various kinds of activities—walking on the road, swimming in the river, lying on the earth. Gazing on them appears to stir within her sexual "roots of desire," but she asserts that she feels no heterosexual attraction to them—"She did not crave men." Rather, Thi-Linh relates to these figures in a maternal, matriarchal way, "as a mother imparts warmth to the buds of suckling nakedness that later become men." Her feminine, nurturing affection for young Indochinese males eschews sexual connection for intergenerational and ethnic kinship—also quite different from the white-Asian, male-dominated structure of her relationships with French men and Garstin. By attributing to Thi-Linh a temporally expansive significance in this scene—the narration describes her here as "old with the age of forgotten years" (77)— *Congaï* gives Thi-Linh a relevance that stretches across time, a durability that contrasts with the social and historical liminality and neglect that accompany being a *métisse*. Breaking from colonials' timeless fetishization of her difference, the notion of an Indochinese past, present, and future imbues Thi-Linh with a historicity that retemporalizes her abstract commodification within networks of *métissage*. The emergence of temporal multivalence through feminine-led, age-differentiated bonding fractures paternalistic teleologies of Euro-American imperial time and opens up different, divergent paths for *Congaï*'s conclusion.

The social reimaginings that result from Thi-Linh's exploration of various forms of non-normative desire and affiliation presage a dramatic, sexually charged scene involving Justin Jr. in which Thi-Linh's hope for sexual and historical fulfillment come together. After her tryst with Garstin, Thi-Linh returns to the home of Chauvet. Now in his teenage years, Justin Jr. unexpectedly arrives to report that Mama Thi-Bao has died. When he appears, he is so strikingly dressed that Thi-Linh has difficulty focusing on their conversation. Instead, she turns her eyes to his powdered face and polished dress—his "Norfolk jacket, full white trousers, . . . tie of bright blue" that give him a disconcerting "air of authentic breeding and reserved assurance"—the very things that would, in theory, legally qualify him for French citizenship as a *métis* (299). The narrative's focus is thus formally divided—split between Thi-Linh's ostensible concern over Justin Jr.'s apparent assimilation and an eroticism cutting through the scene. Even at the news of her mother's death, Thi-Linh quickly returns to the way her son looks and, in a striking moment of passion, imagines "her hands [moving] hungrily over his face . . . to kiss him again and again" (302). At one point when Justin Jr. rises to kiss her, the narration reveals that he does so "on the mouth," causing "the pounding in her temples [to mount] fiercely" (304). These erotic interactions are sparse and overpowered by the jagged, prolonged narrative style that appears fixated on Thi-Linh's ostensible worry that France is eviscerating Justin Jr.'s Annamite identity. Torn between her attraction to her Europeanized son and her resistance to things European that her embryonic anticolonial feeling has generated, Thi-Linh's passions explored in the earlier episodes—sexual yearning outside *métissage* and want of intergenerational longevity—merge in an instant of disturbing incestuous desire.

The eroticization of ethnic sameness, generational difference, and mixed-race familialism sets the stage for and even seems essential to the novel's climactic moment of rescue that promptly follows. As Thi-Linh rapturously responds to her son, Chauvet, a director at the Banque de l'Indochine and thus in charge of much of French Indochina's capital, suddenly returns home. To avoid encountering the hot-tempered Frenchman, Justin Jr. hides in an adjacent room. Following minutes of tense pleasantries, a drunk and jealous Chauvet shouts at Thi-Linh for being a "whore" and strikes her for the affair with Garstin, which he has learned about through networks of gossip (309). Justin Jr. runs in to defend his mother, inadvertently killing Chauvet through means that Hervey leaves vague, elided in an elliptical narration that offers only the image of porcelain shards as evidence of physical conflict.

This defining act of violence that immediately follows on the heels of

Thi-Linh and Justin's sexualized embraces establishes anticolonial action against the figure of imperial finance as the final form of rescue in *Congaï*. Liberation emerges as driven by the coordinated, embodied will and action of mixed-race Indochinese subjects: "her dark blood pouring back into Indo-China through Justin, . . . torrents of blood swelling the anemic veins of Indo-China . . . the tawny triumph of Asia" (311). The explicit language of revolt indicates that the cycle of melodrama has brought Thi-Linh salvation, overturned the social norms of imperial melodrama, and upended Euro-American terms of virtue and justice at the same time that the sexual charge between Thi-Linh and Justin Jr. continues to permeate this scene. The sequence of events suggests that the incestuous kinship between the two characters mobilizes and legitimates Indochinese feeling and agency to activate a new, intergenerational version of anticolonial melodrama.

However, despite the political symbolism of the killing, Justin Jr. expresses a lack of political intention, fissuring the cross-generational, ethnic solidarity that Thi-Linh envisions has followed their impassioned reunion. He describes the killing as an apolitical accident, an unintended consequence of conflict between male colonizer and colonized: "'I didn't mean . . . I heard you quarreling . . . and I pushed'" (310). The dramatic but short-lived moment of anticolonial coaction dissolves, suspending yet again the return to justice that *Congaï* as a melodrama sets up. Hervey then reins in the novel's volatile political energy and contracts the narrative's expanding horizon to return to Thi-Linh's individual situation, defaulting to the sartorial and social norms with which the novel begins. Immediately registering that the punishment for murder in French Indochina is "the guillotine" (310), Thi-Linh directs Justin Jr. to leave and turns herself in to the police in his stead, devising a plan to become the prefect of police's mistress in exchange for her son's immunity. In a final sartorial staging that carries high legal stakes, Thi-Linh manipulates dress codes to convince the prefect of Justin Jr.'s innocence and her fabricated guilt. Approaching the prefect with a "calm" and "remarkably composed" demeanor, she enacts need through a color-coded appearance, a "dress [that] was soft and gray, accentuating the golden tint of her skin" (315). With the assistance of the vibrant sun, Thi-Linh accents the "flecks of gold" in her eyes (316), exuding a cinematic illumination that highlights her return to legibility in the eyes of French law and articulates one last time sartorialism's function as a code through which empires bestow and deny rights. In a pronounced moment of meta-generic commentary, *Congaï* questions whether Thi-Linh can "rise above the nauseating melodrama of this scene"—a self-reflexive reference to Thi-Linh's separation from her son, her continued suffering, and Justin Jr.'s disappearance into an unknown future (307).

Erotic and political desire converge in Thi-Linh and Justin Jr.'s meeting to promise a dismantling of norms of race, gender, sexuality, and family that uphold ideals of imperial familialism, as well as of melodramas of empire. But these efforts ultimately fail. The novel relegates both characters to realms of melodramatic alterity, splintering the narrative into subordinated *ir*resolutions, or what Susan Gillman calls melodrama's "occult histories."[80] The novel's surface ending is, hence, presented as an unjust one, as the accumulation of failed rescues makes salvation a precarious and unstable requisite of melodrama. Concomitantly, Thi-Linh's inability to exceed the formal and social constraints of colonial melodrama and the novel's recourse to the genre's dichotomies illustrate the power of polarized representations of conflict. Hervey's braiding of the erotic and the political results in a narrative retrenchment that returns to the social hierarchies that undergird colonial melodrama and that delegitimize Indochinese anticolonial thought and agency and the much more varied forms of kinship that constitute colonial society. Put differently, depicting intersectional justice emerges as a narrative problem in *Congaï*.

Two factors come into play in considering the challenges that complex relational, intersectional social and political issues pose to American melodramatic form. First, the dynamics of American exceptionalist rhetoric typically collide with the collective, structural premises of anticolonial critique. As Anker argues, American melodramatic practices import French liberal philosophy's belief in personal will and choice but aggrandize the self into a heroic *hyper*-individualism punctuated by an Emersonian *self-sufficiency* standing tall against the odds.[81] That individualized solutions stand in for complex structural problems demonstrates the difficulty of figuring intersectionality, given American melodrama's individualist streak that constrains representation of interconnections. The tendency to privilege individual capability eclipses collective grievances and corresponding structural resolutions that would need to be considered in order to represent anti-imperialism's necessary counterpart, decolonization.

Relatedly, Hervey's depiction of Thi-Linh's racialized, gendered, and classed oppression problematically eroticizes her persecution. In *Congaï*, incestuous desire functions as an intergenerational structure that harnesses a specifically Indochinese anticolonial politics in the present and for the future. However, as Kadji Amin writes, "While erotic attraction may put one into proximity with political movements, . . . erotic, psychic, and affective life nonetheless *obeys a different temporality* than do the political movements that seek to transform social orders."[82] Hervey's literary foray into incest tests the limits of non-normative social relations as a basis for political action. Yet its failure to produce the result Thi-Linh desires also

points to the limits of eroticism as a framework for imagining transformation. The novel critiques Euro-American eroticizations of racial difference,
understanding these narrative strategies as ways to rationalize imperial aspirations. Yet *Congaï*'s sexualization of Indochinese desire, even if for anticolonial purposes, still functions as a mode of eroticizing race that maps the
instantaneousness of sexual yearning over protracted processes of political
thought and action.

Sexualized kinship as a means of connecting to contexts of cultural and
political inequality was not only a concern in Hervey's fiction. It was also a
relation that Hervey explored through nonfiction. In *Travels in French Indo-
China* (1927), which he positions as having generated his ideas for *Congaï*,
Hervey describes a chance meeting with an Indochinese boy with whom
he forges a cross-racial, intergenerational identification that leads to ethical
reflection:

> Hastily I turned off into a side street; I could never formulate the end
> of my story amidst such confusion.
>
> Suddenly a figure stepped out from a black doorway.
>
> "*Bonsoir, monsieur*," said a young voice.
>
> "*Bonsoir*," I returned.
>
> Sandals clattered after me.
>
> "*Pardonnez-moi, monsieur. Vous avez une allumette?*"
>
> I paused and handed the boy a box of matches. As he struck a
> light he smiled; his face was very white, his clothing absurdly French.
>
> "*Merci, monsieur*," he murmured; and I could feel him still smil-
> ing in the darkness. . . .
>
> Certainly the grotesque, pathetic figure of that Annamite boy
> was eloquent. But how could I put him into words?[83]

The detour onto a side street leads to an interracial meeting unfolding in
the shadows and across the space and time of the ellipsis. Hervey's portrayal
of the Indochinese boy as helplessly structured within a homoerotic, age-
differentiated economy of sex work invokes Orientalist discourses of pederasty whereby, as Frank Proschan has shown, Indochinese males relentlessly
pursue intergenerational gay liaisons.[84] Ideologies of pederasty rationalized
diverse forms of imperial conquest, including the moral distinctions that
hierarchized colonist over colonized and the sexual violence that Indochinese temptations reportedly invited.[85] But Hervey expresses his relationship
to the boy in terms of affiliation more than desire. Rather than suggest that
he cannot help but be seduced, Hervey forges what Amin might describe
as "pederastic kinship"—a form of affiliation across age and, often, racial

difference that "takes up the reproductive labor of intergenerational trans- mission and financial, material, and bodily care."[86] For Amin, pederasty af- fords an "indispensable opportunity to *directly theorize the erotics of social structure.*"[87] Hervey's meeting with the boy, who is detached from any form of community, identifies the potentiality of pederastic kinship, as the os- tensibly non-sexual identification Hervey establishes with the youth poses an alternative to colonial society's hetero- and homonormativities. It also compels Hervey to pause over the boy's vulnerability, prompting Hervey to respond to the figure's "grotesque, pathetic," and "eloquent" manner with a pathos that lingers beyond the pages of the book.

Yet other aspects of Hervey's biography locate the potential slippage be- tween kinship and appropriation. Indeed, the photo of Hervey in Orientalist costume reproduces some of the problems of racialized and exoticized sar- torial signification he criticizes (see the Hervey image). It was purportedly taken as Hervey prepared for a theatrical performance in "Asian" dress, real- ized in the photograph as a mixture of dramatic makeup, ornate headdress, fan, textured fabrics, detailed peacock design, and Japanese *geta.*

While crafting an Asian voice in *Congaï* facilitates anticolonial critique and queer representation, however flawed, here "Asia" is an outfit to wear— a costume that "miscegenates" Hervey's whiteness and perhaps links queer and racial alterity while trafficking in Orientalist tropes. Evocative of writers such as Loti and Rudyard Kipling,[88] who often mediated queer representa- tion through the Asiatic, Hervey linked gay identity and the "Oriental," typi- cally through tropes of "splendid oriental dresses, clothes, shawls, and fabrics"; motifs of bodily cladding often acted as narrative cover for the taboo topic of queerness.[89] Certain aspects of French Indochina, for instance, were for Hervey embodiments of sexual freedom, including homoerotic carvings he saw at Angkor Wat.[90] In the photo, an uneasy ideological proximity emerges between Hervey's anti-imperial politics and cultural appropriation, conveying the challenge of intersectional awareness in lived experience. Relatedly, one might argue that *Congaï* constitutes an act of passing and places Hervey within a cultural history of impersonations of Asian women in American literature, from Long's "Madame Butterfly" to Claude-Michel Schönberg and Alain Bou- blil's *Miss Saigon* (1989) and Arthur Golden's *Memoirs of a Geisha* (1997).

This brings us to the specificity and contradictions of Hervey's own in- terests in the ills of global colonialism. Beginning in 1939, Hervey claimed in interviews that he wrote because he wanted to fight injustice around the world. Although the United States was poised to succeed Europe in world affairs, it would not be the better, more "virtuous" power but would bring only, in his words, an "injustice more exquisite and subtle"—softer, dressed down, and made alluring.[91] Hervey viewed this as no less true within na-

Harry Hervey in "Asian-inspired costume," 1920s. (Photograph of Harry Hervey. Catalogue: MS 1695-VM01-10-03, Carleton Hildreth and Harry Hervey Papers. Courtesy of the Georgia Historical Society, www.georgiahistory.com.)

tional space. When others found out Hervey was gay during his brief residence in Charleston in the mid-1920s, the city "shunned him," publicizing his sexuality as "a contagion that had to be contained." Hervey vowed never to return to Charleston.[92] Perhaps to intimate the homophobia he faced, Hervey claimed an "affinity between Indo-China and myself," identifying with the colony potentially to establish a shared position of subjection and imagine possibilities for dismantling white heteronormativity.[93] For Hervey, discrimination in any form and across disparate spaces worked to serve Euro-American power: "We of the West are humanitarians outside theory until the skin changes colour, then we are altruistic; and our weapon is conversion through acquisition."[94] Hervey would continue to enlist melodrama in other popular works about a range of locations—including Savannah, Tennessee, Borneo, the Caribbean, India, Portugal, and present-day Guinea-Bissau—to draw attention to various examples of national and transnational injustices. A combined biographical and formal reading of his works reveals how Hervey attempted to test what various forms of alternative, non-normative affiliations could do to connect the personal, familial, national, and geopolitical. The fluctuating degrees of success in his efforts reflect the complex erotics, aesthetics, and politics of representing America's Asia.

Analyzing Hervey's works suggests that where melodrama can be most illustrative is where it breaks down into latent, minoritized streams, exemplifying how genre's workings become most apparent precisely when they are being breached. Judgments regarding the question of genre's relationship to geopolitics—the extent to which melodrama enables and constrains the depiction of overlapping Vietnamese, French, and American contexts and rhetorical dressing—would carry over into discussions related to *Congaï*'s stage and screen versions. The novel's juggling of different intersectional concerns would be reflected in the reception of various versions of *Congaï*, where audiences became preoccupied with certain social and political relations over others—a revelatory discussion to which I now turn to demonstrate further melodrama's importance in shaping attitudes about not only America's Vietnam but also Americanized empire.

Congaï on Broadway and (Not) in Hollywood

Congaï received a good deal of publicity when it was published (see the image of the novel's dust jacket). Advertisements regularly appeared throughout major American newspapers in 1927, and a gloss of the endorsements on the back cover of the first edition reveals that *Congaï*'s marketing catered to a popular demand for stories about locations perceived to be foreign and exotic. Comments note the novel's "sultriness, warm colors," and "clinging odors," as well as its more sinister "dark intensity" and Indochinese morals that would be "startling to the Western Mind." While many readers evaluated the novel favorably, these assessments also served an ideological purpose by differentiating among the normative, civil, and moral in the United States in contrast with French Indochina.

Hervey upped the political ante in his play and film versions of *Congaï*, portraying Indochinese anticolonialism as unapologetic and collective, to which theater critics and Hollywood censors responded by downplaying the story's revolutionary traces. The theater version of *Congaï* toured San Francisco; Chicago; Washington, DC; Atlantic City; and other major American cities. On November 27, 1928, the Broadway production premiered with the rising star Rouben Mamoulian as director—seven years before his influential direction of *Porgy and Bess* and *Becky Sharp*[95]—and Cleon Throckmorton as set designer. Throckmorton's deliberately dull and monochromatic staging of French barracks in contrast to the vibrancy of his vision of French Indochina helped Mamoulian capitalize on Hervey's attention to decorative materials to produce the sensual, atmospheric experience for which Mamoulian would become famous: "incense burned from pots onstage and throughout the theater" along with "a symphony of whining pipes and menacing drums and fantastic shadows arising from the mists of the rice fields."[96] Mamoulian and Throckmorton's color and sound techniques combined onstage to give French imperial destruction of Indochinese vitality the appropriate aesthetic look.

While some reviews suggested that the Broadway season that began in fall 1928 was not extraordinary, many considered *Congaï* Mamoulian's "biggest hit of the year" and one of the season's best productions.[97] It led to lively discussions in American newspapers concerning the generative effects of colonial Indochina's circulation in American popular consciousness—from the contemplation about colonial affairs it provoked to excitement about new ideas for feminine fashion that the play's costumes inspired. Numerous critics cited one of *Congaï*'s chief merits as the novelty of its subject matter, "moving with atmosphere new to Broadway," while others noted that some of the production's multiethnic actors, "a cast of many names," set the play apart from other productions. Several critics appreciated the broad cultural and political appeal of Hervey's steamy story. Percy Hammond of the *Los Angeles Times* commented that *Congaï* had "all the world of Broadway" astir, noting his long wait to get a ticket because the show was typically sold out.[98]

However, Hammond, along with some other reviewers, faulted Hervey's take on heroes and villains, which allegedly focused too much on sex: "The play, as all the world of Broadway knows, is a dramatization of Harry Hervey's novel of the sex life of Indo-China with the amorous French invaders

Dust jacket of *Congaï*, 1927. (Photograph by Harlan Greene. Courtesy of Harlan Greene.)

plying their casual romances among the defenseless native women. Their practice, both soldier and civilian, is to rent a village belle for the season and to walk out on her without the customary two weeks' notice. . . . *Congaï* is not a bad play and one hesitates timidly to add that it is not a good one."[99] Suggesting that French sexual exploits were old news and undeserving of the sustained attention that Hervey gave them, Hammond reduced *Congaï*'s plot to a sordid tale about "the sex life of Indo-China." Similarly, a *New York Times* critic praised the production's attention to detail—"the atmospheric tropical settings, the costumes of (probably) precisely the correct Oriental cut and local color"—but critiqued the insistence on Thi-Linh's suffering while leaving them unresolved, "a constant striving after something that it could never reach." Lightly applauding the play's willingness to interrogate French colonialism, the critic used the metaphor of a failed salad to lament *Congaï*'s poor attempt at melodrama: "Sophisticated melodrama is a salad that takes expert mixing. . . . The authors of '*Congaï*' have tried to mix the same sort of dish with hands much less expert, with taste less sure."[100]

The stage production's more explicit treatment of Indochinese solidarity perhaps helps to explain why critics responded sourly to Hervey and Hildreth's adaptation. Whereas in the novel Garstin and Justin Jr. offer disparate, failed forms of rescue to leave the position of rescuer open, in the play Thi-Linh and Kim Khouan meet again in the third act and plot to run away together. Their conspiracy theatricalizes stronger collective anticolonial will than in the novel. Thi-Linh's son also assumes more symbolic significance in the stage version of *Congaï*. Not only is he renamed Quyen, heightening his Indochinese identity, but toward the end of the play Thi-Linh makes a comment about him that does not appear in the novel: "I am going to send my son back to the jungle." Her son no longer disappears simply for safety; he vanishes into unmappable, uncontainable space. Perhaps the most striking change in the play is the elimination of Garstin as a character, totally removing America as a possible savior not only for Hervey's Thi-Linh but also for French Indochina itself.[101]

Theater critics' concerns about *Congaï*'s aesthetic qualities as a melodrama thus were not simply about how well the play executed the form. They were also articulations of how American melodrama should relate genre and empire—preferably by staging a melodrama that was literally and symbolically beautifully dressed to affirm America's exceptionalist role as a hero for those suffering under European rule. These were especially pertinent questions given America's self-defined role as a "nation of nations" committed to soft imperial tactics and anticolonial rhetoric. The *Times* reviewer elaborated that Thi-Linh's "native patriotism" was "unrationalized" and that the narrative's irresolution—its failure to articulate American rescue—prevented a compelling treatment of the more serious issue at hand: "the white man's dealing with the little brown brother and sister, . . . a very sore subject [that received] a very ill turn." American audiences would have recognized "little brown brother" as a reference to Filipinos, likely connecting *Congaï*'s anti-colonial themes to realities of war in the Philippines—hence, the review in *Billboard* in which Wilfred Riley wrote, "Evidently it is the intention of the authors to show that colonization is not good for those it subjects and that colonization only brings ruin and vice."[102] By attributing *Congaï*'s failure to an amateurish handling of melodrama, these critics turned the play's engagement with questions of race, nation, and empire toward questions of aesthetic taste to suggest that American melodrama should be pro-colonial, exposing the impetus behind official U.S. anticolonial rhetoric.[103]

In a striking parallel to *Congaï*'s anticolonial themes as also a consideration of non-normative desire, public discussions about the play's depiction of empire also covered a queer thread. The Broadway production starred Helen Menken in yellowface as Thi-Linh, her first major role after she had been taken into custody for playing the lesbian character Irene in Edouard Bourdet's *The Captive*.[104] Along with the casts of other plays that were deemed immoral, the actors involved in *The Captive* were arrested, causing the show to close. A couple of months after the controversy, the State of New York banned theater "'depicting or dealing with, the subject of sex degeneracy, or sex perversion.'"[105] This widely known controversy was not much discussed in reviews of *Congaï*, despite the fact that not even a year had passed between the scandal that embroiled Menken and her debut in *Congaï*. Critics' focus on Hervey's play as a potential archetype for a nationalist form of American melodrama demonstrates how not only cultural production but also cultural criticism shape how we think about geopolitical discourses' significant reliance on genre.

Hervey's screenplay version of *Congaï* brings into further relief the conditions under which French Indochina emerges in early twentieth-century American culture. The movie was slated for production by Paramount Studios, with a number of actresses lined up to play Thi-Linh, including Jean Harlow, Myrna Loy, and Dolores del Río, who had craved Helen Menken's stage role.[106] But the project was abandoned after numerous revisions; Hervey and the studio were "unable to cool the piece off sufficiently to assure freedom from censorship."[107] The Motion Picture Producers and Distributors of America (also known as the Hays Office) had just circulated its list of "Don'ts and Be Carefuls" in 1927, and number six on that list was a clause prohibiting the portrayal of miscegenation (defined as black and white).[108] Memos from the Hays Office indicate concern about Thi-Linh's "disloyalty to her white lover" and cite *Congaï*'s portrayal of miscegenation as the core

Actress Helen Menken as Thi-Linh with "rickshaw driver" in scene from the stage production of *Congaï*, 1928–1929. (Photograph by Vandamm Studio. © Billy Rose Theatre Division. Courtesy of the New York Public Library for the Performing Arts.)

of its "dangerous material."[109] But also likely at play was the script's undertone of revolution—described in the memo as the story's "general disparagement of the White Man and of civilization *as opposed to the jungle and jungle emotions.*"[110]

In some correspondence, this warning was interpreted in more pointed terms that claimed that the real problem was *Congaï*'s implication that "dark blood" would defeat white blood—an ending that would stoke fears about mixed-race anticolonial revolt.[111] As a circulating film, Hervey's melodrama might expose the myth of American exceptionalism too widely, and the film's censorship suggests that one way to circumvent certain problems of empire and foreclose reflection on consequences of U.S. colonialism in Asia was to avoid representing racial discontent unaccompanied by the promise of American salvation. Consider that in 1901 Oscar P. Austin, chief of the Bureau of Statistics in the U.S. Department of Commerce and Labor, wrote, "On the whole, there is hardly a phase of the Philippine problem not already illustrated in the history of Indo-China."[112] Americans also feared an anticolonial revolt driven by mixed-race populations. A U.S. report on the colonies titled "Difficulties in Governing Mixed Races" warned, "The descendants of mixed races at some period have deposed their European fathers as the ruling class and instituted a despotic, unstable, and changing misgovernment. . . . Cuba and the Philippines are examples of the above-described desire for freedom."[113] Of course, the real danger for the United States was the obstruction of U.S. capitalist expansion. President William Howard Taft remarked that if Filipinos gained independence, "capital would be driven from the islands," and that "itself requires us [the United States] to stay here."[114] Discussions about *Congaï* as a melodrama not only concerned evolving geopolitical power but also harked to the possibility of mixed-race revolution and the threat it posed to U.S. capitalist interests.

Congaï's staging of possible revolution to come informs why theater critics and film censors negatively critiqued its practice of melodrama. Conversations about aesthetics and genre were entwined with the question of global empire: how might artists represent the emerging role of the United States in the world in good taste and *as* good taste? Hervey's audience deemed the theme of Indochina exciting and new, but the kind of telos that many wanted *Congaï* to convey onstage and on the screen—a more conclusive, decisive story of U.S. ascendance in Southeast Asia—was not Hervey's message. Reviewers wanted French Indochina to be *America's* Vietnam and to feel good about a happy ending, which the genre of melodrama, according to them, should have fulfilled. Consequently, several of Hervey's cinematic projects did not come to fruition. Among his twenty-seven original screenplays, three were set in Vietnam: *Prestige* (1932), *Indo-China* (circa 1934), and *Saigon* (1943).[115] Although Hervey was championed by influential industry figures such as Frances Marion, an Academy Award–winning screenwriter and film director, only *Prestige* was produced.[116] Hervey's most famous but relatively unacknowledged contributions in Hollywood would be as story provider or writer for a remake of *The Cheat* (1931), *Shanghai Express* (1932), and *Road to Singapore* (1940).

The complexities of Hervey's career in fiction, on Broadway, and in Hollywood compels an understanding of genre in terms of its internal formal qualities and institutional contexts. Melodramas are produced, edited, expunged, and used for different ideological ends, variously—or simultaneously—critiquing and advancing imperial hegemony. The business of theater reviews and film censorship are part and parcel of melodramas of America's Asia. Their consideration gives us a more nuanced look at melodrama as a genre of not only feelings and objects but also systems of power—part of a cultural industry that has substantially shaped the making and erasing of America's Vietnam. Hervey's works and public discussions about them show that anticolonialism in French Indochina emerged in early twentieth-century American public consciousness on the condition that it was thematized in a way that supported American exceptionalism and imperialism (rhetorically clothed as American anti-imperialism) and did not endorse decolonization. Within this ideology, America *was* decolonization, and melodrama often gave this story formal shape.[117]

The degree to which Hervey turned to other Asian spaces because of the censorship issues his melodramas of Indochina raised is a compelling question that warrants further investigation, as is the question of whether French Indochina is a subtext in other melodramas of the era. The next chapter continues an examination of how genre reveals the force and fault lines of American imperial logics by turning to Monique Truong's and Alice B. Toklas's approaches to the cookbook and their differing portrayals of Vietnamese servitude that helped sustain the famous household of Toklas and Gertrude Stein's. I develop more fully the politics of another complex context of queer alterity and historically elided Vietnamese-American encounter by moving to the metropole to bring into focus invisible conditions of labor and migration that shaped the mundane lives of Vietnamese cooks who worked for Toklas and Stein in modernism's most famous cultural capital, Paris.

WHO SERVED UP MODERNISM?

Vietnamese Labor and Anticolonialism in Modernist Paris

M onique Truong's *The Book of Salt* (2003) begins with an ending—Alice B. Toklas and Gertrude Stein are swathed in camera flashes before departing the Gare du Nord for one of Stein's lecture tours in America.[1] Binh, their Vietnamese cook and the story's narrator, remains in the background, a mere shadow behind the public presence of his famous Mesdames. As a colonized subject who describes the scene but whose words neither his employers nor the press will ever hear, Binh offers a different perspective on the legacy of Toklas and Stein, one in which the language and labor of Vietnamese servants help to generate the literary innovations that define modernist Paris.

Binh is a composite of two Vietnamese cooks, Nguyen and Trac, who worked for Toklas and Stein Paris in the 1930s and are initially characterized by Toklas in *The Alice B. Toklas Cook Book* (1954).[2] *The Book of Salt* departs from its literary predecessor by presenting Binh as the narrative voice, rather than the narrative's object, and in observing a story of modernism from a twenty-first-century Asian American lens. In Toklas's cookbook, the culinary mastery of her Vietnamese servants, Trac and Nguyen, is a pleasure to behold, the repetitions of their pidgin French an amusing novelty to hear. In Truong's reimagining, the cooks' linguistic experiments and cooking skills are reframed through Binh, the novel's protagonist, whose verbal repetitions and culinary servitude exist in uneven circuits of imperial power. *The Book of Salt* suggests that Toklas and Stein extract creative possibility from their

Vietnamese servants while eliding the colonial context that brings these laboring bodies to France.

This chapter comparatively analyzes Toklas's and Truong's texts to understand how these authors enlist the cookbook genre in different ways to animate varied aspects of food and labor under empire. Through the prism of Southeast Asia, the Vietnamese figures' linguistic characteristics are no longer an amusing pidgin but mark the unrecognized colonial labor that supports modernist cultural production in the metropole. The previous chapter examined American pluralism as central to emerging discourses of American empire, while here that pluralist ideology generates modernist innovations at the same time that it erases Euro-American hegemonies that make "diverse" encounters possible. Relatedly, extending Chapter 1's interest in the problem of intersectional representation, in this chapter Truong's reimagining of Toklas's world points to the boundaries of Toklas's and Stein's queer politics, as *The Book of Salt* refracts their white bourgeois perspective by fusing queer with decolonizing critique. At the same time, Truong's novelization of Toklas's text occludes the history of Vietnamese revolutionary networks in Paris even as it evokes this context, outlining the limited extent to which *The Book of Salt* can broach anticolonial themes in the contemporary multiethnic literary marketplace.

Coupe Grimaldi I

In its strictest definition, a cookbook comprises recipes that each provide a list of ingredients followed by clean and concise instructions for how to prepare a dish.[3] Recipe instructions typically have a universalist bent, written in an accessible way so that readers at varied skill levels can complete the recipes and produce the final product.[4] Cookbooks are also often professedly "nonliterary." Toklas's publisher, for instance, notes in prefatory remarks to the *Cook Book* that, when asked whether she would "write a book about her life and Gertrude Stein," Toklas refused, stating instead, "What I could do . . . is a cook book" (vii). As if to underscore the ostensibly nonliterary thrust of cookbooks, Toklas notes in the last line of the text, "As if a cook-book had anything to do with writing" (280).

Cookbooks are, of course, much more plastic and constitute their own genre worthy of inquiry. As in other literary forms, cookbook authors construct personas and casts of characters, involve interlocutors in the form of other cooks or readers, use figurative means to tell stories, and solicit audience participation by forging grounds for conversation and even argumentation. In Doris Witt's transformative reading of cookbooks, *Black Hunger* (1999), cookbooks are layered narratives—contested sites of gendered and racialized difference and political asymmetry.[5] Moreover, with the recent rise of food studies, as Anita Mannur, Robert Ku, and Martin Manalansan note, a critical approach to food contexts must attend to inequalities of race, class, and gender that infuse food writing more generally.[6]

Weaving together recipes with vignettes of memorable figures Toklas and Stein encountered during their life together in France, the *Cook Book* incorporates conventional and unconventional cookbook elements to present a narrative that is part cookbook, part memoir, part history, and part elegy to Stein.[7] In chapter 10, "Servants of France," Toklas sketches a history of mostly foreign women she and Stein hired, capturing their quirks and tastes through brief literary portraits enlivened by specific recipes. While the frequent turnover of servants results in a series of domestic transitions and character shifts, the returning figure of servitude constitutes the chapter's unifying thread, making possible the continuity of not only Toklas's narrative voice but also the domestic operations of 27 Rue de Fleurus.

While living in Paris, Toklas and Stein employed a number of Vietnamese cooks. Toklas favors two, Nguyen and Trac, and includes three of Nguyen's recipes, highlighting Vietnamese presence in the historical and cultural milieu of modernism. "Coupe Grimaldi" seems to be a relatively straightforward recipe, reflecting the whimsy and artistry that cookbooks insert into daily life:[8]

COUPE GRIMALDI
Fresh pineapple cut in inch squares is macerated in kirsch for 1 hour, drained, placed in a glass and covered with mandarin orange or tangerine *sorbet*, decorated with sweetened but unflavoured whipped cream and crystallised violets.

With its succinct instructions for how to make the dessert, "Coupe Grimaldi" is impersonal and to the point. But read as a layered narrative, it raises more questions than it answers, as there is a lot going on in this seemingly simple one-sentence text. Specifying only five ingredients—pineapple, kirsch, mandarin orange or tangerine sorbet, whipped cream, and violets—the recipe stipulates six different actions: to cut, macerate, drain, place, cover, and decorate. There is also much more to these ingredients and actions than meets the eye. To "cut" pineapple is more complicated than it may sound. To "decorate" with whipped cream and violets would require a skill and artisanship satisfactory to the discriminating Toklas and Stein. It is also unclear how the whipped cream is produced; Toklas merely notes in a preceding paragraph that Nguyen always ensures that "a provision of whipped cream" is available. Further, there is no mention of how Nguyen crystallizes the flowers.

The recipe also reveals other telling details only obliquely: its name and ingredients map a provocative Vietnamese-French-Italian-American cultural nexus, while its preparation hints at the intangible aspects of Nguyen's labor, such as his measured approach to culinary flourish (the violets are crystallized, the whipped cream sweetened) and moderation (the whipped cream is unflavored).

Within the field of literary food studies, the recipe has increasingly become a fertile subgenre for literary studies, as its narrative qualities and complex plays with space and time serve as rich points for cultural analysis. Kyla Wazana Tompkins points out that, through the recipe, cookbook authors construct a temporalized structure of power whereby an "eternal present tense" subjects readers to the "command" of the past. This cross-temporal, hierarchical relationship is open-ended, however, as recipes and the food networks they depend on are provisional, undergoing inter- and intragenerational change.[9]

"Coupe Grimaldi" illustrates the literariness and temporalized hierarchy of recipes that Tompkins describes. Toklas links her past to our reading present, speaking to us with the knowledge of a unique recipe and inscribing her past into our future. But the gaps in her relationships with servants make Toklas's narrative authority vulnerable. A former servant for Indochina's governor-general, Nguyen is elsewhere described as a singular cook— "inventive, deft, a wizard" (188). He prepares dishes "to perfection," displaying an innovative yet disciplined creativity that admittedly escapes Toklas's pen (190). His skill in the kitchen also seems unsurpassable, with "movements . . . more rapid than the eye could follow" (188). Nguyen outstrips Toklas's watchful gaze and exceeds her literary representation. In revealing that she is not privy to the colonized subject's culinary expertise, Toklas upends her own authorship, an inversion syntactically marked by Toklas's use of the passive past tense instead of the present tense, which diffuses the command of her voice. In a cookbook whose recipes are also authored by servants, the cookbook author's power is subverted by the heteroglossia of figures of servitude.[10] Toklas's text is striking in how much attention she gives to minor characters.[11] We might say that it is not only Toklas who speaks to us from the past but also, indirectly, Nguyen.

Yet while Toklas hints at the dish's unknowns, such as Nguyen's silent mental preparation and secret methods she cannot access, "Coupe Grimaldi" attests to a dynamic by which such ambiguities provide a glimpse of subaltern subjectivity but ultimately cede to cookbooks' principal players: the recipes. Toklas reasserts culinary authority and re-secures authorial power, evident in what Janet Malcolm describes as Toklas's overall "magisterial tone," her dominating class "hauteur."[12] Consider how Toklas narratively bookends Nguyen's three recipes. She introduces them with the disclaimer, "It was not from Nguyen that I learned, but this must have been the way he made [Fruit Sorbet]," exposing the fiction that recipes in cookbooks are voluntarily and mutually exchanged. Yet she closes out the recipes with a charge of Nguyen's possible theft: "Those were the names he gave these desserts, but are they or were they his inventions?" (189–190). Toklas suggests Nguyen's thievery of others' recipes, as if this is a logical response to a cook's withholding of culinary knowledge. But as Witt points out, there is a long, "lesser known history" of white appropriation of the recipes of cooks of color.[13] As food and its preparation open the cookbook to the labor that forms the backbone of Toklas's narrative, servant subplots also emerge, but they recede as quickly as they come into relief.

In addition to recipes' temporality—their hierarchical structure that subjects the present to the authority of the past—the unequal social status of Toklas's cooks produces a fractured temporality and culinary conscious-ness.[14] The past that Toklas attempts to recall is not fully available to her, because the trajectories of servitude that constitute "Servants of France" are partly obfuscated by her narrative voice. Her *Cook Book*'s layered narratives reveal how cookbooks transmit historical lacunae as much as they pass on instructions for how to prepare a dish. In the *Cook Book*, a central historical discrepancy concerns Toklas's elision of her relationship to French empire, which is foundational to her life in Paris but that she contains within her ideologically attenuated approach to the cookbook genre as homage to her, and Stein's, life in the 1920s imperial city.

Cookbooks as Narratives of Labor

Coeval with Toklas's *Cook Book* was an output of 1920s–1930s American nonfiction about Vietnam that Orientalized Vietnamese character and his-tory. Quite different from Harry Hervey's politicized fiction about French Indochina discussed in Chapter 1, ethnographic writings of the 1920s–1930s posited Vietnamese outdatedness and lack of political motivation.[15] Echoing John White's observation in the 1820s of Vietnamese stasis and isolation-ism, the political scientist Virginia Thompson wrote in a 1937 study that Vietnamese language had an inherent backwardness that explained stunted Vietnamese character: "Annamite language . . . is adapted to the mentality of a primitive people. The vocabulary is limited and lacking in words to express the major emotions and complex ideas." Thompson proceeds, "If one suc-ceeds in understanding a single *nhaqué*, or peasant, one understands them all," further noting that the "wealth of the colony [French Indochina] lies in its labor."[16] In 1939, the American journalist Mona Gardner described the Vietnamese as "too finely bred" and, hence, unfit for manual labor, elaborating that they were fatigued from French colonialism's interruption of a long and dynamic history of Vietnamese civilization.[17] Gardner implied that extracting colonized subjects from the paralyzing grip of European imperialism would return them to physical robustness—or, put differently, restore their ability to work.

While these two arguments seem antipodal in their differing content—one suggests that the Vietnamese are primitive and crude, while the other asserts their refinement and modern potential—both position the Vietnamese as potentially refractory subjects of colonialism. In these assessments, Vietnamese suffer from a historical and political inertia, an inability to change with time, that French colonialism has largely exacerbated. Such reified distinctions between telic modernity and primitive, premodern pasts are premised on a notion of American imperial time positioned as superior to—more modern than—that of the European world, as Chapter 1 illustrated. If a byproduct of European, class-bound modernity is the backwardness of its colonized, as Thompson and Gardner suggest, the latent argument is that a democratic America can save the Vietnamese by more effectively bringing them into the most modern modernity. As in Hervey's *Congaï*, melodramatic rescue structures American imperial interests, narrating American salvation of the colonized from the cultural, political, and economic failures of European empires.

In contrast to social-science approaches that reify Vietnamese history as static, premodern, and primitive, James Clifford argues that radical cultural production in early twentieth-century Paris offers complex, open-ended treatments of modern life, esteeming "a continuous play of the familiar and the strange," an uprooting of form from fixity that resists forcing legible wholes out of parts. Radical ethnographic practices engage the "generalized experience of dislocation" to resist capitalist homogenization.[18] One could say that, in using the cookbook genre to tell a story about a transnational cast of characters passing through 27 Rue du Fleurus, Toklas does what most coeval American nonfiction about Vietnam does not: she brings Vietnamese subjects into the American home and imbues them with personal idiosyncrasies rather than generalizing them as a faceless Asiatic horde. Read this way, the *Cook Book*'s engagement with figures of difference and migration shuns the standardizing effects of imperialist expansion.

Toklas's recognition of the social underclass recalls the relationship she and Stein had to social and cultural alterity. Although Toklas was instrumental to Stein's success as a writer, her role in the partnership has often been narrated in terms of convention and marginality—the "domestic servant" in the Toklas-Stein pair; "pussy" to her more masculine "lovey"; the half that typed, edited, and "cooked and served" Stein.[19] Stein, though now lauded for her avant-garde, anti-patriarchal practice of literary repetition—a technique she valued for its ability to undo conventional hierarchies of language—was regularly mocked by many male authors who deemed her an incomprehensible writer.[20] To them, she was "a language freak, or a joke."[21] Her writing did not resonate with the U.S. public, from whom she remained more or less cut off,[22] and a range of critics, from literary figures to doctors, pathologized her writing as symptomatic of a mental or bodily disorder.[23] Toklas and Stein were even considered too unconventional within Paris's queer communities.[24]

Toklas's incorporation of laboring bodies such as the Vietnamese servants could be read as a recognition of their overlap with her own and Stein's experiences of gendered marginalization and labor. These linkages might also inform her more admiring portrayals of Nguyen and Trac, whose multiple displacements and ties to domesticity echo aspects of Toklas's life. Moreover, Toklas's portrayal of Vietnamese culinary inventiveness illustrates radical modernism's investment in food objects as texts that constantly generate meaning rather than as exchangeable commodities with fixed values; Nguyen and Trac contribute to 27 Rue du Fleurus's aura of craft, intimacy, and slow pace, as opposed to the homogeneity, anonymity, and high velocity of a globalizing economy. And given Toklas's actual reconstitution of the home's conventional hierarchies of power, domestic work does not merely signal absolute disempowerment. It is a constitutive, generative force. Toklas reveals that Stein insists on the value of the servants' imperfections linked to their dislocation: "Gertrude Stein liked to remind me that if they did not have such faults, they would not be working for us" (173). Trac's and Nguyen's social and political alterity as colonial laborers are partly why Toklas and Stein like them in the first place.

Yet Toklas's memoirist approach to food writing does not acknowledge the colonial context that underpins her employment of Vietnamese cooks. One scene in particular from Toklas's Cook Book captures a dynamic to her text whereby food motifs illuminate and obscure the imperial context of her book. Here she reveals that what brings Vietnamese cooks into 27 Rue du Fleurus is a logistical problem that uproots Toklas from her legendary position as mistress of the house: "When it was evident that connections in the quarter were no longer able to find a servant for us, it was necessary to go to the employment office. That was indeed a humiliating experience, from which I withdrew not certain whether it was more so for me or for the applicants" (186). One sentence longer than the "Coupe Grimaldi" recipe, these lines reveal that Toklas and Stein are having trouble finding servants, perhaps because they are facing a time of strained social and financial resources. Toklas must then venture to the unfamiliar and disorienting space of the employment office, where she finds herself face-to-face with a mass of the unemployed in a context of labor exchange. In contrast to the bourgeois bohemian condescension that Malcolm associates with the *Cook Book*, here Toklas is uneasy about her encounter with the harsh conditions of labor in the metropole, exposed in her fleeting sympathy for masses of humans who are hungry for available work.

In an abrupt withdrawal from the scene of social need, Toklas immediately retreats from the space of mass unemployment—from the abstract labor that is a marker of the homogenizing force of modernity—by recalling the pleasures of Vietnamese character. Foregoing the agency's services, Toklas instead places an ad in a newspaper. Her destabilizing encounter with the commodification of working-class bodies becomes rewritten as mere prefatory matter, a fortuitous moment that heralds the arrival of the Vietnamese cooks: "It was then that we commenced our insecure, unstable, unreliable but thoroughly enjoyable experiences with the Indo-Chinese" (186). Toklas disassociates from the social difference of the employment office and quickly takes readers—and her new Vietnamese servants—to the comforts and securities of her American home set against the context of labor in imperial France.

Several other examples show how Toklas reimagines realities of Vietnamese colonized labor as proto-multicultural novelty. For instance, Trac consistently produces "delicious" dishes, compelling Toklas to relinquish her legendary dominion of the culinary sphere to designate him "master in his kitchen" (187). Despite this admiration and the inversion of the mistress-servant relationship he effects, however, Toklas includes none of his recipes. Rather, Trac's defining trait is his pidgin French, referring to most things by negation or association. "Not a cherry" substitutes for a strawberry, a lobster becomes "a small crawfish," and "a pear not a pear" stands in for a pineapple (186). When reprimanded for purchasing a cake instead of making one himself, Trac responds to Toklas with the amusing repetition, "Me know, me know" (187). These linguistic repetitions echo Stein's penchant for literary repetitions, but Toklas casts them as infantilizing and feminizing expressions of Trac's core subjectivity—his simplicity of feeling, "his childish joy," his "gayest, most innocent and infectious laughter" (187). And in one moment that stands out for its depiction of Nguyen's colonized corporeality, Toklas describes his bodily deterioration as an effect of alcoholism. Nguyen reassures her that it "should not be a worry" and appears to nurse himself back to health, continuing to "[produce] his marvellous cooking all through the summer" (188). Coupled with the scene at the employment office, this episode implies that Toklas and Stein's material resources and hospitality help to save figures such as Nguyen from the contingencies of the labor market and the dangers of their own devices. While melodrama is not the genre at work in

Toklas's memoir, the melodramatic mode threads it by suggesting that the famous couple and the comfortable domestic life they have secured provide liberalist protection from the dangers of the external world.

Trac enchants Toklas and Stein so much that the American couple subsequently hires a succession of Vietnamese cooks in an effort to replicate a range of reified Vietnamese features—their uniquely "delicate, varied, and nourishing" dishes and overall culinary sensibility (186). Stein's depiction of Vietnamese servants in letters to Carl Van Vechten exhibit a logic of exchangeability that contrasts with her conception of non-exchangeable literary repetition. Stein recounts Trac's daily enthusiasms and activities, including his visit to a circus and his excitement at receiving a photograph Van Vechten took of him. She also explains how her disappointment at the loss of Trac leads her to hire more Vietnamese to replace their "one china boy": "Now we have two, they replace each other so sweetly that we have no responsibility and hardly have to learn their names."[25] Her interchangeable cooks are like interchangeable parts, as both food and Vietnamese laboring bodies become unacknowledged commodities in these letters. For Toklas, Trac, as a servant to her, Stein, and their famous guests, becomes an object for aesthetic contemplation and consumption: "To see Trac, immaculate in white, slicing in lightning quick strokes vegetables and fruits was an appetiser" (186–187). Outpacing the speed of modern life, Trac becomes that which he makes, as Toklas relishes his gradual transformation from a colonized laborer into an arresting figure in a tableau. She and Stein draw aesthetic value from the colonized labor on which their household depends, but it is a logic that Toklas and Stein disavow. Vietnamese servitude becomes a source of proto-multicultural difference and aesthetic reverie, similar to how Vietnamese anticolonialism in *Congaï* becomes an exotic backdrop for American bourgeois theatergoers.

If Trac and Nguyen could talk to us directly, what would they say? What were some of the secrets that Toklas admits Trac and Nguyen had—cooking and otherwise? Truong, intrigued by this minor story of American literary modernism, questions cookbooks' privileging of food by foregrounding the colonial politics of language and food as observed from the fictionalized purview of a Vietnamese servant, whom she suggests not only cooked in a house of modernism but helped cook up modernism itself.

Coupe Grimaldi II

The Book of Salt shifts the narrative reference point of Toklas's story, turning the *Cook Book* from the inside out to map the racial and sexual politics of modernist Paris from the perspective of a queer Vietnamese colonized subject. A servant of France, as well as of his "American Mesdames," Binh, like Trac and Nguyen, is an architect of taste, anticipating and manipulating the gastronomic desires of his Mesdames, as well as of their famous guests. In Truong's novelization, Binh moves to France after he is fired from the governor-general's house for having an affair with the French head chef. His father, whom we discover is not Binh's biological father, subsequently banishes him from home in Saigon, ashamed of Binh's professional failure and homosexuality. Leaving behind his father's gendered and sexualized notions of family and nation, Binh departs Vietnam and heads to France, working as a galley hand at sea to cross the waters. He responds to Toklas's ad for a cook, and when the legendary doors of 27 Rue du Fleurus open, Toklas appears and proclaims, "'I am Alice B. Toklas, and who are you?'"[26] With equal confidence, Binh responds, "'I am the cook you are looking for,'" to which Toklas replies, "'Of course'" (26). So begins Binh's life as a servant to the famous American pair, bringing a psychological force and linguistic breadth to the narrative of Vietnamese servitude that Toklas briefly cites.

As several scholars have noted, *The Book of Salt*'s take on Vietnamese servitude is not an act of reclamation in which a colonized subject "speaks against" figures of Euro-American power. If anything, the novel exhibits a postmodernist skepticism about authoritative and authentic historical narratives. Y-Dang Troeung and Catherine Fung suggest that although the novel offers an internal life and social landscape vaster than Toklas's and Stein's spare representations of Nguyen and Trac, the novel is not interested in recovering the story of Vietnamese servitude to fill in historical gaps.[27] Rather than reify history as verifiable, *The Book of Salt* presupposes that history is unstable and discursive,[28] putting pressure on the premise that we can know and represent material history and exposing the power differentials that render subjects variously present and absent within it.

A number of textual specifics suggest that the novel is not an act of historical rewriting but, instead, aligns with postmodernist appraisals that we cannot know, reference, and represent the past. For instance, a key character in *The Book of Salt* is "the man on the bridge"—who turns out to be Nguyễn Ái Quốc, or the future Hồ Chí Minh—who is briefly named in the novel and is also queered. As David Eng asserts, by not naming the man on the bridge as Hồ Chí Minh and by suggesting that this historical icon *could* have been gay, Truong highlights that dominant representations of history sublimate the myriad ways in which any historical narrative can be told.[29] *The Book of Salt*'s destabilization of historical understanding also emerges in the novel's postmodernist auto-referentiality, bringing the story to a close by negating Binh himself. We discover that Binh is "not Binh"—it is not his real name; therefore, we cannot "know" Binh.[30] By working against the disciplining dynamics of history and identity, *The Book of Salt* opens up the realm of the possible rather than hewing to the knowable.

My focus is slightly different, as I interpret the novel as illustrative not of the impossibility of historical reference but, rather, of the importance and provisionality of historicized literary inquiry. If Toklas's text is a work of nonfiction threaded with historical circumventions, Truong's novel enlists fiction to re-historicize the *Cook Book*. As Crystal Parikh argues, "minor literatures" can "self-consciously enact historical recoveries of that which has proven heterogeneous to the time and space of the modern state."[31] In my reading, *The Book of Salt* does not reject narrative possibilities for historical representation but, indeed, self-consciously engages the material past—a professed attempt to offer a story of the Vietnamese cooks who "must have seen everything" in Toklas and Stein's household, as Truong puts it, yet have been rendered "a minor footnote," or mere scenery, to this iconic story.[32] The literary traces of colonized Vietnamese labor that lace Toklas's and Stein's works serve as starting points for Truong's twenty-first-century reimagining of American modernism, in turn rerouting American literary history through dynamic, contingent material histories of colonization and decolonization in Southeast Asia.[33]

As a formal springboard for *The Book of Salt*, the cookbook genre plays a significant role in Truong's act of re-creation. Consider how food and food markers take on an entirely different character in *The Book of Salt*. In a nod to Toklas's Trac, Binh draws on similar rhetorical devices to identify food objects whose names he does not know or cannot recall: "'Madame, I want to buy a pear . . . not a pear'" (35). Like Trac, Binh references food relationally, relying on linguistic equations in which playful but complex negations, reconstituted signs, and dislodged referents give deductive rise to meaning. However, *The Book of Salt* makes three important changes. First, it inserts ellipses where they do not appear in Toklas's *Cook Book*. Evocative of Theresa Hak Kyung Cha's treatment of the pained, embodied labor of speech under empire in *Dictée* (1982), inserted punctuation here marks the mental and physical expenditure of colonized Vietnamese when communicating in a foreign tongue. Second, the phrase's present tense temporalizes linguistic labor as a constant, changing process of negotiation. If cookbooks posit an ongoing connection among the past, present, and future, the relationship that *The Book of Salt* passes on is anchored in the labor of subaltern subjects that makes bourgeois epicurean worlds possible. Third, the semantic shift from Toklas's "a pineapple was a pear not a pear" to Truong's "'Madame, I want to buy a pear . . . not a pear'" punctuates the Vietnamese cook's social subjugation. The assertion of desire—"'I want'"—is desire unfulfilled, as what Binh wants is what he cannot communicate.

Binh's belabored attempt to name a pineapple enlists linguistic instability to dramatize the varied kinds of labor that the colonized carry out. The temporal lag that the ellipsis indicates records the power asymmetries that make his request so difficult—including the dominance of French language as the imperial tongue and Toklas's ability to give or deny what Binh wants and needs. Binh's effort to identify the fruit also opens up a peripheral perspective that elaborates a complex Vietnamese subjectivity. The statement "I want to buy a pear . . . not a pear" is and is not about a pineapple, encompassing an elaborate interiority that contrasts with the brevity of Binh's verbalized request:

> I wanted that afternoon to ask Miss Toklas whether the household budget would allow for the purchase of two pineapples for a dinner to which my Mesdames had invited two guests. I wanted to tell her that I would cut the first pineapple into paper-thin rounds and sauté them with shallots and slices of beef; that the sugar in the pineapple would caramelize during cooking, imparting a faint smokiness that is addictive; that the dish is a refined variation on my mother's favorite. I wanted to tell her that I would cut the second pineapple into bite-sized pieces, soak them in kirsch, make them into a drunken bed for spoonfuls of tangerine sorbet; that I would pipe unsweetened cream around the edges, a ring of ivory-colored rosettes. . . . I wanted to tell her that I would scatter on top the petals of candied violets, their sugar crystals sparkling. (34–35)

This passage extensively modifies Nguyen's "Coupe Grimaldi" recipe from Toklas's *Cook Book* by "Vietnamizing" the French version, as the main entrée described here is a familiar Vietnamese dish. Binh's recipe-memory pursues the gaps and fissures that Toklas's one-sentence recipe leaves open, amplifying the details of Nguyen's colonized mental and physical labor. What I described as Nguyen's measured approach to culinary flourish and moderation manifests here as Binh's carefully gauged planning that must take into account time, resources, and a sense of the occasion, with attention paid to the aesthetic effects of culinary craft.[34] The range of speeds and tasks—cutting, sautéing, caramelizing, soaking, piping, and scattering—show that such acts are as much a matter of form as feeding, as Binh must orchestrate complementary shapes and tastes to tie dishes together into a conceptually cohesive and aesthetically pleasing whole.

While Toklas and GertrudeStein (I use this designation hereafter to distinguish between the historical Stein and Truong's character GertrudeStein) take pleasure in consuming Vietnamese dishes, as well as the visual and linguistic novelty of their servants, Truong, by contrast, highlights the invisible labor that produces modernist proto-multicultural experience. But what is perhaps most telling about this scene is its delineation of layered narratives that emerge simultaneously. In spurring Binh's flashback to a memory of his mother, the recipe reveals the buried temporalities that compose a single narrative instant. Toklas sees Binh only with fingers "spread like two erect, partially opened fans . . . the embodiment of 'a-pear-not-a-pear'" (35). She does not recognize the accumulation of unrecognized Vietnamese histories, desires, and intentions come and gone—something the passage's past tense and stacked anaphoric incantations of "I wanted to" communicate. As such, Binh's intergenerational, transnational story is muted in the version of American modernism that *The Book of Salt* suggests we have come to know (and perhaps not know), one in which Toklas and GertrudeStein see Binh as without a history and are simply bemused at his linguistic shortcomings, delighted to consume his charade of "'a-pear-not-a-pear.'"

As this scene shows, language's variations are not simply postmodernist plays with signs that indicate the limits of narrative authenticity and authority. Formal experimentation in and of itself is an inadequate mode of critique, for here it becomes a rationale for historical and political evasion; Toklas and GertrudeStein subordinate conditions of colonial servitude under the very *cover* of linguistic turns, which is transformed from a sign of Binh's displacement into a source of American pleasure and surprise. *The Book of Salt*'s deliberate destabilization of language, narrative, and identities may exhibit a distinctly postmodernist turn—understandably suspicious of "historical" understanding, given imperialism's censoring of the archive and marginalization of subaltern histories. In Amy J. Elias's terms, post-1960s fiction is concerned with "whether history is knowable, how it is possible to speak the historical," and what relationship language has to history.[35] Yet Truong's materialist and historicist novel pointedly engages historical context and experience through worlds of objects and language, reaching toward the recoveries that, according to postmodernist ideology, inevitably eludes our grasp. We might position postmodern literature and history dialectically rather than placing them at odds, understanding both as embroiled in the same conundrum of the politics of literary-historical representation.

Breaking perceived impasses between postmodern literary and historical approaches can move us toward a generative approach to literary history. A cross-disciplinary lens coupled with a long historicist view encourages us to read food objects in *The Book of Salt* as material traces of history that assert an empirical presence and articulate how food and labor have long been tools of imperial dispossession.[36] Offering an alternative framing of the *Cook*

Book, *The Book of Salt* rereads Toklas's ostensible interest in food as, instead, ruptured by deep histories of Vietnamese-American encounter. By portraying the invisibility of subaltern culinary labor, *The Book of Salt* demonstrates how circuits of Vietnamese food and bodies in imperial France implicate American modernism in networks of global empire.

Producing Food for Thought

To situate my reading of Truong's novel as a critical lens on the cloaked colonial framework of Toklas's *Cook Book*, it is necessary to understand the means by which foodways—food's production, circulation, and consumption—were instrumental to French colonial power and thus made modernist Paris a participant in these material realities. For instance, when Toklas and Truong invoke Vietnamese preparation of pineapple, they recall one of the most prominent food commodities of colonial history. As Gary Okihiro has shown, pineapples have long played a significant role in the history of Euro-American colonialism. Imperial networks brought the pineapple from South America to the United States and to the European continent, at once mapping and disrupting reifications of a world geography divided into tropical and temperate zones. In the American context, the Dole Hawaiian Pineapple Company developed technologies, canneries, and slick advertising to market the fruit as a desirable, exotic commodity whose processed forms could easily be transported into American homes.[37] "The princess of fruits and a sign of conspicuous consumption and wealth," the pineapple's marketing erased the product's exploitation as a food object of empire—stolen, transplanted, and cultivated through plantation labor.[38]

Portrayals of pineapples as exotic, desirable fruits thread literary and historical narratives of Vietnam, where the pineapple likely first arrived via the Spanish-occupied Philippines. In 1631, Father Christoforo Borri, an Italian Jesuit priest, astronomer, and mathematician whose *An Account of Cochin China* (1633) was the first published European account of Vietnam, noted the preponderance of pineapples in the southern part of the country. The fruit was entirely new to him, and he found its look, feel, and taste thoroughly intriguing: "The fruit is like a cylinder, a span long, and so thick that it requires both hands to grasp it. The pulp within is close, and like a radish, the rind somewhat hard, scaly like a fish. When ripe, it is yellow both within and without, is par'd with a knife, and eaten raw, the taste of it an eager sweet, and as soft as a full ripe *bergamot* pear."[39] Borri's description situates the Vietnamese cooks' association of pineapples and pears in the *Cook Book* and *The Book of Salt* within a much longer history of cultural translation via simile and metaphor, highlighting how comprehending the new can occur by evoking resonant shapes of the familiar and evincing the scalar, formal possibilities of quotidian materials. Even though pineapple's introduction across parts of Vietnam resulted in illnesses and even deaths,[40] by the turn of the century the pineapple was cited as a valuable Southeast Asian export commodity in the official guide to the Colonial Exposition of 1906 in Marseille.[41]

The appearance of pineapple in *The Book of Salt*—an object over which Binh labors in physical and linguistic ways—connects to a broader colonial context in which France overhauled food practices and production in Indochina. Vietnamese fruits were often the only foods that French colonials openly acknowledged they ate regularly, and pineapples were considered a luxury item—one of the few ingredients from the colony incorporated in French colonial menus that were dominated by French dishes.[42] "Mousse ananas," for instance, lent a French banquet the cosmopolitan aura of culinary hybridity.[43] Otherwise, Vietnamese food, since the earliest days of French missionary accounts, had been deemed putrid, inefficiently or unhygienically prepared and distributed, or simply unpalatable—not up to par with standards of French national cuisine and modern techniques. French assessments of Vietnamese food regimes were based on simplistic observations of village practices, which were quite diverse but simplified in French writings as a diet of rice, fish, fish sauce, and, for fancier occasions, pork.[44]

While the notion of an identifiable national food culture was itself a turn-of-the-century construct in both Vietnam and France, French ideas of inferior Vietnamese cuisine conveniently supported French takeovers of major commodity markets and infrastructure under the banner of modernization. These included the highly lucrative salt and alcohol markets, which were targeted as reliable sources of revenue because they were so important to Vietnamese cultural and economic life. Along with opium, salt and alcohol were heavily taxed and secured as French monopolies, a consolidation that edged out long-standing Vietnamese and Chinese networks of production and distribution, eliminated multiple actors in trade, and altered the population's relationships to these products.[45] For example, the brothers Lucien and Alphonse Raphael Fontaine transformed the production of rice alcohol in Indochina through technology developed by Dr. Albert Calmette, a student of Louis Pasteur. Arguing that Vietnamese distillation techniques were "primitive," "unhygienic," and "less civilized," the Fontaine brothers promoted factory-based production and promised a cleaner, purer alcohol with lower production costs. In actuality, the industrialization of rice alcohol effectively homogenized its taste, reflecting a French perception that Vietnamese palates were so simple that they would accept the new concoction, even though historically Vietnamese rice alcohol had come in a wide range of types and grades. Reflecting France's attempt to secure economic control by constructing hierarchies of food culture, Governor-General Albert Sar-raut (1911–1914, 1917–1919) reframed French food agendas as health pro-grams, claiming that the Fontaines' distilling procedures mobilized modern science to promote the hygiene of the people.[46] Toklas's depiction of Trac's deteriorating health due to his putative alcoholism is ironic, given France's claims that its superior distillation methods delivered healthier results.

These aspects of Vietnamese food history under empire highlight how the French reconfigured foodways in Indochina to standardize taste and time. French monopolies reorganized commodity production and distribu-tion in ways that changed Vietnamese expectations about how and where a commodity was produced and how and when one could get it. French con-trol of salt, for example, meant that populations sometimes lacked access to it for years, which could be devastating, given how much salt figured into daily life not only as a flavoring but also as a preservative.[47] Observers noted that those with limited access to salt would mix rice with ashes as a substi-tute;[48] the title of Truong's novel evokes the multilayered significance of salt as an important ingredient for Vietnamese survival that French colonists exploited and monopolized for capitalist profit, with the potential effect of malnourishing the colonized. One of the biggest effects of restructured food networks in Indochina was villagers' awareness that they might have to wait indefinitely for a product that was once available to them in familiar forms, from familiar people, and through familiar processes, even in times of drought or famine. Cultural hierarchizing of food reified French supe-riority, collapsing heterogeneous food milieus and histories into a singular timeline of culinary modernization.

Toklas and GertrudeStein are not colonists. But *The Book of Salt* shows how the temporal rhythms of 27 Rue de Fleurus, while open to different tastes and cultural practices, align with the imperial standardizations out-lined above. Food objects in the novel implicate Toklas and GertrudeStein in the circulation and regulation of colonial commodities and labor; they "ate" both. We can push this reading further, as Binh's linguistic experiments are also commodities—food—for GertrudeStein. While Binh watches Gertrude-Stein consume his performed "embodiment of a-pear-not-a-pear," he notes, "I remember seeing GertrudeStein smile. Already, my Madame was amus-ing herself with my French. She was wrapping my words around her tongue, saving them for a later, more careful study of their mutations" (35). Binh's labor is shown here to extend beyond the kitchen and asks us to consider the imperial context of his pidgin French. While his linguistic shortcomings are inspirational semiotic experiments that GertrudeStein consumes, they are also symptomatic of the dismal realities of French colonial education. Only a few elite Vietnamese had formal access to it due to a combination of ill-conceived colonial educational policies, French protests against Vietnamese education, and long distances to schools.[49] By the mid-1920s, the literacy rate among Vietnamese was about 5 percent.[50] The linguistic errors that are culturally generative for GertrudeStein also index the unmentioned structural inequalities of French colonial power.

This systemic asymmetry is the foundation on which Binh's pidgin French acquires literary value on GertrudeStein's body, becoming ripe for her word play and rendering Binh her muse. His words invisibly enter American culture as they envelop GertrudeStein's tongue as tactile, raw materials for the linguistic experiments that will make their mark on literary history. Yet the words of the servant compete vigorously with the body of the mistress as the impinging possessives—"my Madame," "my French," "my words," "her tongue"—stage an unevenly leveraged linguistic sphere. GertrudeStein emerges as Binh's word wrangler, her tongue the agent that affixes, translates, and claims his words. In marshaling them toward an avant-garde poetics, she abstracts these inventive phrases from the colonized laboring body and the colonial system that displaces that body. While the ingestion of Binh's words nourishes GertrudeStein's literary practice, Binh is left empty-handed. The spontaneity of the word game is only so for GertrudeStein, since Binh must always be available to her, even after all his kitchen labor is done: "The dinner dishes have been cleared and washed, and I have been again summoned to the studio. Surely after four years of this game, I think, there cannot be anything left in this apartment that we have not named" (36). It is not only Binh's labor as a cook that defines his domestic servitude but also his un-clocked, uncompensated labor as a provider of tantalizing cultural difference for modernist form. Truong suggests that the Vietnamese servants who cooked in Toklas and GertrudeStein's kitchen also helped cook up American modernism itself.

Binh thus must be efficient in the kitchen, but he must also perform the informal, slow labor of an on-call word chef, providing food for thought, consumption, and literary invention. As the two Mesdames like to consume his dishes, so GertrudeStein consumes Binh's language experiments as commodities that feed her genius status but whose source will go unnoted in American literary history. French networks of food and labor sustain and even inspire the American duo's world of not only gastronomy but also modernist aesthetics. In turn, GertrudeStein enacts empire's temporal unevenness—what Sarah Sharma terms global capital's "power chronography"[51]—that reveals time as an instrument of power, requiring colonized subjects to sync their rhythms to masters and mistresses. As Binh puts it, "The irony of acquiring a foreign tongue is that I have amassed just enough cheap, serviceable words to fuel my desires and never, never enough lavish, imprudent ones to feed them" (18–19).

Revolutionary Cooks

Only in Binh's queer desires does a sense of personal gratification from a life of colonized servitude transpire. His relationship with Marcus Lattimore, a mixed-race American iridologist from the South who passes as white and is a guest at 27 Rue de Fleurus, suggests that in queer desire the two can cease playing the roles of charming Indochinese cook and attentive white iridologist, instead attending to their own wants: "We are on the floor, fumbling for buttons, flaps of fabric, until we are skin on skin, a prayer for the Buddha with the fire in his heart" (109). Yet Toklas and GertrudeStein's power chronography emerges even in this most private and pleasurable of spaces. Binh's affair with Lattimore occurs on Sunday—Binh's day off, his down time— but their relationship nevertheless follows a predictable "routine" whereby Binh arrives early in the day, cooks, and leaves early the next morning; each meeting lasts for fewer than twenty-four hours because Binh must get back to work (110). Moreover, it is Toklas and GertrudeStein who orchestrate the affair, hiring Binh out to Lattimore as a cook because they want to determine Lattimore's racial identity: "'Is Lattimore a Negro?'" (189). While 27 Rue de Fleurus values difference, it also manages those differences and their disruptive rhythms, as Toklas and GertrudeStein socially manage bodies to satisfy a curiosity about queer, racial others—to "be absolutely sure" (189) about them by staging a modernist "interracial party" where the stereotypical black primitive meets the abstract Asiatic laborer.[52] While America at the time is steeped in lynching and legal exclusion of Asians, in France Toklas and GertrudeStein view their project as simply a form of entertainment.

The relationship between Lattimore and Binh establishes a structure of comparative gazing in which a queer couple of color's gaze looks back on that of Toklas and GertrudeStein; questions of empire are explicitly brought to bear on the American couple's expatriatism. This act of queering Asian America, as Eng and Alice Y. Hom might put it, attends to intersections of race and sexuality in a transnational frame,[53] through which what Eng calls a "queer diaspora" surfaces—formations that do not fit nationalist, normative conventions of time, space, and social relations.[54] I would specify that a queer diasporic lens must also be joined by a decolonizing approach to understand the implications of what it means to reframe American modernism within a context of colonialism in French Indochina. While most analyses of Binh's relationship with Lattimore focus on the importance of his affective desires, what is equally significant is the structural alignment of French and American hegemonies that the relationship brings into relief. As one of America's most famous queer couples, Toklas and Stein have left a powerful legacy of cultural innovation emerging from spaces of social alterity, but their domestic comfort and aesthetic play are seen to reproduce social hierarchies. Fusing queer with decolonizing critique brings to the fore how Truong suggests that Toklas and Stein's queering of literary modernism is itself limited by their white bourgeois gaze that refuses to see how they capitalize on colonized labor.

The Book of Salt's decolonizing theme becomes explicit when we see that the only relationship that gives Binh a sense of pleasure free of a power differential is his romance with "the man on the bridge." The two meet in 1927 and immediately strike a chord, discovering that they have both served as galley hands at sea and as cooks in illustrious settings—Binh at 27 Rue de Fleurus and Nguyễn at the Drayton Court Hotel in London under the famous chef Escoffier (86). Referring to each other using the familiar term *bạn* (friend), they reveal language as a conduit that cements their bond. In *The Book of Salt*, the shared language between Binh and the man on the bridge allows them to speak to each other as if they "shared a secret," exchanging ideas about the "salt of [their] labor" and their interminable migrancy (95).

Binh and Nguyễn's shared position as Vietnamese colonized laborers culminates with their final dinner together at an American restaurant headed by a Vietnamese chef, after which Binh suggests but leaves open the possibility of their one-night affair. The depiction of the meal underscores that it is a night when neither character needs to cook or watch the clock:

> A pink mound of shrimp, all with their shells and their heads still attached. A red sash at the base of their heads, their coral shining through, identified them as females, prized and very dear when available in the markets of this city. There was also a plate on either side. *Haricots verts* sautéed with garlic and ginger were in one, and watercress wilted by a flash of heat were in the other. A compote dish towered above them all, holding white rice, steam rising at topmast. A bottle balanced out the tray, its cork announcing that it was a decisive step up from the decanted bottles of house wine. (96)

The gradations of color, textures of the dishes, and steaming mountain of rice capped by a bottle of wine depict the multisensory effects of a complete and abundant meal. That the dishes are arranged "family style" signals that the guests are mutually invited to partake of the feast and are on equal footing with the chef, who does not charge them for the food. Binh's previously unmet requests are here satiated in a feeling of corporeal plenitude: "Our feet shuffled underneath us, unaccustomed to the weight of a sated body" (99). The sense of embodiment combined with minimal references to time mark a rare occasion in which colonized laborers move through Paris according to their own rhythms, marking the imperial city with their weighted, uncommodified presence.

The emergence of the figure most readers would know as Hồ Chí Minh infuses *The Book of Salt*—and, retroactively, Toklas's *Cook Book*—with Vietnamese revolutionary presence. Some historical context helps clarify the importance of this iconic anti-imperial figure in Truong's novel, one that both evokes and obscures the revolutions with which he is identified. Hồ Chí Minh arrived in Marseille as Nguyễn Tất Thanh in 1911 after working as a kitchen boy on the ship *Latouche Treville*.[55] He had stopped over in New York City in 1912 and settled in England between 1913 and 1914.[56] In 1919, Nguyễn Tất Thanh presented a petition titled "The Claims of the People of Annam" to world leaders in Paris after World War I. The petition drew from the language of President Woodrow Wilson who, as discussed in Chapter 1, had positioned himself as a champion of self-determination for the colonized world. The young Nguyễn Tất Thanh, who was the son of a mandarin, requested a meeting with Wilson, but the meeting never occurred. Nguyễn Tất Thanh joined the French Communist Party shortly thereafter.[57]

Nguyễn Tất Thanh finally returned to France in 1919 as Nguyễn Ái Quốc.[58] He traveled throughout Russia, China, Belgium, and France as an active member of the Comintern and French Communist Party and an outspoken proponent of decolonization, although he would continue to solicit U.S. support.[59] In *The Book of Salt*, the character Nguyễn Ái Quốc discloses his residence as Rue des Gobelins (93), referencing the well-known address of 6 Villa des Gobelins—a counterpoint to 27 Rue de Fleurus and the address where Nguyễn Ái Quốc and other Vietnamese agitators lived in Paris. As discussed in the previous chapter, the French Indochina of the 1920s that Toklas's Nguyen and Trac—and Truong's Binh and his dinner companion, the future Hồ Chí Minh—would have known was a time of boycotts, attempted assassinations of French officials, protests against Franco-Vietnamese collaboration, and numerous anti-imperial movements. Those who lived at 6 Villa des Gobelins were considered the most dangerous Vietnamese at the time in the French Sûreté's 250 files.[60]

Nguyễn Ái Quốc and his housemates were part of a broader population of about 3,500 Vietnamese laborers and students living in France. Some of them, in turn, were among the 48,995 Indochinese, out of 222,793 documented colonized workers, who went to France during World War I.[61] Many of them were members of Vietnamese professional organizations, and several of the organizations centered on the food industry—for instance, the

Association des Cuisiniers, founded in 1922, and Travailleurs Manuels, founded in 1923. These groups carved out a social, financial, and political lifeline for Vietnamese in France, and their members typically met in cafés and restaurants to catch up on the latest gossip and news, discuss financial and political concerns or the latest deals in drug trafficking, or just share opium and cocaine. These groups were by no means socially or politically homogeneous. For instance, at a meeting of the Association des Cuisiniers held in 1927 at a Parisian café, a drama of personal jabs, accusations of embezzlement, and fights between French girlfriends followed the association's decision to reject a proposal to merge with a student group. Such divisions bring into relief the personal and organizational rifts that ran within and across Vietnamese expatriate communities, particularly between laborers and students/intellectuals.[62] Nevertheless, by the early 1930s French police reports were expressing general concern over Vietnamese activities taking place in Vietnamese food milieus, noting drug use, miscegenation, and political activity: "They carry on an active revolutionary propaganda, in close collaboration with European and black militants, going on board all the ships coming in to port and inciting their compatriots to revolt."[63] These food contexts contributed to the emergence in French popular consciousness of the Vietnamese student as the quintessential figure of revolution.[64]

Any of Toklas and Stein's cooks could have been a revolutionary. Thus, in Truong's novel Toklas and GertrudeStein's expatriate lives appear somewhat provincial compared to the anticolonial activities that may have trafficked in and around their famous home. Whereas Toklas carefully watches over 27 Rue de Fleurus as "a guardian of their temple" (30–31), the man on the bridge is a curious "philosopher" (87) and a "scholar-prince" (100). GertrudeStein's removal from America allows her to "[grow] more intimate with the language of her birth," lifting American English from its "everyday" usages to a language "reserved for genius and creation" (30). Yet she possesses only a "common" knowledge of French, while Nguyễn Ái Quốc speaks and writes French fluently and with agility, developing a reputation as an elegant, multilingual letter writer who offers his services to other Vietnamese by appointment (33). We know from our twenty-first-century hindsight that this character is a man on the move, his travels mapping a complex geography of adaptive Vietnamese anticolonialism. The Book of Salt throws into relief the limits of Toklas and GertrudeStein's queer, bourgeois bohemian American modernism, inflecting their expatriate lives with a decolonizing, even revolutionary, gaze.

The bridge figure's cultural and political worldliness connects Binh to a broader Vietnamese political community. But similar to Congai's episodic references to and ultimate excision of collective Vietnamese anticolonial agitation, Nguyễn Ái Quốc simply disappears in The Book of Salt. To contemporary audiences, he is synonymous with Vietnamese revolution, but that thread is not pursued. After the rendezvous, the man on the bridge proceeds to the train station, leaving Binh to long for him thereafter: "I have looked for him on the avenues, on the quays, on the park benches of this city. I have even gone back to the restaurant" (243). The telos of political change that Nguyễn Ái Quốc promises remains unrealized, as evidenced by Binh's indefinitely benighted wandering.[65] By the end of *The Book of Salt*, Binh's identity has unraveled in a pattern of repetition and negation that resembles his speech. To repeat a point alluded to earlier, we discover that Binh is not Binh—this is not his real name. He continues to occupy an alternative temporal plane that, Truong suggests, Toklas's *Cook Book* suppresses: "Time that refuses to be translated into a tangible thing, time without a number or an ordinal assigned to it, is often said to be 'lost.' In a city that always looks better in a memory, time lost can make the night seem eternal and full of stars" (99).

The Missing Picture: Cooking and Empire in Mid-century America

The tempering of Vietnamese revolution in Toklas's and Truong's texts becomes especially notable given that the *Cook Book* was published in 1954, the year the Việt Minh defeated the French at Điện Biên Phủ under General Võ Nguyên Giáp, inspiring revolutionary movements across the colonized world. During this time, the United States funded 85–90 percent of France's effort to maintain control of Indochina (discussed further in Chapter 3). While Toklas undoubtedly wrote her manuscript before this event, Vietnamese liberation movements leading up to it were of global significance. For instance, prior to North Vietnam's victory at Điện Biên Phủ, Hồ Chí Minh declared Vietnam's independence in 1945 during a brief power vacuum in Indochina after World War II. His speech, the "Declaration of Independence of the Democratic Republic of Vietnam," was modeled after America's 1776 version. Neither the 1945 nor the 1954 watershed moment is compatible with the nostalgia of Toklas's *Cook Book*.

It is not that Toklas willfully neglects the fact of empire in her writing. At the beginning of her "Beautiful Soup" chapter in the *Cook Book*, she prefaces four recipes for gazpacho with a comment on imperial gastronomy. Realizing that the French view gazpacho as a poor or tasteless person's dish—"only eaten in Spain by peasants and Americans"—Toklas emphasizes that food is about power and entwined with empire.[66] She elaborates, "It was as a result of eating *gazpacho* in Spain lately that I came to the conclusion that recipes through conquests and occupations have travelled far" (49). Toklas also delves into the challenges of food conservation during the Nazi occupation in France but suggests that wartime rations did not affect her and Stein too adversely. Without mentioning their collaboration with Vichy regime figures who likely helped them survive during this period, as Malcolm has argued, Toklas states, "We were really very well off" (203).[67] For the most part, imperial battles are part of the past in the Cook Book. A narrative about a life of food already lived, Toklas specifies that the book's points of focus are acts of wistful remembrance during a time of illness—"written as an escape from the narrow diet and monotony of illness [and also from] nostalgia for old days and old ways."[68]

However, the importance of 1954 as the year of the Cook Book's publication opens up the mid-century as a significant period not only of Vietnamese decolonization but also of Americans' own changing foodways as means for increasing hegemony. The post–World War II moment was a time of contradictory food messages in the United States in a post-food rationing era. By the end of the war, America was "the world's food superpower,'" committed to high food production and export under the logic of commodification and consumption.[69] Government officials encouraged restraint and conservation while advancing agribusiness and the industrialization and transnationalization of food, redefining food in terms of profit and not as a human necessity that should be available to everyone in healthy forms.[70] By the time of the Cook Book's publication, Americans consumed "more food than any other country per capita,"[71] even if the end of the war made the "potentially endless state of hunger" a reality for many in the world.[72] And as Mark Padoongpatt shows, American food hegemony was substantially exercised through the Pacific frontier, becoming a site for rhetoric of culinary "diversification."[73] Mid-century America built on existing notions of U.S. pluralism by promoting the literal ingestion of difference—at the same time that U.S. mass-produced and industrialized food homogenized this "difference"—to support American global expansion.

That Toklas and Stein never seem to go hungry accords more with a mid-century era of American gastronomic plenitude and intersects with this critical moment of American food nationalism. The first pages of the Cook Book differentiate French from American culinary attitudes, as Toklas writes that the French maintain a regrettably "strict conservative attitude" that does not allow for "the slightest deviation in a seasoning or the suppression of a single ingredient" (3). By contrast, Americans have a culinary "ingenuity" that recognizes the benefits of gastronomic flexibility, enabling "new directions and . . . a fresh and absorbing interest in everything pertaining to the kitchen" (4). Suggestive of America's postwar proto-multicultural hegemony, she also applauds American food technology—its "time- and labour-saving devices"—that encourage "imaginative" and "exotic" culinary inventions (4). Her attention to the modernity and creativity of Vietnamese servants would seem to match America's supposed openness to new foods. But to get that point across, Toklas detaches from the colonial realities and deprivations that underpin her fascination with Vietnamese food makers and admiration for America's mid-century food power. She omits much of what might be disruptive, "distasteful," or outside the *Cook Book*'s "diet" of proto-multicultural pleasure. Through a food-focused lens, Toklas polarizes European and American culinary practices and does not acknowledge their overlapping nationalist and imperialist motives, minimizing the fact of empire as an ongoing, ever changing present.

Yet *The Book of Salt* also mutes the topic of Vietnamese decolonization, compelling us to consider what appetite postmodern audiences have for this complicated and disruptive history. In Truong's novel, the man on the bridge leaves a lasting impression on Binh as "a traveler whose heart has wisely never left home"—the expatriate who gets it right by maintaining a strong sense of Vietnamese identity across borders (247). His purposeful internationalism supplements and more overtly politicizes Binh's diffuse, aimless wandering. A master trickster who had many aliases throughout his life, Nguyễn Ái Quốc is in many ways an appropriate figure for writing outside dominant cultural frames. However, there is a tinge of nostalgia and romanticization in Binh's reading of the bridge character that seems a little too neat, even uncharacteristic for a self-reflexive Binh, whose own banishment evidences sexualized and gendered notions of Vietnamese national piety. Their affair productively frustrates American melodramatic romances that historically depoliticize liaisons with Asia, but Nguyễn Ái Quốc is in many ways too exemplary a figure of resistance—an obvious iconic historical touchstone, a quintessential figure of revolution. As Hồ Chí Minh, Nguyễn Ái Quốc would be politically marginalized and silenced by the Communist Party by the start of the U.S.-Vietnamese war, yet he is no less the personification of emotional and political agency in *The Book of Salt*. The novel's shift away from his revolutionary legacy toward a more speculative, prerevolution depiction suggests Truong's choice to show a "Vietnam" that is relatively free of explicit political conflict. As she notes in an interview, "There are no military conflicts in my novel, there are no soldiers, there are no weapons. I suppose it is no coincidence that the first long-distance flight of my imagination as a writer would take me to a time in history when Vietnam was more or less at peace."[74]

Truong's presentation of 1920s–1930s Vietnam as a time of relative peace suggests an awareness of audience that must be situated within the dynamics of the literary market. As Viet Thanh Nguyen argues, ethnic literature "is *collaborative* in its relationship to American culture." For Nguyen, Vietnamese American writing in particular "can raise the troublesome past of war and even the difficult present of racial inequality, so long as it also promises or hopes for reconciliation and refuge."[75] We might complement Nguyen's point with John Carlos Rowe's assertion that the American novel, particularly after the Vietnam War, has managed to evade trenchantly critiquing U.S. imperialism in Vietnam, which bolsters the American novel form's already nationalist, middle-class, English-language limitations.[76] In stopping short of thematizing Vietnamese attempts to change colonial conditions systematically—in broaching but bracketing this decolonizing history—the novel might be said to perform the elisions and reconciliations that Nguyen and Rowe describe. If, as the previous chapter shows, anti-imperialism has been a recurring theme in American literature, it is mainly so as a rhetoric that veils U.S. hegemonic practices. Decolonization—processes of imagining and practicing structural dismantling of (neo)imperial systems in ways that are complicated, comprehensive, and sometimes contradictory—tends to be unapproachable subject matter.

However, read as a materialist, historicist Asian American novel, *The Book of Salt* broadens domestic frames in ways that transform Southeast Asian American cultural studies in particular. *The Book of Salt* subverts the Americanist loyalty that the literary industry expects by delineating extended colonized disaffection and grievance across the long twentieth century and demonstrating how fiction can retroactively reconstitute a familiar account of a famous American cultural milieu. Consequently, Truong's novel stresses "transnational ties or repressed histories of dispossession," to borrow Susan Koshy's description of Asian American fiction that is invested in contexts of colonialism.[77] *The Book of Salt* also transfigures American literary history by drawing from but revising Toklas to explore the under-studied topic of Vietnamese presence in an epicenter of literary modernism: Paris's imperial circulations of food and labor that the *Cook Book*'s narrower points of focus obscure. In not resurrecting details of Vietnamese resistance, whether from the early twentieth century or the mid-century, *The Book of Salt* displays some political ambivalence, and this is perhaps what marks its contemporaneity most strongly—its suggestion that the language and vision of past Vietnamese revolutions do not correspond to the intersectional challenges of our neoliberal, neo-imperial present. The narrative that Harry Hervey foregrounds as a hidden history in the 1920s–1930s, as discussed in Chapter 1—the incomplete story of social and political change in French Indochina—occupies center stage in Truong's 2003 novel yet is still unresolved. Thus, Vietnamese American literature bears a relationship to a long history of Vietnamese decolonization and America's role in that story, but what that relationship is remains unclear. (Furthermore, as the next chapter shows,

Vietnamese decolonization itself is a fraught topic.) *The Book of Salt*'s approach is to focus on small-scale negotiations of life under empire, marking how revolutions are not simply terminal and "won." The modulated way in which decolonization emerges in *The Book of Salt* arguably marks the ideological limit of this particular Asian American novel's depiction of that topic within the uneven dynamics of the literary marketplace. Nevertheless, the novel shatters a number of interpretive paradigms, including understandings of American modernism that disconnect from French colonialism in Southeast Asia, and Vietnamese American literary studies models that occlude a long twentieth-century trajectory.

In light of this volume's similar spirit of opening the literary and historical archive of Vietnamese-American encounters, I conclude the chapter with a reading of *The Book of Salt*'s ambiguous ending. Toklas and GertrudeStein present Binh with an envelope on a silver tray. It is the only correspondence Binh has received during his five-year stint as their live-in cook, and this is the first and only time that Binh will be served by his Mesdames at 27 Rue de Fleurus. As Toklas and GertrudeStein prepare to head off to America, Binh imagines that the envelope contains his letter of dismissal: "'Marvelous cook but clumsy when inebriated and has on occasion been known to pilfer'" (226–227). Envisioning his American mistresses paying homage to his cooking skills, Binh also imagines them painting a picture of a more debauched Binh—a wonderful cook, but also an occasional drunk, a self-proclaimed thief. Yet Toklas and GertrudeStein are more amused that Binh has received a letter at all than concerned with its urgent contents, dispatched from Vietnam. The Vietnamese vices and linguistic forms on which Toklas and GertrudeStein's proto-multicultural proclivities capitalize will make their way into American literature, but Binh's own future, like that of his fellow laborers, remains uncertain and in the shadows. Mesdames and Vietnamese servant, having "served" American modernism, are thus poised to part ways, raising the question of what conditions will allow the Vietnamese subject reentry not only into the twentieth-century American house but also into American literary history. In the next chapter, I show that a condition for this is war, as the United States definitively supplants France as the "modern" colonial power, and the Vietnamese body reemerges as a body in pieces.

3

VIETNAM WAR EXCEPTIONALISM

Dismembering and
Disremembering Vietnam

Michael Herr spent almost ten years working on *Dispatches* (1977), even though most of it had already been written.[1] Between 1967 and 1968, Herr covered the Vietnam War from Saigon for *Esquire*, the magazine that "had attitude before attitude came into vogue."[2] The idea of a weekly column was scrapped, however. Herr believed that the imposed deadlines and formal conventions of traditional war reporting could not do justice to his experience in Vietnam. Later refusing affinities with the American press, Herr professed that he "was never a part of them" and that, while journalism could gather the facts, it "never found a way to report meaningfully about death, which of course was really what it was all about."[3]

The articles that Herr wrote for *Esquire, New American Review,* and *Rolling Stone* eventually became the chapters of *Dispatches* and set the tone for American cultural discourses of the Vietnam War specifically and of Vietnam more generally.[4] His direct critique of American political figures and foreign policy; his eclectic use of language that ranges from poetic meditations on war to profane denouncements of it; and the diverse voices that compose his text catapulted Herr to instant fame. In popularizing an alternative mode for war representation—one that mixed the language of "cool," rock-and-roll, war movies, the military-industrial complex, and soldiers' slang on the ground—Herr became a central architect of America's Vietnam War discourse, identified as a new and exciting practitioner of New Journalism who could tell it like it was. The American public anxiously awaited the publication of Herr's articles in book form, but in the years that followed his time in Vietnam, Herr experienced a series of debilitating setbacks. He was broke, smoked marijuana regularly, and suffered from trauma and writer's block before analysis helped him break through his inability to write. When *Dispatches* was finally published in 1977, it was immediately placed on several "best" lists, a standing that has been cemented in popular and academic discourses over time.[5] His screenwriting work for *Apocalypse Now* (1979) and *Full Metal Jacket* (1987) bolstered his cultural stature, which will likely extend beyond his death in 2016.

Since its publication, many critics have agreed that *Dispatches* is not only a quintessential Vietnam War text but also an exemplary postmodern one. Others, including Susan Jeffords, have taken *Dispatches* to task for the re-masculinization it tries to establish after devastating military loss.[6] Yet very little scholarship exists on the text's intersections of form, history, and race, despite its almost coeval publication with Edward Said's *Orientalism* (1978). This chapter revisits some of the formal qualities for which *Dispatches* is famous—most notably, its linguistic and syntactic fragmentations—to argue that these literary innovations depend on haunting depictions of the Vietnamese body in pieces, making ghostly renderings of Vietnamese dismemberment inherent to Herr's experiential "truth." Through its incorporation of journalism, gothicism, and memoir, *Dispatches* is actually a generically mixed text, exhibiting a hybridity of form that relates Herr's attempt to cross the spectrum of objective and subjective representation to convey what he posits is the conflict's singularity. But even with a multitude of genres, Herr repeatedly asserts the unrepresentability of the war, suggestive of how *Dispatches* exceptionalizes, and thereby de-historicizes "Vietnam."

Drawing from a range of Vietnamese perspectives on twentieth-century conflicts in Vietnam, including writings by Trần Đức Thảo, a Vietnamese philosopher and student of Maurice Merleau-Ponty, and the contemporary Vietnamese American poet Ocean Vuong, I analyze *Dispatches* comparatively to diffuse Herr's sensationalized portrayal of violated Vietnamese bodies and deconstruct prevailing interpretations of the text as a work of New Journalism that is faithful to the experience of postmodern war. By refracting *Dispatches* cross-culturally and cross-temporally, we can de-exceptionalize Herr's Vietnam to understand Vietnam War violence from American and Vietnamese perspectives. By analyzing the text cross-generically, we can attend to its non-journalistic forms to observe Herr's reproduction of imperial tropes and his claim to subjective truth that cannot be conflated with historical veracity; genre emerges in this chapter not only as a practice of writing but also an interpretive frame that shapes how we read "Vietnam." Herr's use of fragments of Vietnamese flesh as the impetus for literary innovation works to dismember and disremember Vietnam, indicating authorial angst about how to depict America's role in ongoing histories of empire in Southeast Asia. Restoring historicity and formal variation to Vietnam War literature places *Dispatches* within a longer cultural tradition and resituates the conflict as part of an unfinished process of decolonization.

Rendering the War Inscrutable

"We had this gook and we was gonna skin him" (a grunt told me), "I mean he was already dead and everything, and the lieutenant comes over and says, 'Hey asshole, there's a reporter in the TOC [tactical operations center], you want him to come out and see that? I mean, use your fucking heads, there's a time and place for everything.'" (67)

In this scene from the first section of *Dispatches*, "Breathing In," Herr describes a conversation concerning the timeliness of "skinning" a Vietnamese in plain view of a reporter. The concern is not the ethics of the killing, a matter rendered null and void anyway because the "gook," whose political affiliation is unclear, is "already dead." The issue is, rather, who will bear witness to the scene should it be documented and circulate widely before the American public. What matters for the lieutenant is that the marines' conduct not reveal what Herr has in fact just exposed: the banality of killing that has become characteristic of the Vietnam War.

In many ways, this scene reveals the central conundrum of *Dispatches*: how to represent a war that does not make sense to Herr on any level and when inherited modes of narrating war and history fail. In South Vietnam, Herr takes part in almost every activity possible—smoking pot with soldiers, improvising as medic, viewing Vietnam from the air, participating in battle on the ground. Yet his experiential range and spatial coverage fail to produce a conclusive understanding of the war and his relationship to it. As a military operation, the war is, for Herr, fueled by a series of "objectiveless" missions shrouded in incomprehensible code names (156); as an exercise in American foreign policy, the war reveals only that "we never announced any policy at all" (153); as a psychic experience, the war guarantees only intense psychological duress—"Going crazy was built into the tour" (59); and as literary labor, Herr can classify his text only by identifying what it is not: "My book is in no way a journalistic book. . . . It's not a political, historical or moral take on Vietnam."[7] Herr arrives in South Vietnam believing that he can penetrate the U.S. war machine to obtain a more authentic understanding of the conflict in a way that other reporters, who ask only "bullshit questions," cannot (37). Yet while he "went to cover the war," he finds that "the war covered [him]" instead (20). Rather than demystifying his object of knowledge, Herr finds himself impotent before it and, as a result, renders the war *inscrutable*.

Herr's professed failure at journalistic representation is also what has constituted *Dispatches'* success. It is precisely his self-reflexive admission of authorial futility that scholars, reviewers, and the public have repeatedly noted in their high praise for *Dispatches*—a text widely viewed as an *accurate* depiction of the social, political, and military confusions that are now synonymous with the Vietnam War. Herr continues to be cited as a defining figure of mid-century New Journalism, praised for his deep skepticism about what journalistic content and form can and cannot do. If, according to Tom Wolfe, New Journalism incorporates scene-by-scene description as opposed to narration, realistic dialogue, a distinct perspective anchored in writers' immersion in their subject matter, and "status life" (realistic details that convey a strong sense of character and context),[8] for most critics, Herr hits and even transcends all of these points.[9] As John Le Carré writes in his endorsement, found on the cover of many editions of *Dispatches*, for many it is "the best book . . . on men and war in our time."

Fredric Jameson perhaps most famously conceptualizes the new formal turn that *Dispatches* takes. In *Postmodernism, or, The Cultural Logic of Late Capitalism* (1991), Jameson references Herr early on as an example of the challenges of literary representation in the postmodern era when no generic precedent for portraying a historical context exists:

> The extraordinary linguistic innovations of this work may still be considered postmodern, in the eclectic way in which its language impersonally fuses a whole range of contemporary collective idiolects, most notably rock language and black language: but the fusion is dictated by problems of content. This terrible first postmodern war cannot be told in any of the traditional paradigms of the war novel or movie—indeed, that breakdown of all previous narrative paradigms is, along with the breakdown of any shared language through which a veteran might convey such experience, among the principle subjects of the book and may be said to open up the place of a whole new reflexivity.[10]

Jameson's oft-quoted remarks suggest that *Dispatches* both describes and enacts a formal and thematic breakdown, as the war's peculiarities are not assimilable to extant literary forms. However, whereas other scholars view Herr as breaking with conventional journalistic standards of truth and objectivity, Jameson's presuppositions are different. He submits that Herr's antecedents are not journalism or even nonfiction but, rather, the fictional war novel and war movie.

That fiction may be the only appropriate basis from which to write a Vietnam War narrative indicates the scope of the conflict's perceived opacity and the level of imagination required to represent it. America's high-tech military operation in Southeast Asia is so total—encompassing all geographies on, above, and below the ground—that one cannot comprehend its scale or workings, let alone authentically depict them. As the U.S. state stubbornly pursues its abstract, universalizing project of modernization regardless of local specificities, traditional journalism's commitment to the "facts" becomes fundamentally compromised. Hence, Herr's text marks a new kind of narrative in American literary history, one oriented around an "in motion" modality whereby portrayals of movements and events as they occur in the present tense, without causal connection, become the stuff of news.[11] As Herr writes, "Some of us moved around the war like crazy people until we couldn't see which way the run was even taking us anymore, only the war all over its surface" (8).

Yet proposing American war novels and films as the formal premises for Herr's nonfictional war story risks dematerializing Vietnamese contexts and reproducing American war culture's mythologizing power. I suggest that gothicism and memoir, under-studied dimensions of *Dispatches*, also frame Herr's text to create the kind of legitimacy that journalism and fiction cannot deliver. Gothicism gives formal shape to what eludes Herr's cognitive and representational grasp. Memoir, as a genre that is episodic, self-reflexively reconstructive, and rooted in subjective "truth," releases Herr from being bound to verifiable facts while still imbuing his text with the aura of authenticity. Read as a generically complex work, *Dispatches* embodies a formal dilemma resulting from the contradiction between the war's supposed inscrutability—its exceptionality—and the latent recognition that the conflict can and must be understood within a long history of imperial wars and violent, racialized exterminations.

Herr's Exceptional Vietnam

In *Dispatches*, the crises of representation Herr continually faces are aesthetically generative. Formal failure becomes formal innovation and, more important, creates possibilities for a new kind of political critique, a new kind of literary language. *Dispatches'* literary inventiveness born of experiential aporia returns us to the scene of skinning "the gook," whose disorienting effects hinge on the work that the Vietnamese body part performs. In relating the casualness with which the marine expresses an excessive desire to disassemble an already dead Vietnamese body, the image of Vietnamese skin communicates the dark depths and murderous logic of late twentieth-century

American warfare. On another level, Herr suggests that the moral quandary evident in this scene has a foundational racial component. Given the racialized etymology of "gook" in U.S. culture—skinning as a racist construction tied to Native Americans in the American ideology of settler colonialism, and "gook" as a racist epithet referring to Asians beginning with the Philippine-American War (1899–1902)—the marine's comments articulate a disturbing wish to enact ongoing Orientalist violence on the Asian body. While this historical racial context is admitted, Herr supplants it with the fraternal, cross-rank vernacular that is the real focus of the scene.

The skinning episode's dialogic framing highlights the fact that Herr never sees the Vietnamese body he conjures. While bodies like it could be stumbled upon at any moment—"We killed so many gooks it wasn't even funny'" (64)—the Vietnamese figure's presence is more haunting than material, lying on the threshold of Herr's "I"/eye. The seeming immediacy of but actual remoteness from the site of racial harm, however, is largely what defines Herr's signature narrative style. I quote from the scene again to draw attention to Herr's simulacral representation of Vietnamese bodily injury, an echo chamber of sorts that at once emphasizes the obscenity of postmodern death in war while forging perspectival distance from it, even though he is inside the war zone: "'We had this gook and we was gonna skin him' (a grunt told me), 'I mean he was already dead and everything, and the lieutenant comes over and says, 'Hey asshole, there's a reporter in the TOC, you want him to come out and see that?'"

The stacked quotation marks reveal that the act of killing being described has been narratively displaced multiple times, for Herr is telling us a story that a marine told him about a lieutenant trying to censor the marine's narration of a killing that has already occurred. In Herr's sphere of war, the trope of the Vietnamese body in pieces (signified here by Vietnamese skin) generates a narrative style that is equally fragmented and partial. What results is not only disconnection from the original moment of brutal Vietnamese-American encounter but also confusion over who is witnessing what and who is accountable for what and to whom. In subordinating the specific time-space of atrocity to the narrative performances of American confusion and polyvocality, Herr detaches the episode from context and suggests its unrepresentability. He makes the retold tale the historical event worth recounting, not the actual violence committed against the Vietnamese figure.

Herr's Vietnam emerges as a de-historicized corpus in pieces whose fragments of Vietnamese flesh become essential to depicting the altered American experiences of killing and dying that attend technologized destruction. Repeated portrayals of dismembered Vietnamese provide reason for assembling a variety of U.S. voices and vernaculars to evidence the cognitive and linguistic disorientations concomitant with this war and that require a new cultural model for war representation that can effectively signal the breakdown of a "shared language" for perceiving and interpreting military conflict.[12] The disembodied trope of the Vietnamese body in pieces substantially organizes the formal fragmentation of a work that disclaims historical logic, while the Vietnamese subject who is capable of a range of sensations, affects, and discernible politics is excised in Herr's canonical Vietnam War text.

The ghostly Vietnamese body part as indicative of a crisis point in the narration of American power compels attention to the imperial gothic as a shaping aesthetic in *Dispatches*. Peter Brantlinger defines this subgenre as a literary project through which the imperial imagination confronts its dystopic effects while trying to maintain separation from the Other to preserve the imperial self.[13] Gothic forms manage the threat of "racial difference" through portrayals of "species difference" and help to work through the knowledge of imperial vulnerability,[14] for the empire is not simply "over there" but "is apt to come home" and rupture the nation.[15] That is, despite the empire-colony boundaries enabled by gothicizing the Other, the traffic of products, economies, and human connections that accompany imperial relations makes gothicism's boundaries porous, jolting "a complacent nation out of a false sense of security."[16]

In *Dispatches*, gothicized Vietnamese body parts allow Herr to carve difference between the American self and Vietnamese Other by giving narrative space to Vietnamese on the condition that their form is subhuman and mutilated and, in Herr's version of the imperial gothic, that actual contact with them is foreclosed. To do otherwise would attribute potential agency and political desire to Vietnamese, and American imperial rhetoric, as explained in Chapter 1, hinges on the idea of rescuing passive victims around the world from colonial and authoritarian rule. The ghostly shapes of Herr's Vietnamese figures forestall an interactive dynamic with their subjecthood and suspend a mutually animating understanding of the war. Herr's gothic poetics of fragmentation ably undermine the U.S. nation-state's meta-narratives that would suppress the conflict's constant and extreme states of duress but, in turn, construct "Vietnam" as a category that defies historicized depiction.[17]

As a key sign of postmodern warfare's mystique, the Vietnamese body in pieces evoked in an imperial gothic register acts synecdochically, the problems of perception and representation it produces expandable to the effect of "Vietnam" as a whole. That the unrepresentability and, consequently, indecipherability associated with Vietnamese existence applies to Vietnam in general is perhaps most evident in the famous opening scene in *Dispatches* concerning an old French map that hangs in Herr's apartment in Saigon.

Herr writes, "That map was a marvel, especially now that it wasn't real any-more. . . . It was late '67 now, even the most detailed maps didn't reveal much anymore; reading them was like trying to read the faces of the Vietnamese, and that was like trying to read the wind" (3). Combined with the repeated sketches of Vietnamese bodies' silence, biological death, and disfigurement, the naturalized illegibility attributed to the Vietnamese and to Vietnam seem to coerce decontextualization. Moreover, as the conflict stretches in time to the point of becoming old news ("We also knew that for years now there had been no country here but the war" [3]), reality and myth bleed into one another more explicitly ("You couldn't avoid the ways in which things got mixed, the war itself with those parts of the war that were just like the movies, just like *The Quiet American* or *Catch-22*" [210]).[18] Herr excuses his own perpetuation of cultural myth as history by underscoring the seemingly unavoidable problem of postmodernity's warping of reality into spectacle— "This movie is a thing of mine, and I'd done it" (206). Facilitating Herr's delineation of the narrative conundrums, psychological costs, and intracta-bility of contemporary military destruction, battered, gothicized Vietnam-ese in *Dispatches* carry an ideological payoff: they promote a Vietnam War exceptionalism.

While narrative moments such as the skinning episode exhibit a recursive drive to retell stories of violated Vietnamese during the conflict, a scene that follows anticipates how imperial gothic strategies oriented toward Vietnam-ese figures of division will continue to play a crucial role in the portrayal of Vietnam's exceptionality in American memory. Describing the images found in American soldiers' photo albums, Herr writes, the "obligatory Zippo-light-er shot . . . the severed-head shot . . . or a lot of heads, arranged in a row, with a burning cigarette in each of the mouths . . . a picture of a Marine holding an ear or maybe two ears or, as in the case of a guy I knew near Pleiku, a whole necklace made of ears, 'love beads'" (198–199). In Herr's inventory of Vietnam War memory making, Vietnamese body parts function as souvenirs, serving a commemorative purpose comparable to that of a Zippo lighter. The image of severed Vietnamese heads lined up in a queue conveys the routinized ex-hibition of fragmented racial corporeality as wartime spoils. In Chapters 1 and 2, material objects contribute to the racialization of Asian characters; here, Vietnamese have *become* sartorial objects. Resignified as decoration, their domestication in photo album form illustrates what John Carlos Rowe calls a neo-Orientalism that began with the Vietnam War—a new kind of "self-conscious importation" of foreignness into the American imagination, whereby key images, tropes, and terms substitute for "genuine historical dis-cussion" and become readily transferable from one "Orient" to another.[19] By morphing into ornamental attachments, dead Vietnamese evince how U.S.

soldiers—and Herr—renarrate intimate encounters with Vietnamese subjects by objectifying their complexity for the long term. Herr's depiction of Vietnamese as entities that push against but fail to penetrate his story world as social and political beings draws out the notion of exceptional Vietnam War violence into future time.

Interpreted as an example of American imperial gothicism through which writers handle moments of imperial instability, Herr's dismembered Vietnamese exert a haunting that is, nevertheless, consistently contained. He records the marines' fears of the ongoing power of Vietnamese body parts: "'Like they're *lookin* at you, man, it's scary'" (199). The admission of the Vietnamese occult, in turn, obliges management on the part of the soldiers, this time through the racialized and sexualized language of military masculinity used to describe a horrific image that concludes Herr's list of wartime images: "the one we were looking at now, the dead Viet Cong girl with her pajamas stripped off and her legs raised stiffly in the air." A marine attempts to lessen the graphic impact of the image by making a joke: "'No more boom-boom for that mamma-san,' the Marine said, that same, tired remark you heard every time the dead turned out to be women. It was so routine that I don't think he even realized that he'd said it" (199). Herr detaches from the marines' vulgar attempts to "get off" on the war, performing New Journalism's commitment to description rather than narrative manipulation. But his observant self-positioning passively reinvests in the scene's racist vocabulary and visual rape to achieve something few critics have focused on: a moral high ground that exists above the soldiers' inability to recognize their profanity. Herr converts the moral standing he claims through self- estrangement from the marines' disturbing "routine" into literary capital, authoritatively registering a dystopic vision of Vietnam. While the observational acumen and immersion in combat life of Herr's New Journalism lend authenticity to his narrative, imperial gothicism anchors *Dispatches* figuratively in the Vietnamese body in pieces—a trope through which Herr communicates and removes himself from exceptional violence to cement both moral standing and authorial legitimacy.

The unprecedented nature of Vietnam War combat as *Dispatches* presents it raises the question of how the public will respond to this vexed cultural-historical moment. It also, I suggest, compels Herr's turn to memoiristic practice in ways that mold readers' interpretation. While memoir's distinction from other forms of life narrative continues to be debated, we might define memoir through its episodic, focused scope, as opposed to other autobiographical narratives' more encompassing span of an entire life. Memoir is thus a genre whose attention to a particular autobiographical context potentially counteracts dominant histories; personal recollection can contest existing narratives by foregrounding individual remembrances that may speak to collective experiences excised by hegemonic accounts of the past, or even ejected by one's former account of oneself. The conscious engagement with the politics of literary craft gives memoir a meta-narrative quality. As the autobiography scholars Sidonie Smith and Julia Watson note, memoirs exhibit a "density of language and self-reflexivity about the writing process, yoking the author's standing as a professional writer with the work's status as an aesthetic object."[20] I would add that memoir has another potential function in addition to self-referential engagement with the question of authorship, which is to *transmit* personal knowledge with a sense of immediacy and feeling, eroding the separation between authorial truth and readerly experience.[21]

Herr's memoiristic moves forge a direct connection with readers, latently summoning their endorsement of his narrative to authenticate his rendering of the inscrutability and exceptionality of Vietnam. On one level, this singular historical moment has caused a crisis of literary representation: "Disgust doesn't begin to describe what they made me feel, they threw people out of helicopters, tied people up and put the dogs on them. Brutality was just a word in my mouth before that" (67). Herr finds himself at a loss for words, a literary impasse symptomatic of the war's overriding "brutality." On another level, the problems of writing that accompany new forms of violence engender problems of reading, a challenge that Herr confesses he faces. Comparing images of contorted Vietnam War bodies to those of war victims he recalls from old issues of *Life* magazine, Herr writes, "You know how it is, you want to look and you don't want to look. I can remember now the strange feelings I had. . . . I didn't have a language for it then, but I remember now the shame I felt, like looking at first porn" (18).

In this example, memoir's premises of nonfactual authenticity and readerly trust allow Herr to structure intimacy across the page to shape how the public will read the war. The rhetorical shifts between first-person and second-person narration equate "I" with "you" to position audience members as virtual consumers of mutated Vietnamese within a capitalist commodity structure; viewing Vietnamese dismemberment is like viewing porn. While Herr momentarily historicizes the conflict by linking it to other wars, he collapses this flicker of context by enlisting a metaphor of toxic nature to suggest that one cannot help but interpret "Vietnam" itself as a dystopia: "Sitting in Saigon was like sitting inside the folded petals of a poisonous flower, the poison history, fucked in its root no matter how far back you wanted to run your trace" (43). Use of the second-person structure of address in this instance not only enlarges Herr's personalized construction into collective truth; it also joins the theme of Vietnam's inherent doom to elongate the portrayal and interpretation of Vietnam War exceptionality in time for the reading public.

Whereas journalism requires expedient coverage and publication "to insure maximum impact of the information that it provides,"[22] memoir's subjective time liberates the text from such temporal constraints. No longer limited to Herr's and the marines' experience, Vietnam's "poisoned history" becomes a commodity for Americans to experience at large and across the *longue durée*.

Memoiristic elements help to universalize Herr's experiential and emotional point of view, exceeding the kind of individualized legitimacy and literary resonance that journalism and imperial gothicism, respectively, enable Herr to secure. As a self-reflexive genre, memoir in Herr's hands also facilitates neo-Orientalist representation that self-consciously objectifies the Asiatic in ways that reflect back on America; as Rowe writes, America's Vietnam imaginary differs from traditional Orientalism in the assimilation of the other to the U.S. self and nation: "It is all about us, not *them*."[23] In many ways, the prevailing focus on *Dispatches* as a work of New Journalism has impeded analysis of more complex narrative dynamics at work in the text and has shrouded Herr's inheritance of imperial literary practice—namely, the mobilization of the partitioned body as spectacle in historically obscuring and U.S.-centric ways, producing what Guy Debord might describe as the "despotism of a fragment" presented as world "pseudo-knowledge."[24] This tactic can serve capitalist logic by separating subjects from material conditions through the veil of the spectacular fragment. Herr's Vietnam emerges distinctly as a decontextualized site of transhistorical violence in which serial portrayals of dismembered Vietnamese express Vietnam's exceptionalism, undergird *Dispatches*' literary innovations, and obscure the long evolution of America's political and military investments in Southeast Asia. It is a transferrable model for portraying and interpreting the conflict that has endured.

De-exceptionalizing Herr's Vietnam

As Viet Thanh Nguyen asserts, in America's Vietnam War story, which serves as a national memoir in many ways, "The reader does not see himself as enduring being killed or raped, only being the witness to such acts."[25] Herr's depictions of violated Vietnamese bodies invite us to ask, "What is the effect of circulating images that re-present such atrocity over time?" Does such an instance constitute a "just image," or is it "just an image," to borrow Roland Barthes's terms for assessing the ethical and political ramifications of visual culture, particularly when images act as critical flashpoints in a nation's history?[26]

One way to comprehend more critically the implications of the recurrence of Vietnamese body parts in *Dispatches* is through Achille Mbembe's conceptualization of the political landscape undergirding a contemporary necropolitical era. According to Mbembe, power is now based on the "sub-jugation of life to the power of death."[27] "Death-worlds" are where politics take place and where sovereignty is imposed, largely through means of mass terror and killing. Sites of battle encompass the ground and the air, while to-pographies are divvied up and given ideological importance. Violated bodies and body parts—skeletons, corpses, half-alive bodies—are left out in the open and stripped of "bodily integrity."[28] Rather than the threat of death alone characteristic of earlier epochs, in a necropolitical moment the deploy-ment of power turns not on "immediate death" but on the liminal status of the living dead. Necropolitics operates by threatening populations with the possibility of being killed and ripped to pieces, held in indefinite states of potential violation before and after biological expiration.

Interpreting *Dispatches* through a necropolitical lens—specifically, Herr's portrayal of Vietnamese figures as sites of violation or possible violation that are stripped of "bodily integrity"—opens up our reading of the text, for his exceptionalized Vietnam brackets the kind of political history that Mbembe invokes. Bodily dismemberment and mutilation are, of course, not new in the history of aesthetic representation. In her study of the fragmented body in art, the art historian Linda Nochlin argues that the modern, for many artists, is figured *as* the body fragment.[29] Global histories of imperial con-quest and racial violence would seem to make partitioned bodies a condi-tion of politicized cultural engagement. We are compelled to consider why Vietnamese figures must appear in such damaged, not-quite-human forms, as if this is what helps make a war story "good" or "true," as Nguyen notes about American Vietnam War narratives that consistently maim, rape, and kill Vietnamese characters.[30] To investigate the aesthetic and political impli-cations of Herr's portrayal of the Vietnamese body part, we might incorpo-rate an interdisciplinary angle that includes Southeast Asia studies to return historicity to the extracted Vietnamese bodies that permeate U.S. Vietnam War culture.

Herr's sensationalizing trope of Vietnamese dismemberment draws from but sidesteps an extensive history of the Vietnamese body in pieces. Consider the photograph from 1908 showing severed or potentially severed Vietnamese heads, a reproduction of Vietnamese disfigurement that recalls Herr's retellings of stories of fragmented Vietnamese flesh. The image is part of a postcard series by Pierre Dieulefils (1862–1937), a French photog-rapher and postcard entrepreneur, that documents executions carried out by Vietnamese in the early twentieth century under orders of French authori-ties. As exemplified here, Dieulefils's images temporalize public executions by capturing them in progress as well as emphasizing the before and after. The beheaded are often identified by name and crime, and some postcards

3124   TONKIN — Indigènes décapités pendant les troubles de Juillet-Septembre 1908

Postcard by Pierre Dieulefils showing execution of Indochinese in Tonkin, 1908.
(Author's collection.)

take the form of an assemblage, picturing the shamed pre- and post-death, in uniform and then as severed head. Punishment by guillotine in French Indochina, though not pictured in the postcard, was another way to put dissident Vietnamese to death while providing "pageantry" and "spectacle" for the public, as the historian Michael G. Vann points out.[31] Colonial beheading was a "pedagogic" event and commodity, a form of instruction for the colonized and sensationalized entertainment for the public in French Indochina.[32]

While Herr performs perceptual and literary impairment when faced with images of disfigured and decapitated Vietnamese uprooted from space and time, the photos, when they are more properly contextualized, gesture toward a longer history of displays of Vietnamese mutilation that, similar to the photographs gathered in American marines' albums, have long been collected as mementos. Instead of the Vietnam War exceptionality Herr suggests, juxtaposing Herr's text with Dieulefils's postcards marks a continuum of Franco-American empires, as I also demonstrate in Chapters 1–2; both powers have capitalized on constructions and consumptions of the Vietnamese body in pieces. Herr's simulacral, exceptionalized fragments of Vietnamese flesh become palimpsestic when refracted through a longer imperial past, as he elides the *longue durée* of systemic racialized mutilation as it has occurred across Southeast Asia in the nineteenth and twentieth centuries yet builds on and contributes to that cultural history.[33]

Dismembered bodies were not the purview of Euro-American empire in Southeast Asia alone. Between 1940 and 1945, during World War II, Japan occupied French Indochina and gradually increased its armed presence until it overthrew France's administration in a coup on March 9, 1945. Reflecting Indochina's geostrategic importance to multiple empires, Japan's access to bases in the region facilitated military objectives in the Pacific theater, including the bombing of Pearl Harbor. During the Japanese occupation in Indochina, a combination of environmental and policy factors—droughts and floods, French monopolies over key industries, and Japanese policies that required Vietnamese to sell most of their rice crop, among others—resulted in a famine. Below are images from that famine taken by Võ An Ninh, who was one of Vietnam's most famous photographers, although he is relatively unknown outside Vietnam and its diaspora.[34]

The figures in Võ An Ninh's photos may not have been beheaded or severed by human hand, but their emaciated forms have empire's hands on them. The cropped bodies and skulls in these photos point to the masses that starved beyond the frames; an estimated one million to two million people in the north perished, their bodies piled up in the streets.[35] Japan's World War II surrender left a power vacuum that the Việt Minh exploited to assert Viet-

Dead bodies in Hanoi during the 1945 famine, gathered for transportation to burial grounds. (Photograph by Võ An Ninh. Courtesy of the Vietnam National Museum of History.)

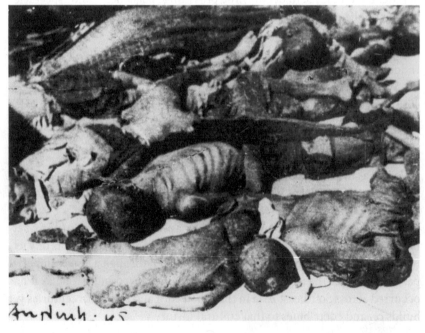

Vietnamese sweeping the roads of Hanoi in search of rice during the 1945 famine. (Photograph by Võ An Ninh. Courtesy of the Vietnam National Museum of History.)

nam's liberation. In his Declaration of Independence of September 2, 1945, modeled after the American declaration, Hồ Chí Minh blamed France and Japan for the famine: "When the Japanese Fascists violated Indochina's territory to establish new bases in their fight against the Allies, the French imperialists went down on their bended knees. . . . [F]rom that date, our people were subjected to the double yoke of the French and the Japanese. . . . [M]ore than two million of our fellow citizens died from starvation."[36] Offering a history lesson as much as a statement of independence, the declaration suggests that the famine was in fact systemic starvation—a war crime. In this context, the spectacle of Vietnamese suffering is mobilized for anti-imperial purposes. However, in turn, these images' official place in contemporary Vietnamese history (they are housed at the Vietnam National Museum of History) clouds another instance of biopolitical management in Vietnam: the mid-century land reform campaign carried out by the communist regime that resulted in three thousand to fifteen thousand executions.[37]

The corporeal legacies of both imperial and anti-imperial appropriations of bodily division demonstrate, to borrow Nochlin's words, "that there are times in the history of modern representation when the dismembered human body exists for the viewer not just as a metaphor but as an historical reality."[38] Attending to inter-imperial and domestic dynamics to include French, Japanese, and Vietnamese governance gives Herr's Vietnamese body parts longer historical pasts and reminds us of the United States' long-standing involvement in this story. Rather than an exception to the rule, corporeal mutilation is a facet of empire that has often found cultural representation. The differences among these depictions—changing contexts of imperialism and responses to it, altered modes of technological reproduction that shape cultural dissemination—help to periodize the evolution of empire across the *longue durée*. In Herr's late twentieth-century Vietnam, generic hybridity creates endless opportunities for reimagining Vietnamese dismemberment, creating a sense of formal and somatic overload that suggests a contemporary inundation of decontextualized spectacle while furthering the notion of inaccessible history. Herr's deterministic rendering of Vietnam's fate as "poisoned history" finds no reason not to continue adapting a system of cultural (re)production that capitalizes on commodified racial body parts.

As Alan Liu argues, a society concerned with the consequences of evolving technologies still "must have its poetics. And that poetics . . . must also be a poetics of historicity."[39] A turn to Vietnamese contexts takes Herr and the Vietnam War culture he shaped out of an exceptionalizing Cold War framework to consider the purview of the Vietnamese. In the next section, I advance a comparative reading of *Dispatches* by considering the materialist philosophy of Trần Đức Thảo (1917–1993), who studied in France and moved back to North Vietnam to support the revolution, as well as other Vietnamese conceptualizations of violence and reconstruction to resituate Herr's Vietnam within a complex and contingent political milieu. I briefly gloss a particular dimension of Frantz Fanon's understanding of violence to lead into Trần Đức Thảo's investigation of violence, which several scholars suggest influenced Fanon, to draw attention to models of Vietnamese decolonization within the broader circulation of postcolonial ideas. I highlight in particular Trần Đức Thảo's notion of imperialism's construction of separate perceptual horizons between colonizer and colonized, employing it as method for rereading *Dispatches* that specifies, in a more finely grained conceptual way, the politics of Herr's poetics of racial fragmentation.

Decolonizing Vietnam: Clashing Visions

In *The Wretched of the Earth* (1961), Frantz Fanon famously considers the question of violence in contexts of decolonization: "National liberation, national reawakening, the restoration of nation to the people or Commonwealth, whatever the name used, whatever the latest expression, decolonization is always a violent event."[40] In Fanon's view, anticolonial violence is integral and necessary to the project of national independence because the Manichean social structure that colonialism installs not only separates colonizer from colonized in spatial and legal terms (self–native, citizen–non-citizen, prestige–contamination, and so forth) but also divides their consciousnesses. Colonialism imposes both physical and psychological violence on the colonized, making anticolonial violence the only recourse for undoing imperial domination and achieving freedom.

Recently, scholars have suggested that Fanon's thinking on anticolonial violence may have been in conversation with the ideas of Trần Đức Thảo, a Vietnamese philosopher who lived in Paris between 1936 and 1951. Trần Đức Thảo was born in Bắc Ninh, outside Hanoi, and arrived in France to study at the École Normale Supérieure, where he later taught. An influential thinker of the time, he was mentored by Jean Cavaillès, a specialist in the philosophy of math and science, and the philosopher and phenomenologist Maurice Merleau-Ponty. Through intensive study of Edmund Husserl's works and unpublished writings held at the Leuven archives in Belgium, Trần Đức Thảo helped inaugurate a new interpretation of phenomenology in France that highlighted its scientific, materialist dimensions, in contradistinction to prevailing humanist interpretations epitomized in the existentialist philosophy of Jean-Paul Sartre. While this innovative reading of phenomenology was also advanced by other French philosophers, such as Jean-François Lyotard and Jean-Toussaint Desanti, it is said to have found its strongest impetus in Trần Đức Thảo—in particular, in his lauded *Phenomenology and Dialectical Materialism* (1951).[41] Among the students who frequented Trần Đức Thảo's courses were Louis Althusser and Jacques Derrida, whose own approaches to phenomenology were significantly shaped by these university experiences.[42] Trần Đức Thảo also contributed to *Les Temps Modernes*, and his analysis of the colonial problem using the example of French Indochina helped to define the publication's anticolonial reputation. These writings illustrate how periodical forms written in the language of the metropole clustered and disseminated emergent decolonizing thought.[43] As Merleau-Ponty wrote about his student, Trần Đức Thảo "questioned not only French domination, but all foreign domination."[44] For Althusser, Trần Đức Thảo, along with Desanti, embodied "the hopes of our generation."[45]

The colonial question took Trần Đức Thảo's phenomenology to Marxism and dialectical materialism, bringing into relief phenomenology's materialist bent. Phenomenology, as the examination of a subject's consciousness and perception in relation to the external, material world, entails a pursuit of knowledge that is intentional in what it seeks to know and that it seeks to know, but this pursuit must adapt to what the material world evidences, or "gives." In Nicholas de Warren's reading, Trần Đức Thảo argued that

Husserl's later writings and unpublished manuscripts gave special though typically unacknowledged primacy to the material, object world—the experienced, sensate realm's impact on intelligibility and consciousness—but Husserl, nevertheless, ultimately returned knowledge and experience to the individual. Husserl, in the end, looped back to the subject as the transcendent arbiter of meaning. Radically attributing this final idealism to Husserl's own limitations as a member of the bourgeois class, Trần Đức Thảo attempted to account for the issue of *genesis*—the historical becoming of one's own subjectivity and of the materials that constitute one's experience.[46]

The question of genesis informs "Sur l'Indochine," published in 1946 in *Les Temps Modernes*, wherein Trần Đức Thảo positioned the French and Indochinese as circumscribed by distinct, separate horizons. He argued that the French imperial horizon claimed universality and thus did not recognize a separate, independent Vietnamese horizon. By contrast, the Vietnamese horizon was premised on independence. Liberation from French colonialism was not simply a theoretical proposition or ideal possibility for Vietnamese, it was a "living and concrete totality."[47] French and Vietnamese inhabited mutually exclusive spheres of existence and consciousness, and their sense of what was politically possible fundamentally differed. In relation to the colonial problem, if the genesis of experience, perception, and interpretation were contingent on how a subject was placed in a concrete lifeworld—which in turn determined one's relationship to that empiricism—and if French empire materially and psychologically hierarchized colonizer over colonized, how could this unequal dynamic be undone? The telos of Vietnamese independence and freedom led Trần Đức Thảo to a reading of Vietnamese historical unfolding that would echo later in Fanon: freedom is inevitable, as is violence. Colonialism—in Trần Đức Thảo's words, "the aggression of one existence over another existence"—must be crushed.[48]

In his writings from the 1940s, Trần Đức Thảo consistently reiterated the inevitability of violence as a means of obtaining freedom. He wrote that the Vietnamese "cannot but revolt" as a means to demonstrate their existence.[49] When asked how the Vietnamese would respond to France's return after World War II, following Japanese occupation, Trần Đức Thảo said, "'We shall welcome them with gun-fire.'"[50] Making a crucial observation concerning French-U.S. inter-imperialism, in the 1940s he questioned the effects of increasing U.S. influence in Vietnam, noting that the United States had already paved the way for an imperial handover through its investments in Vietnam and lend-lease program that indebted postwar France.[51] Understanding Vietnam as one piece in an international, not simply Euro-American, puzzle, he observed that France's post–World War II reconquest of Indochina would primarily benefit China and America. By 1949, when the French had returned after a transitional British occupation, Trần Đức Thảo explained that the psychology of Vietnamese freedom would lead to formal freedom: "Vietnam's independence is, however, already acquired. . . . [M]ilitary operations and political maneuvering may delay, not prevent the realization."[52]

In Chapter 2, my analysis of Monique Truong's novel retroactively turns a critical postmodern lens on American literary modernism. Here, a mid-century Vietnamese philosopher can act as a critical lens on postmodernism's major Vietnam War text. The conundrums Trần Đức Thảo attempted to work out in the 1940s anticipate a key problem that threads *Dispatches* and depictions of America's Vietnam more broadly: how perception and experience in relation to material conditions shape what a subject deems intelligible and the implications that this dynamic has for literary representation, particularly when given a situation in which structures of intelligibility and recognition are not mutual but rather unequal. Put differently, what conditions determine what or who is worthy of recognition? These questions apply not only to Trần Đức Thảo's immediate concern with understanding mutually exclusive French, Japanese, and Vietnamese horizons but also to the relationship between what we might call, following Trần Đức Thảo, American and Vietnamese horizons.

As I have demonstrated, in *Dispatches*, dismembered Vietnamese bodies synecdochically relate the Vietnam War's broader incomprehensibility. Herr's literary approach to the Vietnamese material world generates a discourse of Vietnam's indecipherability to register the scale and reach of U.S. hegemony, but in so doing extinguishes the Vietnamese material world of dialogue and socio-political life. This objectification cancels out the possibility of Vietnamese consciousness—let alone anticolonial consciousness and a philosophy of anticolonial violence—and without consciousness, there can be no mutually recognized horizon. To reference Trần Đức Thảo, Herr's critique of U.S. military-political hubris relies on an uneven perceptual structure of hegemony that flattens out the question of genesis on both sides. In many ways, Herr's mode of bringing multiple genres together confuses historical specificity and evades adapting to what the Vietnamese material world gives, as Trần Đức Thảo might have understood it.

Trần Đức Thảo returned to Vietnam in 1951, although it is unclear whether he left of his own accord or was deported. After completing a Maoist self-criticism and reeducation program organized by the Vietnamese Communist Party, he held a range of official positions, including general secretary of the party and dean of the University of Hanoi. Some of his writings eventually became critical of the communist regime, leading to a forced public confession and silencing by the party.[53] In 1991, he returned to Paris, purportedly exiled by the Vietnamese state. French intellectuals who connected with Trần Đức Thảo during this time describe a disoriented personality on the brink of seeming madness. Paul Ricoeur wrote that his colleague and friend appeared "menaced by death,"[54] while the editor Thierry Marchaisse characterized Trần Đức Thảo as someone enveloped by "a mask of solitude" who "slowly sank away into the past, as if reabsorbed by his time, after having accidentally crossed mine."[55] Marchaisse's metaphor of disguise is perhaps appropriate, as a series of recorded interviews conducted with Trần Đức Thảo in Vietnamese during his final years in Paris suggest a sharp mind whose temporal disjointedness may be read alternatively as a performance to detract from Vietnamese surveillance, which supposedly followed him to France, or as indicating continued concern with not only Vietnamese decolonization but also with problems of Marxist philosophy; he would come to believe that Marxism had fundamental flaws in logic.[56] What Trần Đức Thảo recounted as Vietnamese communism's wrong turns mark the changing nature of empire and the challenging task of modifying models of decolonization in a neoliberal era. Oppositional colonizer-colonized paradigms and binaristic comprehensions of violence could not hold in the late twentieth century, particularly as Vietnam began to open its doors to capitalist development. Trần Đức Thảo died poor and in ill health in Paris in 1993.

It is worth noting other Vietnamese models of decolonization apart from Trần Đức Thảo's to continue dialecticizing investigations of Vietnam War cultures. As Trần Đức Thảo's complicated, nonlinear relationship with the Vietnamese Communist Party reveals, a much more varied and shifting map of political alliances and antagonisms operated in the war zone in Vietnam alongside equally varied ideas about the use of violence, a fact that contrasts with common understandings of Vietnamese anticolonialism as a unified project of common will and determination anchored in communism alone. For instance, Việt Minh resistance during Japan's occupation of Indochina during World War II was briefly supported by the U.S. Office of Strategic Services, which provided Hồ Chí Minh, Võ Nguyên Giáp, and other Vietnamese with weapons training and treated Hồ Chí Minh for malaria, hepatitis, and other maladies.[57] The Việt Minh and the United States, in other words, were allies against Japan during this interval. The United States then shifted its support to France to strengthen Allied ties, funding 85 percent to 90 percent of France's war effort against the Việt Minh.[58] While Hồ Chí Minh has long been an iconic figure of coalesced anticolonial revolution, throughout the 1940s–1950s, North Vietnam's party leaders disagreed vehemently over whether to work toward peaceful reunification or undertake militant reunification through violent struggle in the south, especially after the division of the country in 1954, which produced two different states (the Democratic Republic of Vietnam [DRV] in the north and the Republic of Vietnam

[RVN] in the south).[59] Moscow and Beijing's ideological divergence during the Sino-Soviet split also contributed to conflicting North Vietnamese allegiances to China and the Soviet Union, making for an even thornier drama of revolution.[60] Eventually, two allies, Lê Duẩn and Lê Đức Thọ, would usurp power from and marginalize an old guard in North Vietnam that included Võ Nguyên Giáp and Hồ Chí Minh.[61] Together, the new leaders would accomplish their goal of full-scale war against America, no matter what the cost.[62] This changing geopolitical map precludes easy, absolutist explanations of imperial hegemony and anticolonial resistance in Vietnam.

The south offers a no less complicated picture of Vietnamese decolonization. While violence was a key issue that divided northern leaders and their Sino-Soviet advisers, in the RVN officials attempted to formulate a distinct political ideology in the shadows of American political and military aid. This contradiction is evident in Ngô Đình Diệm's fraught legacies. Conventionally viewed as a "puppet" of the United States, this first president of the RVN, who ruled from 1955 until his assassination in 1963 by a U.S.-backed coup, also had a long anticolonial and anti-American record.[63] He distrusted Hanoi, which he referred to as a "dictatorial regime,"[64] was suspicious of American motives, even though he needed their assistance,[65] and believed that France and the United States both wanted to maintain their hold on Vietnam while giving colonial rule a new faux democratic face.[66] As political adviser, Ngô Đình Nhu, Ngô Đình Diệm's brother, opposed increased U.S. military troops and worried that Americans' misunderstanding of the Southeast Asian political context and their reputation for changing sides would, as history had demonstrated, result in military frustrations and failures, potentially leading to a sudden withdrawal down the road.[67] Authoritarian in their rule, the Ngô brothers also recognized that American modernization projects were top-down forms of hegemony performing as bottom-up efforts—updated examples of America's "dressed-down" imperial rhetoric.[68] The heterogeneous perspectives I have outlined—Trần Đức Thảo's theorization of differentiated consciousnesses under empire, North Vietnamese leaders' disagreement over war or diplomacy as the proper path forward, and the Ngô brothers' formulation of a political paradigm that might solve the problems of democracy and communism—elaborate a range of overlapping and often clashing Vietnamese decolonizing visions.

A U.S.-backed coup on November 2, 1963, resulted in the assassinations of Ngô Đình Diệm and Ngô Đình Nhu. The United States would begin secret talks with North Vietnam in 1969, culminating in a settlement signed in 1973 in Paris between Secretary of State Henry Kissinger and the DRV's Lê Đức Thọ. The agreement allowed North Vietnam's troops to remain in the south while U.S. troops withdrew, terms that infuriated Nguyễn Văn Thiệu, the RVN's president at the time, who stated, "'The South Vietnamese people will assume that we have been sold out by the U.S. and that North Viet-Nam has won the war.'"[69] South Vietnamese leaders lamented trying to fight a war with decreased aid—which resulted in, for instance, lack of adequate ammunition—while Kissinger responded to criticism by asserting that America had "'mortgaged'" its foreign policy to assist South Vietnam.[70] In 1973, Kissinger and Lê Đức Thọ were awarded the Nobel Peace Prize.[71]

The nonsynchronous perspectives outlined above, or differing notions about how to achieve equitable material reorganization,[72] demonstrate how Vietnamese continued to address mutating formations of hegemony in urgent ways at a time when many thinkers and writers began turning to discursive politics and what Lyotard calls "language games."[73] While discursivity was certainly a substantial dimension of Vietnam War experience—an important political and cultural tool for all sides involved—it has often been privileged in cultural critique apart from materialist inquiry.[74] Decolonization generated new questions and problems that Vietnamese had to grapple with concretely and conceptually at the same time that countries such as the United States were well on their way to putting "Vietnam" behind them. In the next section, I return to my examination of *Dispatches* to suggest that, in canceling out decolonizing intricacies in ways that make the Vietnam War a spectacle for consumption, Herr's poetics of fragmentation exemplifies how American popular culture has worked to disremember Vietnam.

Disremembering Vietnam

The dematerialization of Herr's Vietnam in *Dispatches* is perhaps most prominent in the chapter "Khe Sanh." In his view, Khê Sanh, one of the most famous sites of the Vietnam War, dramatizes how a material context comes to acquire purely ideological meaning and thus necessitates abstracted representation. That this perceived abstraction also made Khê Sanh the most reported story of the 1968 Tết Offensive shows how much journalists were attracted to the discursive nature of the Vietnam War and anticipates how American culture would trade on the conflict's discursivity, as opposed to its material history.

A U.S. Marine combat base, Khê Sanh was the target of a seventy-seven-day Northern Liberation Front (NLF) siege beginning on January 21, 1968. American officials, members of the press, and citizens believed Khê Sanh to be the next Điện Biên Phủ, and the story looked something like this: six thousand marines defending an isolated base in the middle of a hilly, mountainous area surrounded by an unseen and unknown number of North Vietnamese soldiers, who were ready to attack at any moment under the leadership of General Võ Nguyên Giáp, the mastermind behind Điện Biên Phủ. Bad weather provided an apt backdrop to American B-52 raids around the area, which eventually unleashed 100,000 tons of munitions and over 150,000 artillery shells, "more than had been exploded on any comparable space in history."[75] According to Peter Braestrup, Khê Sanh had exactly the mystery that made for a compelling story: "The hill outposts of the base[,] . . . where most ground action occurred during the siege and where life was dirty and most dangerous, were largely inaccessible to newsmen. The B-52 strikes were also largely invisible to the press. But the sprawling main base on the Khe Sanh plateau, with its aid station and metal air strip, provided sufficient visual color and drama."[76]

In Herr's account, Khê Sanh is a false narrative of redemption in which the United States hopes to write over prior Euro-American loss at Điện Biên Phủ by preparing for victory at Khê Sanh. Its anticipated climax stretches out before the American public like a slowly unfolding serial. Herr captures the theater of Khê Sanh in his profile of a U.S. battalion commander who nervously points to an imagined NLF presence from his office: "The colonel squinted at the distance for a long time. Then he swept his hand very slowly along the line of jungle, across the hills and ridges running into Cambodia. . . . 'Somewhere out there . . . is the *entire First NVA Division*'" (96). Khê Sanh encapsulates the abstraction of the entire war itself: "Khe Sanh had taken on the proportions of a siege camp and lodged itself as an obsession in the heart of the Command, long before a single round had ever fallen inside the perimeter" (86). A semblance of an impending battle, Khê Sanh epitomizes for Herr the foundational problem of Vietnam War representation, comparable to the centerpiece of Wallace Stevens's poem "Anecdote of the Jar": "Khe Sanh became like the planted jar. . . . It took dominion everywhere" (107). The ideological significance that Herr aptly notes Khê Sanh has acquired is permeating, absorbing anything else that the area might mean.

It is worth providing some background to consider how Herr's striking depiction interacts with historical context. First, while the predicted showdown at Khê Sanh never happened, it did have tactical value as a diversionary ploy strategized by the DRV, with communist forces deliberately using it to preoccupy U.S. troops. As Lien-Hang Nguyen shows, this was part of Lê Duẩn's, not Võ Nguyên Giáp's, broader plan to distract American forces from major areas where the NLF would coordinate guerrilla attacks in violation of the cease-fire for the 1968 Lunar New Year.[77] Vietnamese military strategy, and not U.S. military arrogance alone, contributed to the difficulty of comprehending and portraying sites such as Khê Sanh, as the war itself did not have a clear front line to follow and was more episodic, giving rise to an intractable, "hit-and-run" quality.

Second, while Herr positions U.S. military leaders as the brains behind the Khê Sanh myth, journalistic abstraction was partly inherent in American press operations in South Vietnam and in global reporting more generally. While New Journalism is characterized by embedded reporting for maximum authenticity effects—Hunter Thompson's editor at Random House reportedly said, "'Your method of research is to tie yourself to a railroad track when you know a train is coming to it, and see what happens'"[78]—during the Vietnam War, the infrastructure of news made for fairly disjointed reporting. Journalistic coverage was expensive and risky, with wire services proceeding through a clunky process of fact checking and drafting that typically began with a reporter in the field who would run or hitch a ride (often by helicopter) to the nearest phone, then dictate an often fractured story to the Saigon bureau. Other news snippets would be added to the initial thread, resulting in a sutured, intertextual report that would pass through offices in places such as Tokyo, Manila, and Singapore before going to print. Of all the foreign press offices in Vietnam, only *Time-Life* began coverage with adequate resources, maintaining its own Telex ties to New York and employing a number of Vietnamese.[79]

In addition, in some cases news was deliberately sensationalized. As Rowe notes, "CBS journalists were sent to the war with specific instructions *not* to learn much about the history and culture of Vietnam, so that they could send back fresh impressions."[80] Throughout the late 1960s, foreign journalists had little to no background in Vietnamese language, history, or politics, and at the start of 1968, no American reporters had fluency in Vietnamese. When representatives from the Army of the Republic of Vietnam (ARVN) or Republic of Vietnam Armed Forces (RVNAF) conducted daily briefings, Americans generally did not attend, and foreign journalists would sometimes mock them.[81] Such instances suggest the asymmetrical and racialized dynamic among the American press, the RVN press, and the U.S. and ARVN information ministries that is relatively absent not only from Herr's critique of wartime representation but also from most Vietnam War cultural criticism.[82] In Herr's chapter on Khê Sanh, a kind of renegade journalism recuperates reportage, placing blame for Khê Sanh's inflated ideological weight primarily on the U.S. state. Other factors are minimized, including specific Vietnamese military tactics that complicated warfare for America, logistical and financial hurdles of transnational journalism, and the racialization of news.

The presumed baselessness of Khê Sanh's ideological value circumvents these complexities and returns Herr to the mutilated Vietnamese body trope as an expression of Vietnam's exceptionality. Frank Lentricchia argues that Herr's exposure of the emptiness of America's military operation in Khê

Sanh marks an effort to "undermine discourses of abstraction and domina-tion,"[83] yet the subordination of Khê Sanh's more complex geopolitical im-portance reveals that *Dispatches'* overturning of abstraction pivots on more abstraction. Indeed, Herr's experience at Khê Sanh generates one of the few instances of corporeal proximity to embodied Vietnamese presence, an oc-casion that produces a metaphor of slow and anguished Vietnamese dying as cinematic spectacle. In a nocturnal scene of collective American witness of Vietnamese pain, Herr and some marines listen to the piercing screams of a North Vietnamese soldier caught on a wire forty meters away:

> We heard then what sounded at first like a little girl crying, a sub-dued, delicate wailing, and as we listened it became louder and more intense, taking on pain as it grew until it was a full, piercing shriek. The three of us turned to each other, we could almost feel each other shivering. It was terrible, absorbing every other sound coming from the darkness. Whoever *it* was, he was past caring about anything except the thing he was screaming about. There was a dull pop in the air above us, and an illumination round fell drowsily over the wire. (142, emphasis added)

While a U.S. marine relentlessly fires his weapon as if he "[is] holding off a division," he only has a handful of targets in this scene (140). Flares produced by an intentionally paced M-60 illuminate the round that falls "drowsily over the wire," prolonging the annihilating action that the weaponry per-forms. It is precisely when the flare dims that the dying soldier begins to sob again, leaving no moment unaffected by the repetitive cycle of his cries, whose feminized form seems to insist on tortured extermination. The scene eventually comes to an absolute silence when another marine uses his cus-tomized M-79 grenade launcher to "'put that fucker away'" (143). In this py-rotechnic spectacle, the flare from the marine's fatal blow makes his weapon glisten, reproducing from afar the slow cycle of killing and dying by way of reflecting it on the weapon's shiny surface.[84]

This scene relates U.S. military violence coming face-to-face with itself, but only in mediated form, as it is the reflection on the rifle and not the event itself that projects back to Americans their necropolitical acts. As in the marines' photo albums, dead or dying Vietnamese bodies become objects to hold that illuminate the dark depths of the American self. The materiality of Vietnamese sound and body is figuratively buried by the time another soldier named Mayhew registers what has happened: "Mayhew looked out at the wire again, but the silence of the ground in front of us was really talk-ing to him now. His fingers were limp, touching his face, and he looked like a kid at a scary movie" (143). The event's self-referential cinematic framing emerges to transform Mayhew's—and Herr's—position of active witness to one of passive spectatorship, with the Vietnamese figure morphing from a live, suffering body into a character in a film who must die in order to be seen. Only then does Mayhew peel his protective hands away from his face, now able to watch the "scary movie" that is "Vietnam."

The North Vietnamese soldier's silence speaks all too strongly to Mayhew, but Herr distances himself from the figure through an ocular idiom, noting that he sees nothing: "I couldn't see anything out there" (142). He claims, "We didn't need a translator to tell us what it [the screaming] was," but when asked whether he can believe what has just happened, Herr tritely responds, "It was something, really something" (143). After all is (not) said and done, Herr and Mayhew can only return "to the bunker for some more of that sleep" (143). Repackaged as a cut from a film, the scene anticipates how Vietnamese sensory segmentation, whereby a live Vietnamese figure is variously heard but not seen or is seen but remains unintelligible, stands in for dynamic history to become a consumable commodity beginning in the 1970s.[85]

By outlining the North Vietnamese soldier's expiration in such a way, Herr manages to expel from his narrative politically significant losses of Vietnamese civilians. We might briefly juxtapose his account of the Tết Offensive with Nhã Ca's account *Mourning Headband for Huế*, which focuses on mass South Vietnamese deaths during this season of war from a Huế woman's point of view. Nhã Ca relates how the numbers of unarmed Vietnamese killed by the NLF steadily increased,[86] part of the thousands of civilians who died in a condensed time span. Many were reportedly thrown alive into mass graves, while scores were executed by those whom Nhã Ca describes as NLF members passing as friends and neighbors; bodies continued to be discovered through the fall of 1969. Inhabiting a position of political ambivalence, Nhã Ca states that all involved "deserve pity," but at the same time, all are responsible in some way for this time of bloodshed.[87] The photograph by Denis Stanley Gibbons visualizes aspects of the context portrayed in *Mourning Headband*. Interpreted concomitantly with Nhã Ca's work, its portrayal of Vietnamese mourners and victims multiplies the actors in Herr's politically simplified structure of American Vietnam War spectatorship.

The final scene I examine from *Dispatches* illustrates how the text's predicating of literary authority and truth on physically and sonically distorted Vietnamese bodies exacts severe costs on Herr. In a dream that takes place years after Herr's time in Southeast Asia, he finds himself reliving a moment of encounter with Vietnamese who were killed during the Tết Offensive and must be immediately removed from the grounds:

South Vietnamese mourning the loss of civilians killed by communist forces in Huế, circa February 23, 1969. (Photograph by Denis Stanley Gibbons AM. Courtesy of the Estate Late Denis Stanley Gibbons AM.)

From outside we say that crazy people think they hear voices, but of course *inside* they really hear them. (Who's crazy? What's insane?) One night, like a piece of shrapnel that takes years to work its way out, I dreamed and saw a field that was crowded with dead. I was crossing it with a friend, more than a friend, a guide, and he was making me get down and look at them. They were powdered with dust, bloodied like it had been painted on with a wide brush, some were blown out of their pants, just like they looked that day being thrown onto the truck at Can Tho, and I said, "But I've already seen them." My friend didn't say anything, he just pointed, and I leaned down again and this time I looked into their faces. New York City, 1975, when I got up the next morning I was laughing. (68–69)

Haunting Vietnamese reappear belatedly in Herr's present of 1975. Wondering why they have returned to force another encounter, he realizes that he did not really "see" them the first time around. The coerced recognition—the penetration of his consciousness and horizon—leads Herr to internalize the Vietnamese body in pieces, an experience whose likening to the invasion of shrapnel positions Herr as the one who is wounded. Herr's laughter expresses the disorienting, schizophrenic consequences of foreclosing recognition of Vietnamese horizons, yet the acknowledgment is relegated to a dream fragment that lies elsewhere, in a spatially and temporally disconnected realm, even though it is 1975—the year of Vietnam's reunification and the start of mass-migration of Southeast Asian refugees to the United States (discussed further in Chapter 4). Vietnam as bodily and narrative fragment surfaces as remembrance, but it exists more as paratext—imagined as beyond rather than within Herr's narrative—and consequently is suppressed and disremembered.

Herr's anachronistic experience of war's return—the very thing that imperial gothicism attempts to control—suggests that detaching the Vietnamese body in pieces from historical understanding will not bode well for the American future. Yet Herr's aesthetic investment in Vietnamese fragmentation and unintelligibility as cinemascape and dreamscape, and the continued circulation of these types of depictions as some kind of historical fact, has had lasting power. Francis Ford Coppola unapologetically claimed that *Apocalypse Now* (1979), which Herr co-wrote and is replete with dismembered Vietnamese, was "not about Vietnam," emphasizing, "It is Vietnam." That capitalist commodification is in tune with aestheticizing war as spectacle—even if such representations are critical of the U.S. nation-state, for the impenetrability of power that spectacle often implies encourages historical amnesia and discourages materialist inquiry—emerges in Coppola's admission of capitalist excess getting out of hand: "We had access to too much money, too much equipment, and little by little we went insane."[88] In the next section, which concludes this chapter, I discuss Ocean Vuong's poetry from *Night Sky with Exit Wounds*—in particular, the poem "Notebook Fragments"—to query what a fragmented poetics that contends with de-historicized and commercialized Vietnams looks like in the twenty-first century. Piecing together linguistic shards and material remains of war, Vuong's past and present animate each another to offer an alternative poetics of fragmentation.

Ocean Vuong's Fragments as a Poetics of Genesis

Published approximately forty years after the reunification of Vietnam and the publication of *Dispatches*, Ocean Vuong's *Night Sky with Exit Wounds* (2016) offers a poetics of fragmentation that we might also call a poetics of genesis—an exploration of how subjects get to where they are, as well as how the objects, stories, and events that compose a subject's life continue to emerge and evolve.[89] While Herr likens his dream of belated encounter with dead Vietnamese to "a piece of shrapnel that takes years to work its way out," Vuong elaborates on that comparison by foregrounding how violence becomes threaded in everyday lived experience, interwoven in inescapable ways with ordinary activities and materials. A noticeable use of the present tense tracks dynamics of destruction and creation as they occur in real time, while longer historical arcs are placed in dialogue with the present to relate an ongoing confrontation with conflict, its material effects, and its commodification. If an exit wound is a form of bodily harm inflicted by war weaponry— according to the *Oxford English Dictionary*, it is "a wound made by a bullet or other missile passing out of the body"—Vuong's "night sky" is full of exit wounds that encompass the globe, enveloping the planet to mark it with the enormous scale of such loss.[90]

"Notebook Fragments" from *Night Sky with Exit Wounds* is a poem with an informal tone, structured as a diary of two- and one-line stanzas, with occasional time stamps that move in an exploratory way through series of contemplations, revelations, and discoveries. The mode of address that a diary affords is a conversation with the self; the poem suggests that such a dialogue continually interacts with the self's environment, as the speaker remains permeable to other figures, material objects, and retold tales that were perhaps noted on a Post-it or fragment of paper, then integrated into the poem that we read. Everyday encounters expose how empires' varied effects manifest in unexpected ways, often elided by the passing of time and the overlooking of revelatory details: "In Vietnamese, the word for grenade is 'bom,' from the French 'pomme,' / meaning 'apple.' // Or was it American for 'bomb'?" (69). Imperfect translation, internal rhyme, and visual echo cross these two stanzas to reconnect French, Vietnamese, and American imperialism through linguistic resonances figured as vestiges of sight and sound, with each country given its appropriate defining feature: France, a culinary sign; America, a military signification; and Vietnam, an uncertain negotiation of the two accented by the speaker's transformation of seeming fact into grounds for critical questioning. The lines' resonant yet jarring etymological exercise draws attention to the long history of empires' effects on speech and pronunciation, relating how traces of violence become a normalized part of mundane bodily functions, such as the use of our organs and the connotations of what we eat. Evoking what Toni Morrison describes as the "archeological" work of memory,[91] Vuong excavates the history that is folded into everyday language and things. As a genre of episodic personal consideration less bounded by ideals of narrative continuity and cohesion, the diary form makes room for the significance of what might otherwise be marginalized observation, while a poetic cast gives visual and sonic range to the lyrical voice's working out of war's presence in daily life.

Vuong's juxtaposition of the commonplace and momentous, the private and geopolitical, delineates the work of memory as incomplete, continually contingent on interactions with evolving linguistic milieus, object worlds, and sensory stimuli that embody a historicity and urge recognition. The impulse to take note that a diary encourages emerges in a brief exchange with a grandmother, whose presence makes wartime mutilation a part of ordinary conversation: "Grandma said, *In the war they would grab a baby, a soldier at each ankle, and pull . . . / Just like that*" (68). The visual difference tagged by the use of italics indicates intergenerational and perhaps linguistic difference, intimating that the speaker did not witness the wartime bodily abuse being described yet becomes connected to it through acts of listening, translation, and recording. The speaker then unexpectedly turns to an exuberant moment that jolts us out of the searing image the grandmother has depicted: "It's finally Spring! Daffodils everywhere. / Just like that" (68). Epistrophe ties together the speaker's and grandmother's otherwise disparate remarks to suggest the grandmother's influence on the speaker's modes of utterance and awareness, thereby figuring remembrance as not only cross-temporal and cross-spatial but also dialogic, intersubjective, and dispersed. That the grandmother's colloquial expression becomes the diary's private contents that are, in turn, made public creates a shared situation through which to remember war violence on the level of quotidian practice, even amid feelings of joy, while the transition from a past scene of necropolitical conflict to a current image of renewal effects a chronotopic shift to fragment thought and produce a migratory consciousness in motion.

"Notebook Fragments" not only posits an active form of memory making that is attentive to the transformative potential of seemingly banal materials and interfaces. The dynamic consciousness that emerges is important for the speaker who, as a direct product of war, must forge a perspective open to war's myriad, often conflicting repercussions. As a child of a potential rape of a Vietnamese woman by a U.S. soldier, the speaker faces an epistemological conundrum—the knowledge that destruction and life coexist: "An American soldier fucked a Vietnamese farmgirl. Thus my mother exists. Thus I exist. / Thus no bombs = no family = no me" (70). Multiple assertions of causality thread this two-line stanza that contends with the violence of an individual history that is also constitutive of a more common narrative— one in which numerous Americans "fucked" Vietnamese girls and women disadvantaged by race, class, and multiple nation-states' power. The first line's cause-and-effect syntax, whereby an act of aggression "thus" led to specific effects, proceeds to the second line's counterfactual structure, whereby mathematical symbol expresses hypothetical causality had the events just recounted not happened. The latter mode of reasoning does not get very far, however, for to negate a prior cancellation, to wish that there had been no bombs and resulting ruin, would be to erase the speaker's own existence—

thus, the necessity of confronting not only the fact of violence but also the irreconcilability of its effects. As Cathy Schlund-Vials states about the seemingly limitless scope of Vietnam War excesses, "Measured by hundreds of thousands of air force sorties and millions of tons of munitions, such warfare fulfills by way of mathematical greatness the far-reaching parameters of the military sublime."[92] Condensing actual and counterfactual history, the lines from "Notebook Fragments" consider the imprint of quantitatively configured—and profit-driven—military prowess and war sublimity on lives that have been the target of that weaponry, scaling down historical narrative and scaling up personal remembrance to create a relational structure of remembrance. The speaker's personal-historical awareness evolves in relation to and *as* that which testifies to recurring encounters with war.

The dialectical impetus of "Notebook Fragments" opens up paths for different kinds of cognizance and understanding that are affiliated, even if they are "fragments" that are not wholly synced in formal and thematic terms. I conclude my reading of Vuong's poetry by turning to another poem, "Self-Portrait as Exit Wounds," to investigate its consideration of how one might find creative force out of war's violence, contradictions, and commodification. "Self-Portrait as Exit Wounds" begins by announcing itself as an alternative: "Instead, let it be the echo to every footstep / drowned out by rain, cripple the air like a name" (26). The speaker formulates the ambiguous subject "it" as the trace of what disappears, establishing the poem's postulate of marking historical presence after its dissolution. Initially moving invisibly and quietly, the poem traverses various objects, figures, spaces, and elements that the speaker hopes "it" will affect in varied potent, resonating ways: a "room illuminated / with snow, furnished only with laughter," "a sinking boat," a "refugee camp," the year 1968, Agent Orange, the returning image of "the grandfather fucking / the pregnant farmgirl" (27–28). These are familiar signs of Vietnam War and Vietnamese refugee history that the disembodied speaker illuminates. As the opening line suggests, the poem attempts to reorient these images toward a different kind of war portrait that can account for the losses that war leaves: its exit wounds.

At the same time that "it" perambulates in myriad forms across expansive space and time, the nebulous figure behind similarly shape-shifting movements acquires a clearer outline to address the complicated question of agency after conflict, particularly when war's effects endure and morph. In the last few stanzas, "it" is revealed to be the imagined effects of a weapon that the speaker wishes to wield and turn back on the ills that result from conflict: "Let me weave this deathbeam," with "deathbeam" acting as the source of the actions that "it" performs (27). Yet the contradictions of contending with a long history of war violence emerge as the speaker ostensibly craves the power to inflict death yet also becomes a medium for bodily restoration through the different inflection of "deathbeam" that enjambment affords: "Let me weave this deathbeam / the way a blind woman stitches a flap of skin back // to her daughter's ribs" (28). Diverging markedly from Herr's depiction of Vietnamese skin as a simulacral, fragmented object of injury, Vuong's lines return embodiment to the experience of corporeal dismemberment to create possibilities for survival out of a lethal weapon. War's destruction and construction become a core duality that the speaker must negotiate.

Poetry's accretive effect reveals that the portrayal of the fine line between the power to kill and the power to heal hinges on incorporating one of the most recognizable stereotypes of the Vietnam War—that of the menacing, intractable "Charlie"—to critically mine this figure's intimidating legacy and suggest that alternative renderings of war and refugee history inevitably operate in relation to hegemonic depictions of "Vietnam." Toward the end of the poem, the deathbeam's entwined abilities to inflict death and offer remedy branch off into yet another arc that takes us into the war zone itself and centers the dispersed perspective the poem has taken thus far: "Yes—let me believe I was born / to cock back this rifle, smooth & slick, like a true // Charlie, like the footsteps of ghosts misted through rain" (28). Assuming the role of a stock character central to the American military-industrial complex and Vietnam War cultural industry, this "Charlie" could easily be one of Herr's exterminated Vietnamese but transforms the status of being war's object, its target and stereotype, into a position of agency that acts against the very forces that have created it. Where a conventional account of resistance might end with the idea of Charlie's reclamation of power, however, the poem moves on, taking the speaker's Charlie persona back to the poem's beginning to continue the sense of chronotopic movement and migrating consciousness and foreclose a final ending. In the penultimate stanza, the likening of Charlie's motions to "footsteps of ghosts misted through rain" (28) loops back to the first line of the poem, "Instead, let it be the echo to every footstep / drowned out by rain" (26). The speaker at once limns the details of conflict and is the one who must be limned, the subject who historicizes and the one who must also be historicized. The resonant imagery and rhyme of the poem's opening and closing lines invite the creation of a new couplet from the poem's fragments. As minutiae, the marginal, and the otherwise unsaid continue to emerge, perceptual horizons and material worlds impinge on one another and are continually repopulated and restructured. The poem opts for delineating cognition in progress over presenting one that has already been made, not only mapping the genesis of the speaker's evolving, multisited consciousness but also offering a poetic structure of genesis itself.[93]

The dialectic and nonlinear deliberation in "Self-Portrait as Exit Wounds" becomes an exploration of how to build an awareness able to accommodate the notion that conflict devastates at the same time that new, valuable lives emerge from war, are potentially erased, and then must somehow be re-presented in ways that test existing literary approaches. The extended metaphor of portraiture establishes a comparison among the deathbeam, rifle, and artist's instrument to extend the contradictions of depicting war to the realm of aesthetic production. By incorporating historical affliction into the ongoing work of self-portraiture, the speaker—a product of war—creates an image of the wounded self that is determined by others' fractured bodies and psyches. "Exit wounds" constitute material for artistic endeavor and, in turn, become others' marks also to bear. By portraying war injury as proof of violence and the source of creation, Vuong presents "exit wounds" as the speaker's scar, weapon, and gift. However, while the many injuries collected across the poem motivate corrective destruction on the part of "Charlie," they also relate the fear of what may result; the poem's final lines convey the speaker's deep apprehension about the powers of killing and creating art: "As I lower myself between the sights—& pray // that nothing moves" (28). "Self-Portrait as Exit Wounds" suggests the uncertain consequences, even ambivalence, of the poetic act.

The high critical praise of *Night Sky with Exit Wounds* from multiple literary corners promises to generate further inquiry into the contemporary politics of representing America's Vietnam. Declared a "must read" book in many major reviews, the collection has been described as reminiscent of the poetry of Emily Dickinson and Gerard Manley Hopkins,[94] and Vuong, a graduate of New York University's Master of Fine Arts (MFA) program, has been lauded as "a poet of the American experiment."[95] Vuong's heightened stature seems to put a crack in Junot Díaz's claim in the article "MFA versus POC," published in the *New Yorker*, that "the standard problem of MFA programs," as he experienced it, was that "that shit was *too white*."[96] Yet at times, the particular configurations and interpretations of Vuong's background have assimilated biographical details into familiar trajectories of American multicultural mythology. As Daniel Wenger of the *New Yorker* narrates, "Vuong was born in 1988, on a rice farm outside Saigon; two years later, he and six relatives emigrated to Hartford, Connecticut, where they lived together in a one-bedroom apartment. At school, Vuong was buffeted by English long before he could use it—his family was illiterate, and he didn't learn to read until he was eleven."[97] These details, evocative of an immigrant history and not necessarily a refugee one, forge an upward trajectory of perpetual resilience. In the 2000s, an evident desire for a redemptive "Vietnam" story, as opposed to the dystopic registers of works such as Herr's, appears in several reviews that assert themes of hope and possibility as the principal messages of Vuong's poems. Even the name Ocean becomes associated with an idealized sense of "rebirth and transformation,"[98] while the materialist aspects of his book dissolve into "timeless imagery."[99] While "Notebook Fragments" and "Self-Portrait as Exit Wounds" outline a poetics whereby violence results in both injury and creation, with the trope of exit wounds working to rupture idealized notions of coherence and recovery, the business of book reviews intended for a wide, "cultured" reading public risks downplaying the complex engagement with paradigm fragmentation that makes Vuong's poetry a mobile and engaged poetics of genesis.

Herr went to Vietnam because he was genred, aspiring to "Hemingway-esque adventures and literary achievements."[100] He "came back high," only to face a debilitating crash after that high dissolved. Vuong is a direct product of American "adventures" in Vietnam, turning to genres he notes are perceived as less "legitimate" to mine the margins of war experience and literary canonicity and offer an active, reconnective mode of remembrance.[101] What these two authors share are disparate roles in an uneven system of literary representation and interpretation of the Vietnam War. Herr's life and work have traded on the commodification of Vietnam War dystopia and violence committed against Vietnamese, while Vuong's cultural capital has often been interpreted through both the expectation of being able to overcome historical violence and the idea that a certain literary exceptionalism combined with biographical exceptionalism can forge wholes out of parts. Chapter 4 takes exception to this exceptionalism, examining how Võ Phiến's Vietnamese-language epistolary writings produced in the United States elaborate on the politics of literary structures of address in constructing America's Vietnam. While Vuong turns to the subgenre of the diary as a space where the structure of private conversation can express what is heterogeneous to more commonly recognized Vietnam War narratives and forms, Võ Phiến extends the question of address by turning to epistles to bring a Vietnamese refugee diaspora into being. His writings become an important site for considering how to represent ongoing conditions of war and forced migration, and they periodize the 1970s as an important moment in the emergence of Vietnamese American letters.

4

CRITICAL REFUGEE STUDIES
AND THE EMERGENCE OF
VIETNAMESE AMERICAN LETTERS

C hapter 3 analyzed how Michael Herr's *Dispatches* (1977) reduces the Vietnam War to an exceptionalist narrative of the Vietnamese body in pieces, and it concluded with a consideration of Ocean Vuong's poetics of fragmentation that, read historically and transnationally, turns itself into a critical poetics of genesis. This chapter extends my examination of Vietnamese American literature to consider Vietnamese-language writings by Võ Phiến, a prominent author who left South Vietnam in 1975 and resettled in Los Angeles. As scholars including Lan Duong, Yen Le Espiritu, and Viet Thanh Nguyen demonstrate, Asian Americanist critique benefits from nuanced consideration of non-English language works, and they have carved out this path by incorporating Vietnamese-language materials in their reexaminations of Vietnam War-related culture.[1] I contribute to these alternative literary genealogies by focusing on Võ Phiến's use of the epistolary form, developing how it helped refugees narrate, imagine, and create a diasporic community after war and migration. Written in Vietnamese, these works critique the new American national narrative that emerged after the war, one that emphasized America's noble, ethical concern for refugees while erasing realities of Vietnamese subjects' negotiation of postcolonial concerns and ongoing conditions of forced displacement.

Võ Phiến's *Thư Gửi Bạn* (*Letters to a Friend*, 1976) and *Lại Thư Gửi Bạn* (*Again, Letters to a Friend*, 1979) are among the earliest attempts to conceptualize Vietnamese diasporic experience in America.[2] What importance do letters hold for Vietnamese refugees attempting to create communities after migration and the refugee camp? Published a mere year after the end of the war, Võ Phiến's interest in everyday materials and modes of communication illustrate nascent efforts to define what it means to be a "Vietnamese American." As a mode of diaspora creation, epistolary circulation shows how Vietnam War refugees were scattered across the globe and delineate the literary means that they took to reconnect with one another.[3] Examined in their variable forms, epistles record loss and the unmourned, and they articulate the tensions that have long characterized private and public Asian American lives.

Emergent Vietnamese Americans

In *Letters to a Friend* and *Again, Letters to a Friend*, Võ Phiến creates an epistolary relationship that encompasses himself and an anonymous addressee. He toggles between the plural and singular structures of address, at times writing to a collective entity and at others exchanging dialogue with a specific but unnamed letter writer. To summarize the main difference between the two works, *Letters to a Friend* recalls the days before resettlement, lingering over immediate details of life in the refugee camp. *Again, Letters to a Friend* concerns post-camp life and survival, as refugees must adjust quickly to American social and legal codes while still assessing the conditions under which they became refugees.

In one section from *Letters to a Friend* titled "Vietnamese Americans," Võ Phiến considers the implications of cultural nationalism as Vietnamese begin to disperse across the globe. He recalls that in Saigon, South Vietnam, many citizens turned away from Vietnamese cultural practices, including folk music, classical opera, and popular opera. They tuned in to American rock and pop songs, even dressing and acting the part: "from their hair to their beards and clothing, even the way they shrugged their shoulders, their interactions with siblings and parents" (*Again, Letters*, 81). In other cases, Vietnamese preferred Chinese and French restaurants to Vietnamese cuisine and culinary practices. In seemingly mundane ruminations, Võ Phiến depicts Saigon as a long-standing space of cultural hybridity—what Lisa Lowe defines as "the formation of cultural objects and practices that are produced by the histories of uneven and unsynthetic power relations."[4] For Lowe, it is necessary to understand cultural hybridity not in terms of assimilation but as a mode of survival within asymmetrical power relations. In this light, the culturally hybrid practices Võ Phiến describes take place in a Republic of Vietnam whose social and cultural histories, as I have shown throughout this book, have been shaped by multiple international influences across centuries. The coexistence of varied cultural options speaks to the dissemination of culture that happens under foreign occupation and attends international trade. As Võ Phiến puts it, "One need not leave one's country, or go far" to experience the dynamics of inter-continental encounter (*Letters*, 81).

Võ Phiến finds irony in the fact that, as Vietnam War refugees begin new lives in America, some turn to an essentialist language of roots and origins in response to the assimilationist imperatives of the host country. He ostensibly admires his addressee's commitment to Vietnamese language and cultural rituals within the new spatial and cultural coordinates of the United States, such as cooking with shrimp paste and duck eggs—ingredients deemed unseemly and unappetizing by dominant cultures but that, as Sau-ling Cynthia Wong might argue, signify "the ability to cope with the constraints and persecutions Asian Americans have had to endure as immigrants and racial minorities."[5] Extending this claim to the specificity of Southeast Asian refugees, Võ Phiến's portrayal of Vietnamese food acts in America in 1976 sets up the quotidian as a site of contestation. In Chapter 2 in this volume, culinary tropes map geographies of food and labor under empire; in the late twentieth-century postcolonial moment, they "[mark] ethnicity for communities that live through and against the vagaries of diasporized realities," as Anita Mannur puts it.[6] Hence, Võ Phiến writes, "I concede to you my friend. You are someone with an incredibly strong foundation" (*Letters*, 81). While Vietnamese have long negotiated heterogeneous cultural practices, they now find themselves placing a higher value on Vietnamese words and food objects that can circulate only in the private spaces of their new American homes.

The arc of Võ Phiến's life is rather expansive and worth elaborating to trace the genesis of his desire to create a refugee diaspora through literature. Võ Phiến's biography will help us to understand how the epistolary form threads the global with the local, as his observations concerning the perceived foreignness of everyday Vietnamese objects and practices in America mark an attempt to create a new U.S.-based context for diasporic practice and refugee politics. With a personal history spanning multiple changes in regime and refugee experiences. Võ Phiến held a variety of positions that gave him a complex political perspective, including acting as a government official for the information ministries of opposing political parties and working as an influential and prolific writer in Vietnam and the United States. Võ Phiến was born Đoàn Thế Nhơn in 1925 in Trà Bình, a small village in central Vietnam's Bình Định Province. His father was a teacher who left Bình Định to teach in southern Vietnam, where Võ Phiến's mother joined him in 1934. Võ Phiến saw his parents only intermittently until he reunited with them in 1955. Raised by his paternal grandmother after his mother left for the south, Võ Phiến was heavily influenced by her stories, and they would emerge in many of his writings later on. In 1959, the family moved to Saigon.[7]

From an early age, Võ Phiến's thinking and writing were inspired by some of Vietnam's best-known literary figures. He attended Franco-Vietnamese secondary schools in Qui Nhơn, Huế, and Hanoi, where he came into contact with several important Vietnamese teachers and writers working in different genres. Included in this group were Lâm Giang, a memoirist and dictionary author, and Chế Lan Viên, a well-known romantic poet of the New Poetry School (Thơ Mới) of the 1930s, who later became a revolutionary poet.[8] Võ Phiến acquired proficiency in Chinese and French; he also read a range of American writers, including Ernest Hemingway, John Steinbeck, and William Faulkner, after increased U.S. presence in the second half of the century brought more attention to American authors in South Vietnamese culture, extending familiarity with literary works that had already come to Vietnam by way of French translations. Having grown up in Bình Định, a Communist Party stronghold and target of both French and U.S. military operations during the First and Second Indochina Wars, Võ Phiến witnessed and fled the destruction of his heavily bombed village. In support of the liberation movement, he worked in various capacities as a mail carrier, propaganda team member, and teacher to Việt Minh cadres. In 1948, he married Võ Thị Viễn Phố, about whom very little has been written.[9]

By the early 1950s, Võ Phiến had become disillusioned with the communists and broke with the regime. A cousin and some of Võ Phiến's acquaintances tried to turn him toward the Vietnam Nationalist Party (Quốc Dân Đảng), but Võ Phiến never declared allegiance. Because of his indirect association with the organization, however, the Việt Minh arrested Võ Phiến in 1952 and sentenced him to five years in prison. Võ Phiến's cousin was executed. After his release, Võ Phiến disguised himself as a peasant to avoid detection as he made his way to noncommunist Huế. John C. Schafer writes that Võ Phiến refrained from discussing this period of political and geographical transition, glossing it simply as a "painful time of his life."[10]

In Bình Định, Võ Phiến had worked as director of information, but he made an important move to Saigon in 1959. There he worked as a civil servant for the Ministry of Information under Ngô Đình Diệm's regime and in radio for Mother Vietnam (Mẹ Việt Nam), a U.S.-funded propaganda station broadcast into North Vietnam.[11] Throughout the post–Geneva Accords period, Võ Phiến wrote while he worked, gaining recognition first for his short stories and then for his essays.[12] He became part of Saigon's established literati, whose members came from all over Vietnam, and his stories, criticism, translations, and other writings helped shape South Vietnam's emerging and vibrant literary journal scene. He eventually created the publishing house New Times (Thời Mới) in 1962.

On April 22, 1975, eight days before what has become known as the "fall of Saigon," Võ Phiến left South Vietnam for the United States, along with his wife and daughter, arriving at the refugee camp at Fort Indiantown Gap, Pennsylvania, then resettling in Minneapolis under the sponsorship of a family. Several of the writers with whom he worked but who were unable to leave South Vietnam were sent to reeducation camps. Some died there, while others came to the United States later, under the Orderly Departure Program, which the United Nations High Commissioner for Refugees and the Socialist Republic of Vietnam signed into action in 1979 to facilitate legal emigration of Vietnamese. Võ Phiến's family eventually moved to Los Angeles. As before, Võ Phiến worked as a civil servant while writing on the side, and in 1978 he co-founded *Literary Studies and Art* (*Văn Học Nghệ Thuật*), the first Vietnamese diasporic journal of literary criticism.[13] Võ Phiến also spent years trying to track down Vietnamese literary materials that refugees brought with them to the United States in an effort to reconstruct what was left of South Vietnam's literary archive in the diaspora.[14] He died in 2015.

Võ Phiến's biography exemplifies the complex ways in which the personal and political interact across the *longue durée*. Vietnamese American cultural politics emerges as shifting rather than narrowly anticommunist, and, when interpreted through Vietnamese cultural and political contexts such as those that Võ Phiến's life story illuminates, encourages analyzing Vietnamese American literature through Southeast Asian milieus that complement Asian American literary historical frames. He played an integral role in central and southern Vietnamese attempts to envision and define a distinct culture for a newly emerged nation-state; his prominent role in the world of South Vietnamese letters certainly facilitated his literary efforts in America. Audiences continue to view his writings as holding cultural and political purchase across contentious and uncertain times.[15] As a refugee describing and enacting the creation of a Vietnamese American literature after war and migration, Võ Phiến demonstrates, to borrow Homi Bhabha's terms, how a "state of emergency is also always a state of emergence."[16] Furthermore, his elaborations of refugee experience as ongoing, in contrast to public perceptions of refugeeism as a temporary, finite condition, point to notions of crisis and emergency as flawed premises for understanding what it means to be a refugee. Võ Phiến's texts are a neglected contribution to Vietnamese American literary studies even though they are a part of the field—that is, if we view the field through a genealogy that includes its development in the late 1970s in Vietnamese.

Narrating Refugees as Immigrants

The *Letters to a Friend* series is concerned with refugees who left South Vietnam in 1975 and may have resettled by April 1976, when the first book was published. In the years immediately after his arrival in America, there were no Vietnamese ethnic enclaves, which explains why Vietnamese cultural and historical practices take place for Võ Phiến primarily in the private sphere. In an American frame, they have become anomalous and anachronistic. The portrayal of the privatization of Vietnamese language and food shows how an immigrant narrative quickly reframes refugee experiences in the immediate postwar period. A long history of U.S. political and military involvement in Southeast Asia that results in late twentieth-century forced migrations is repackaged as a narrative about the essential foreignness and eventual assimilation of the Vietnamese. However, that Võ Phiến writes in Vietnamese in epistolary form suggests how a sense of shared, minoritized identification among displaced Vietnamese is being forged across geographic distance and as external to English-speaking and English-reading publics.

Rather than succumb to an Americanist telos of inclusion premised on the idea that Vietnamese cultural practices are out of place and out of time, Võ Phiến situates the new context of Southeast Asian "refugeeness" within long historical terms—one moment in the history of American assimilation. Mainstream media and U.S. state narratives depict refugees as suddenly appearing on America' shores, requiring quick, pragmatic solutions and in melodramatic need of assimilation. But Võ Phiến dissects these melodramatic narrative logics, submitting that assimilationist rhetoric is a means of rewriting refugee histories as multicultural phenomena—a sleight of hand that promotes an ideology of self-transformation through Americanization. Accordingly, many Southeast Asian refugees have adopted this euphemistic logic: "Assimilation—the term is difficult to hear, thus many of our people prefer to translate it as 'integration.' It is not because they want to abstain: 'assimilation' [đồng hóa] is just too painful" (*Again, Letters*, 82).[17]

Although "integration" becomes the preferred term for many displaced people to ameliorate painful realities of refugee subjection within an emerging global narrative that expunges their massive losses, Võ Phiến refuses to accept and reproduce this practice. He traces the violent history of American assimilation that underlies depoliticized ideals of the United States as a nation that welcomes immigrants. Tracing a clear line from early twentieth-century American nativism to late twentieth-century refugee contexts, Võ Phiến references Theodore Roosevelt's assimilationist rhetoric that, in Roosevelt's words, aimed to cultivate "builders of this republic"—a program of ethnoracial and historical homogenization at all costs. Roosevelt's phrase was part of a wartime appeal to advance what the *New York Times* described as a "race fusion."[18] Corresponding with early twentieth-century U.S. imperial rhetoric that asserted a shared American consciousness circling the globe (discussed in Chapter 1), Roosevelt's assimilation required immigrants to renounce "the lands from which they or their forefathers came." He expanded, "Any force which attempts to retard that assimilative process is a force hostile to the highest interests of [the] country."[19]

Tracking the shifting vocabulary of race in America across the twentieth century, Võ Phiến couples his reading of Roosevelt with an analysis of John Steinbeck's *Travels with Charley: In Search of America* (1962) to consider how ideologies of assimilation evolve into a subtler form during the mid-century. Interrogating changing, arbitrary reifications of American national identity, he questions what exactly it takes, how far one must go, and how one knows when one has actually become "American." While Roosevelt blatantly calls for assimilation and disconnection from one's past, Steinbeck looks to the American landscape as a metaphor for the smooth incorporation of multi-cultural elements: "Steinbeck suddenly got the idea that he needed to travel all around the country, see with his own eyes every hill, every river, hear with his own ears the different voices of people from different regions, smell with his own nose the scent of the trees and grass of the country, that he must interact directly in order to learn truly about his land" (*Again, Letters*, 83). Võ Phiến interprets Steinbeck's literary multiculturalism as seeming vulnerability to myriad forms of difference that suggest Steinbeck is more friend than foe to human heterogeneity. Yet Võ Phiến's depiction puzzles over Steinbeck's figuration of human variability in terms of sound rather than bodily forms; difference can easily settle itself when abstracted from embodied presence.

Steinbeck's views on race were, of course, not simple. His travels to the U.S. South revealed the virulence of racism that would deeply disturb him and truncate his journey. *Travels with Charley* is full of contradictions result-ing from Steinbeck's attempt to describe the America he sees while knowing that "finding" America also means discursively creating it. Nevertheless, Võ Phiến zeroes in on one of Steinbeck's most crystallized efforts in that text to name what it is that Americans share. In Steinbeck's words: "For all of our enormous geographic range, for all of our sectionalism, for all of our inter-woven breeds drawn from every part of the ethnic world, we are a nation, a new breed. . . . [Americans] have more in common than they have apart. And this is the more remarkable because it has happened so quickly."[20] For Võ Phiến, Steinbeck's kind of variety recognizes particularities but digests them into an Americanized unity. Extending Alice B. Toklas's portrayal of Vietnamese servants as a tableau of multiethnicity and anticipating how, in war, Herr would aestheticize racialized difference by depicting Vietnamese body fragments as wartime scenery, Steinbeck's view of America appreciates variety but ultimately dissolves it into a pleasing, panoramic whole; his America is fundamentally picturesque and serene, sublimating U.S. colonial dynamics that have been culturally and historically submerged across the century. Moreover, that Steinbeck praises the *efficiency* with which ethnics have achieved a shared American identity glosses over the violence of the process. His projection of human multiplicity as assimilated, harmonious sound works hard to reconcile the potential discordance of difference, redirecting underlying realities of war and empire through a transcendent sonic metaphor.

In 1967, Steinbeck traveled to Vietnam as a reporter for *Newsday* and wrote about Vietnamese in strikingly similar terms of sound: "There are a few small restaurants in Can Tho where Viet people, always with their children, go to eat and talk in their language, which sounds like singing."[21] Surrounded by living Vietnamese bodies, Steinbeck notices most the musicality of their voices. Colleen Lye argues that in Steinbeck's prewar agricultural fiction, Asian character "exerts more of an aural than a visual presence," placing the sonic, ghostly Asiatic as a "spectral figure on the margins of narrative vision."[22] Similarly, as a trope of successful ethnic assimilation in *Travels with Charley*, sound carries over into Steinbeck's Vietnam to signify the presence of ethnic bodies while removing Vietnamese flesh and contexts from view. In Võ Phiến's gloss of Steinbeck, Steinbeck believes that, despite their various differences, "Americans do indeed resemble one another"; Võ Phiến, however, reinterprets this conclusion, instead linking Steinbeck to Roosevelt to outline a long, morphing genealogy of American assimilationist ideology, from overt homogenization to a more subtly problematic liberal-multiculturalist assimilationism. The latter incarnation celebrates diverse histories, cultures, and identities but nevertheless forces them to find common ground, defined as the overarching success of American hegemony (*Again, Letters*, 83). Võ Phiến articulates a transitional moment in assimilationist ideology that, decades later, Alfredo Valladão would describe as the "salad bowl" metaphor, a supplantation of the early twentieth century's "melting pot": Steinbeck's distinct hills and rivers still look like distinct hills and rivers.[23]

Võ Phiến looks to the canon of American history and literature as sources for critiquing the nation's ethnocentric ideologies. While Jodi Kim locates "Cold War epistemology" as defining how "Asian Americans have come to know their very selves,"[24] Võ Phiến decolonizes Cold War epistemological foundations as they shape Vietnamese diasporic self-understanding. Linking Cold War contexts back to the 1910s, he outlines different manifestations of assimilation across the twentieth century, which have worked to flatten specific geopolitical conditions within which subjects arrive in the United States; Võ Phiến de-exceptionalizes and re-historicizes "Vietnam" by providing elided context to refugees' flight. Thus, although many Vietnamese refugees use "integration" to describe their resettlement experiences, implying their belief in eventual and equal participation in U.S. social and political life, Võ Phiến rejects this move and its premises of telos and progress, asserting that it softens the coercive force of assimilation that refugees know is at play. American imperatives of assimilation and the speed with which individuals are expected to achieve it will prove to be central conundrums for Vietnamese refugees, whom social scientists, mainstream media, and political figures were quickly re-narrating and mystifying as immigrants, thereby eliding the changing geopolitical circumstances in Southeast Asia that produced them.

Toward a Refugee Literary History

Following Kim's claim that "Asian American cultural productions critically reframe the Cold War," recent studies of Vietnam War refugees have interrogated central tropes of Cold War discourse concerning Southeast Asian Americans.[25] Some of the most trenchant critiques in what has emerged as critical refugee studies have deconstructed the telic narrative of U.S. rescue that surrounds displaced people to understand the refugee figure as an *idea* that does heavy ideological work rather than as strictly a legal category. American state and cultural narratives often attach a sense of ethical urgency to addressing refugee situations, positioning refugees as a problem to be solved and, consequently, shrouding the long history of commercial, political, and military activities in Southeast Asia that contextualize a refugee "crisis." At the same time, refugees are a *solution*, as Espiritu notes, "deployed to 'rescue' the Vietnam War for Americans."[26] For Mimi Thi Nguyen, the refuge and citizenship that America extends to displaced people works toward this new script, but it places refugees in a position of debt, requiring of them a constant expression of gratitude for the "gift of freedom" they receive.[27]

Letters to a Friend illustrates how much the performance of gratitude required by America's emergent identity as global savior of refugees determines Vietnamese diasporic day-to-day life.[28] For instance, Vietnamese constantly face pressures of religious conversion. Võ Phiến writes: "Men and women from the sponsoring churches take turns insistently inviting refugees to go to service, take turns driving the entire family to church every Sunday, . . . advise the household to go to confession. [Vietnamese f]amilies that have practiced ancestor worship for many generations now find themselves confused and worried, for if their children concede to this religious influence, how will they perform their worship?" (11). This question is ostensibly about cultural practice. But as Viet Thanh Nguyen writes, the Vietnam War—as the "bad war, a syndrome, a quagmire" that serves "as a metonym for the problem of war and memory"—entwines Vietnamese cultural practice with the politics of memory and recollecting history.[29] Võ Phiến's comment amounts to a concern about how Vietnam War refugees will be mourned and how and whose history will be remembered in the future.

In another letter, Võ Phiến identifies the importance of conversational Vietnamese to demonstrate how language becomes a milieu through which Vietnamese rehearse refugees' indebtedness on an everyday level. He describes how two Vietnamese women who have just met initiate an excited dialogue in Vietnamese, having had few chances to speak their language since life after the camp. Yet they find themselves interrupting their exchange to apologize to the American woman who has introduced them, even as they privately question why they are taking such care to perform this gratuitous courtesy. Võ Phiến wishes that they could have carried on uninterrupted without feeling so surveilled: "keep talking, regardless of courtesy." For Võ Phiến, "We have paid them a very high price," an explicit reversal of the imperialist logic that places others in debt to the empire (10). Dismissing American platitudes and norms of civility, Võ Phiến identifies the gap between public perceptions of refugees' indebtedness and private Vietnamese sentiments that these perceptions skew actual historical relations; the United States has already cheated those whom they are "saving"—a rebuttal to Henry Kissinger's assertion that the United States "mortgaged" its foreign policy to aid South Vietnam, as discussed in Chapter 3. Võ Phiến remarks on the hegemonic circularity of refugees' debt and payment that will never be made in full; refugees have already "paid" more than ever will be publicly—and historically—acknowledged.

Vietnamese Americans' tailoring of the public self toward American expectations of gratitude compels a conception of what we might call more broadly a *refugee literary history*. Võ Phiến's treatment of assimilation and tropes of debt resonates with Hannah Arendt's "We Refugees" (1943), an essay that conceptualizes refugees' subjectivity as entailing performance according to the expectations of the new country, which international protocols and relief groups reinforce. Echoing Võ Phiến's claim that many Vietnamese Americans prefer the term "integration" to "assimilation" to explain their refugee condition, Arendt writes, "We don't like to be called 'refugees.' We ourselves call each other 'newcomers' or 'immigrants.'"[30] She adds that the "insane optimism" one might associate with refugees "is next door to despair," for the refugee has lost all powers of choice: "The less we are free to decide who we are or to live as we like, the more we try to put up a front, to hide the facts, to play roles."[31] "Refugee" is the category that gains displaced persons legal recognition, yet it is also an identity that refugees must work to shed because of the nationalist, assimilationist expectations of the resettlement country. Ultimately, refugees must continuously "prove our loyalty," becoming complicit in the public erasure of their own grievances and histories.[32]

Arendt shows that the dynamic of refugee performance will repeat itself in the contemporary world. She writes, it is "the same story all over the world, repeated again and again."[33] As their recognition is premised on the threat of exclusion and persecution, refugees are figures through whom nation-states redefine sovereignty, citizenship, and rights in the twentieth century in relation to ongoing national and geopolitical shifts. "Refugees driven from country to country," Arendt writes, "represent the vanguard of their peoples."[34]

We might read Võ Phiến's epistolary writings as examples of how the geographic scattering of Vietnam War refugees marks an important phase in global refugee history. Paralleling Arendt's observation that refugees are *unsettling* even as they are being *resettled* because they embody and thus expose the geopolitical power plays that produce displaced people, Võ Phiến notes that American discourse conflates different kinds of migration by viewing them as equivalent examples of human movement. He writes that after May 1975, the United States "probably did not have any intention of reviewing its immigration policy or setting in place a policy particular to those honored guests who came from Vietnam" (*Again, Letters,* 82). Refugees then must negotiate the binaristic "choice" that U.S. assimilationist ideology has installed across the *longue durée*: "on the one hand extracting one's roots, on the other maintaining one's roots." As a de-historicizing mechanism that collapses immigrant and refugee contexts, "assimilation" constructs absolutist notions of identity that foreclose cultural, historical, and political complexity. It disallows the particular temporal and spatial multivalence that is inherent to experiences of war and consequent displacement. While Vietnamese refugees have lived through a war that I characterized in Chapter 3 as one of the body in pieces, here their surviving bodies house deep emotional devastation and fragmentation stemming from U.S. imperatives of assimilation, wherein Americanization attempts to exorcise other cultural and national attachments: "It can't but be gutwrenching"—an irreparable, forced division that American rhetoric of rescue purportedly helps to heal and reunify (*Again, Letters*, 82).

While Võ Phiến recounts how rapidly refugees were expected not only to re-narrate but also reconstitute themselves as immigrants to secure the possibility of becoming U.S. citizens, *Letters* is threaded with unresolved historical and political issues that reveal the density of refugee politics that cannot be consolidated within clear-cut political categories. On this point, Võ Phiến's continued grappling with South Vietnamese and North Vietnamese geopolitics in the present takes a rhizomatic contour rather than defaulting to absolutist and closed understandings. For instance, his assessment of the conflict as an international affair framed in deep time and space brings into view not only the United States, the Soviet Union, and China, but also the war's relationship to geopolitical currents in Israel, Cuba, Angola, and North and South Korea (*Letters*, 76–83). Võ Phiến does not expand on this nexus of connections, but that the extensive geopolitical mapping he broaches has yet to register in American public consciousness when it comes to the conflict demonstrates how works such as Võ Phiến's epistolary series embed details that can serve as grounds for new critical histories of the war.

Moreover, Võ Phiến overturns stereotypes that Vietnam War refugees are perpetually in gratitude to America and Americans. In her field-defining call for a critical refugee studies attuned to the dynamics of forcibly displaced people's active personhood, Espiritu notes that Vietnamese refugees have "a complex political subjectivity" in which anticommunist sentiments and "gratitude" for resettlement can combine with sharp critiques of U.S. "rescue" efforts and imperial histories.[35] Relatedly, Schafer describes Võ Phiến's writings on America as having no "good things to say about" American culture and "[failing] to express gratitude for the assistance provided his family and many other Vietnamese families by the U.S. government." They are "unrelenting" in their scathing critiques of U.S. culture and empire.[36] In an interview conducted in 2001, Võ Phiến reveals the perpetually performative nature of Vietnamese American self-representation, noting that if Vietnamese Americans have scaled back their critiques, they have done so only because "having lived here longer, . . . we don't dare talk carelessly anymore."[37] Võ Phiến demonstrates how American discourses of Vietnam that emerged after the war distanced public memory and history from U.S. state and military intervention in Southeast Asia and the specifics of refugee production, which was significantly linked to the refugee camp, a crucial site for Southeast Asians' recoding.

Refugee Production

Although we take it for granted that people displaced by the Vietnam War were refugees, this assumption obscures the *production* of refugees and refugee resettlement, which are ongoing processes that take varied forms. While conditions of refugee resettlement have been increasingly studied with more detail, a brief recapitulation of them here emphasizes how different institutional structures operated in the legal, military, and pedagogical making of refugees. The journey for refugees involved several sites both off and on the mainland. From South Vietnam, refugees were transported to an overseas American base at Utapo, Thailand, or Subic Bay or Clark Field in the Philippines. Next came Wake Island or Guam, where reception centers with a capacity for up to fifty thousand refugees had been set up. When it became clear that the hastily built facilities could not handle the large number of refugees, four camps were built on demand on the U.S. mainland: Camp Pendleton, a U.S. Marine base in California; Fort Chaffee, a U.S. Army base in Arkansas; Eglin Air Force Base in Florida; and Fort Indiantown Gap, Pennsylvania, which was also a U.S. Army base.[38]

The camps themselves were built to be relocation centers—that familiar phrase from Japanese American internment—and, as in the past, the government often avoided using the term "refugee camp."[39] At the facilities, which were operated by the U.S. military and Interagency Task Force (IATF), Southeast Asian subjects were recoded through data collection and new forms of identification.[40] The day after they arrived, refugees underwent physical exams, immunizations, X-rays, and screening for communicable diseases. They were also examined for possible security threats using both U.S. and South Vietnamese files.[41] Space in tents or barracks would then be assigned, and Social Security and registration numbers were issued. Refugees then signed up with the Department of Commerce for work and with a Voluntary Agency (VOLAG). These processes typically took twenty-four to seventy-two hours.[42]

The IATF delineated four ways to leave the camp: Third World resettlement, repatriation, financial proof of self-sufficiency, and sponsorship. The first three options were not viable for the majority of refugees, so sponsorship by an organization or family constituted the most common way to leave the camp.[43] The VOLAGs were under contract to resettle refugees within forty-five days, while sponsors were required to offer fiscal and personal responsibility for the refugee family for up to two years. The IATF officially paid each organization $500 per refugee, and the average overall sponsorship cost per refugee was $5,601.[44] Essentially, sponsors were responsible for providing basic needs such as shelter, food, and clothing, as well as helping with employment, education, and social and cultural adjustment until refugees were deemed ready to strike out on their own.[45]

Official rhetoric often resorted to a state-of-emergency logic to narrate the refugee situation, relying on themes of expediency and eventual Vietnamese self-sufficiency to project into a future moment that would succeed the refugee "crisis." This paradigm of emergency naturalized what was transpiring, focusing on efficient action and "problem-solving" tactics while obscuring the development of refugees, as well as the long history that had led up to the "crisis." The term "refugee" itself was complicated, as refugees from the conflict were actually parolees when the U.S. government admitted them, meaning that their stay was temporary until legislation could be passed to change their legal status to refugees. While they were in the camps, they could not go beyond their borders, because this would shift their classification from parolee to illegal alien, opening up the possibility of prosecution.[46] The *legal* production of the refugee was joined by the *military* making of refugees. All four mainland camps were military bases, and refugees' journeys were facilitated by existing U.S. military presence throughout Southeast Asia and the Pacific. As Espiritu argues, in addition to the military's role in the wars that produce displaced people, its hand in refugee resettlement inflects refugeeness with a martial frame.[47] Last, as all phases of refugee resettlement entailed some form of instruction whereby refugees learned about American cultural and social norms, the camps served a *pedagogical* function that sought to Americanize refugees.

The emergence of the refugee camp coincides with a moment of crisis for the modern nation-state, compelling the state to find new ways to sustain the biological life of the nation. According to Giorgio Agamben, the order of the modern nation-state, once premised on the functioning unity of land (locale), the state (political order), and the nation or birth (what indicates life) now finds itself faced with the disconnection of that trinity, whose forms and relations are no longer clear.[48] States of exception erupt to mark the momentary blurring of juridico-political lines wherein order fundamentally unravels: "every possibility of clearly distinguishing between membership and inclusion, between what is outside and what is inside, between exception and rule" is thrown into question.[49] The refugee camp becomes a way to manage the consequences of ongoing warfare and other kinds of economic, political, and environmental conflict. Even as refugee rhetoric oriented around assumptions of statelessness and citizenship presuppose the stability of the nation-state, the mere existence of continual flows of refugees ruptures the nation-state form.

Under U.S. sovereignty but "outside the normal juridical order,"[50] postwar refugee camps mark a point of crisis by housing refugee bodies that are also threshold lives. As "limit figures" who exceed existing contours of land, state, and nation and who force the suspension of the law, these threshold lives index historical moments when "the law enters into relation with that which has no legal standing" and must decide how and on what terms "bare life" will enter the realm of inclusion and the rule, as well as what conditions will define the norm and rule.[51] As discussed in Chapter 1, the mixed-race body of the early twentieth-century acts as a limit figure that tests imperial nation-states' rationale for determining citizenship in the colony. The colonized hybrid anticipates the condition of the refugee, whose future lies in the hands of international refugee organizations, countries of asylum, and nations of resettlement—many of which contribute to or create the condition of statelessness they then try to resolve. As a limit figure, the refugee reveals how questions of citizenship and the norms that define it continue to be posed as immediate, nation-state problems, even though they are of a fully long historical, international scale. In the Vietnam War context, the supposed time-space compression threading official discourse concerning forced displacement manifests in the emergency use of sites off the U.S. mainland for quickly resettling transnational refugee subjects, exhibiting what David Palumbo-Liu describes as a practice of "[dispatching] history to the margins of visibility, to erase the effects of colonization and neocolonial policies in Asia."[52] Simultaneously, the notion of having to retrain refugees to accept American norms overshadowed histories of what Jana Lipman refers to as the "professional and physical proximity" between Southeast Asians and Americans that existed before the refugees' migration and that Võ Phiến delineates in his writings.[53]

State rhetoric concerning whether and how to incorporate refugee limit figures into the fold of everyday American life spilled over into public conversations. One area coordinator argued that a history of war in Southeast Asia had long scattered Vietnamese so that their social structure was already one of dispersal; as a result, they "had no sense of community responsibility" and needed the intervention of "a foreign intermediary" to curb their belligerence. In his words, refugees needed strict discipline so they "would *learn to live together* under the auspices of camp management."[54] This comment evokes Achille Mbembe's idea that built spaces for victims of war are a form of governmentality, exerting "tight control over bodies" in order to process them for passage to the new destination.[55] The camp has a preemptive function by disciplining refugees, interpellating them as pliant, assimilating subjects. In addition to the psychological conditioning of refugees, a desire to sanitize refugee bodies demonstrated an American fear of the kind of corporeality the conflict brought home. A *Los Angeles Times* article posited that the influx of Southeast Asian refugees threatened all domains of social and biological life, from job competition to disease. "Thousands of Americans" living near the refugee camps bemoaned their new neighbors, who were viewed as "a threat to the economy and health of their communities." Democratic Congressman Thomas M. Rees from Beverly Hills expressed exasperation with racist perceptions of refugees as "nothing but diseased job-seekers," while Dean Brown, the California official who managed the state's evacuation process, had to comfort residents that most arrivals were healthy, stating, "Only 48 of the first 38,000 refugees evacuated required hospital care."[56]

A sense of urgency stemming from perceived threats of job takeover and disease suffuses these news snippets, which mute contexts of war and the camp to victimize and pathologize Southeast Asian refugee bodies. American imperial melodrama, discussed in Chapter 1, takes a neoliberal turn, as the rhetoric of rescue and aid obfuscates the ailing refugee's production by interested national and international parties. And despite the "problem-solving" protocols that statesmen and officials typically call for in refugee situations, in some cases essential services were never set up.[57] Refugee camps frequently acted independently, left to the discretion of multiple political authorities and organizations that could tweak stated federal goals as they saw fit. California's Governor Jerry Brown and Arkansas's Governor David Pryor, for instance, neglected to appoint officials to assist Vietnamese in registering for work.[58] Representative Norman Mineta of San Jose noted that he was barred from attending a bipartisan meeting of the California House held to "clarify" the refugee situation, suggesting the racialization of not only refugees but also the decision-making process concerning them.[59]

The need to "clarify" America's stance on refugees was perhaps most evident in changes made to existing law, which redirected the conversation from the war to the "pragmatic" issue of changing citizenship parameters for the country's newest incoming group.[60] Recall that refugees were initially considered parolees, granted only temporary asylum by the McCarran-Walter Act of 1952.[61] When the Adjustment of Status Clause (H.R. 7769, Public Law 95–144) of 1977, an amendment that changed the status of Vietnam War parolees to permanent residents, was signed, Senator Edward Kennedy and President Jimmy Carter emphasized the social and economic benefits of permanently accepting America's new arrivals.[62] Affirming the ideological worthiness of Southeast Asian displaced people, Kennedy stated that they had "shown their commitment to the ideals of this Nation, their willingness to participate in our country." A teleological reversal emerges whereby Kennedy suggests that the future-tense loyal citizen already exists in the present.[63] Consequently, the bill is a mere formality that inscribes the "good" Southeast Asian refugee within the domain of the law.

Carter asserted that making refugees eligible for citizenship was an act of American patriotism: "Although the citizenship procedure takes 5 years, it puts them on an equal basis with others who come to our country with renewed hope for their lives." He looked ahead to the end of the camps, whose closings would complete the American rescue of refugees—a "conclusion" that would affirm how refugees had "assimilated into our society," or, put differently, how refugee camps had successfully prepared inhabitants to become loyal and compliant citizens and workers. Kennedy thanked Carter for affirming America's history as a "humanitarian nation," while Carter forged kinship between Southeast Asians and Americans in the name of "human rights" and "human freedoms."[64] Together, their remarks demonstrate how melodrama stretches across twentieth-century American empire to formalize a dominant refugee aesthetic, reifying forces of good and evil and infantilizing and feminizing Vietnamese as victims needing rescue from a heroic, remasculinizing America.

In the post–Vietnam War era, the United States needed a way to rebuild its political and military standing. The Cold War practice of using the refugee as "a moral-political tactic" strengthened in the late twentieth century, allowing America to claim moral rectitude by positioning Southeast Asian refugees as the starting point for a U.S.-led global humanitarian future.[65] The dominant image of mass-migration that circulated in the media—in 1975, most of the refugees left in the span of a week, between April 25 and May 1—impressed on American popular consciousness racialized dramas of powerless, vulnerable Vietnamese void of their own varied decolonizing politics. These representations called on displaced people of the Vietnam War to act as what Liisa Malkki terms "speechless emissaries,"[66] interpellated to help craft a new narrative of American exceptionalism oriented not around sensationalized dismembered victims of war, as in Herr's *Dispatches*, but around America's swift actions in response to defenseless figures in the face of what was "the largest mass departure of asylum seekers by sea in modern history."[67] In some ways, American cultural narratives such as Herr's that portrayed Vietnamese bodies as excessively violated aided the story of their needed salvation by America. Enforcing a state-of-emergency logic, dramatic images of spatial drift and desperate bodies re-politicized refugees by appealing to emotion and downplaying geopolitical context to deflect American responsibility for refugee production.[68] Put differently, metalepsis prevailed as refugees became the cause, rather than the effects, of U.S. "care." The assertion that refugee bodies and camps were unprecedented and, according to a U.S. Marine Corps document, unlikely to happen again erased from view a long history of racially mapping America through policies of relocation, concentration, dispersal, or extermination.[69]

We might say that post–Vietnam War refugee discourse has contributed to an enduring late twentieth-century form of melodrama: American neoliberal melodrama, an updated use of the genre that renews American exceptionalism. By "saving" refugees, the nation refashions its role as agent of war to humanitarian leader, and military capability displaces military loss through a focus on its humanitarian work, even as the complex subjectivity—the "humanness"—of forcibly displaced people is erased. This narrative feat, in turn, "saves" the nation from a legacy of trauma and defeat, from the paralysis of the Vietnam syndrome. By "rescuing" refugees, America rescues its "free world" image of itself and latently legitimates its political-economic system through the use of refugee rescue as national capital. The desperation of Southeast Asians, as speechless emissaries caught in a state of emergency, to reach American shores proves that any disciplinary measures taken are worth the gifts of American freedom and citizenship; their supposed willingness to assimilate advertises the kind of idealized subjects that people from areas of conflict can become if their countries undergo American-style democratization.[70] Americanization of displaced people predicated on the idea of voluntary self-transformation—a model that was entrenched by the turn of the twentieth century, as discussed in Chapter 1—serves a powerful and flexible ideology from the late twentieth century onward, affirming American multicultural ideals and offering national redemption, even after devastating wars.

By systematically distributing refugees across national space, America's Vietnam War refugee model illustrates how stateless subjects constitute crucial sites through which the United States redefines its role as an international power after the Vietnam War. Saving displaced people enables America to recuperate its status as a "nation of refuge,"[71] a "nation of immigrants," rather than admitting that it produces refugees. However, the reality that U.S. wars contribute to refugee production and that U.S. officials play a large role in determining who is a refugee surfaced in the attorney-general's decisions to exercise parole authority—that is, the ability to grant aliens temporary entry into the United States—a total of fourteen times.[72] By 1978, 170,698 Vietnamese were living in all U.S. states, Guam, the Virgin Islands, and Puerto Rico. The southern and western areas of the United States resettled one-third of refugees; the north-central region, 20 percent; and the northeastern region, 10 percent.[73] Records show that refugees also ended up in Bangladesh, Iran, Ivory Coast, Martinique, New Caledonia, and Senegal—a range of geographies and political contexts that attest not to the neat conclusion of refugeeism but to the spatially expansive and temporally elongated process of refugee production and resettlement.[74] For Vietnamese who were waiting inside the camps, the end of the "crisis" was not necessarily desired, as leaving meant bidding farewell to this "'last bit of Vietnam.'"[75]

Epistolary Networks: Refuge from Refugeeism

U.S. refugee discourse recodes conditions of war and refugee experience to advance a telos of progression and American citizenship more typical of the immigrant narrative. In light of the U.S. nation-state's variant of refugee aesthetics, diasporic epistles written to anonymous readers become a form through which Võ Phiến attempts to bring a diasporic community into being—a form of refuge wherein subjects might articulate their own complex cultures and politics as distinct from prevailing paradigms of Vietnam War refugeeism centered on U.S. salvation and Southeast Asian refugee indebtedness. Vietnamese-language spaces offer literary and critical refuge from the commodification of stateless people that renews U.S. exceptionalism; at the same time, they create an important forum through which to mark the losses that will never be officially recorded.

As noted, Võ Phiến himself was a product of the Fort Indiantown Gap refugee camp, which, he observes, housed eighteen thousand persons (*Letters*, 21). He thus lived through America's program of refugee camp life, followed by sponsorship and dispersal. The moniker of the camp itself marks a long history of forced displacement in the United States, as Fort Indiantown Gap is an Army and National Guard training facility whose name evokes the regional presence of the Delaware, Shawnee, Lenape, and Susquehannock Native Americans and, especially, recalls Susquehannock resistance to colonists in the eighteenth century, which led to the construction of the American fortifications.[76] Upon arrival, Võ Phiến observes the camp border, over which he sets his sights and imagines an ecology of diaspora: "Looking into the forest nearby: the brilliantly white rhodenias recall the yellow flowers around the fence at home" (*Letters*, 20). While the ITAF aimed to resettle refugees efficiently, Võ Phiến describes how refugees initially acted out this imperative but eventually did not want to leave: "When they first arrived at the camp, everyone frantically looked for a sponsor. Three months later, when sponsors from different states reached out to refugees, many in Indiantown shook their heads . . . finding reasons to decline, to delay: perhaps they were waiting for relatives to arrive from Hong Kong or Malaysia, or a wife was about to give birth . . . or an elderly mother was sick. . . . The camp authorities panicked that their program would fail" (*Letters*, 21).

Võ Phiến articulates the tension between the IATF's goal of efficacy and refugees' material circumstances. Refugees' transnational ties and complex politics—which encompass both American contexts and multiple phases in Vietnamese political history and are not reducible to Cold War binaries—fill camp life with a density of emotions, histories, and futurities that the camps' logic of rapid dispersal and resettlement will terminate. Võ Phiến describes how front-page articles in the bilingual daily newspaper at Fort Indiantown, *Healed Land* (Đất Lành), attempt to manipulate readers according to this camp logic through rhetoric: they "entreat and soothe. . . . [T]hen . . . they threaten and forcefully urge refugees to go out and start a new life" (*Letters*, 21). Toward this end, one front-page article, titled "And Why Not Malawi?" is accompanied by a map and description of the similarities between Vietnam's and Malawi's climates in an effort to clear refugee camps of its inhabitants.⁷⁷

While the camp is meant to be a way station to stable resettlement, Võ Phiến writes that the camp itself has become a "new homeland" (*quê hương mới*). Refugees already exist in a state of split subjectivity—in his words, refugees want to find a place to "live freely, *send our bodies temporarily*" (*gửi thân tạm*). Understanding the camp as an interim space rather than a path to permanent refuge, refugees reconfigure the camp culturally and economically. Across the barracks, one can hear "the sounds of Vietnamese speech and laughter" and Vietnamese songs playing on an old cassette tape or borrowed guitar. Worries about the future or one's fate can be assuaged by chatting with the fortune-teller nearby. Refugees also buy goods from and sell goods to one another, re-creating a sense of their former markets and economies and exemplifying how the refugee camp is not simply an abject space but also one of dynamic, constituted cultures and politics (*Again, Letters*, 82).

In light of U.S. policies of post-camp dispersal, Võ Phiến considers the value of letters for emergent Vietnamese diasporic culture. A mere three months after arrival, in September 1975, Võ Phiến notes, only a little more than eight thousand refugees are left in the camp, a marker of time's passing that will break up the community that has formed. While the camp is a built environment that clusters refugees to prepare them for separation, Võ Phiến redefines the border that outlines the camp's perimeter to describe the condition of statelessness in terms of a fragile "thread of shared, invisible affection" among refugees, one that will soon be lost but that prompts Võ Phiến to consider the purpose of establishing a literary diaspora and, simultaneously, a diasporic literature. Anticipating the question "Why write letters now?" he notes that audiences might view such acts as impractical when refugees are both struggling to survive and globally scattered without stable addresses. Võ Phiến estimates that overseas readership for Vietnamese-language materials in the United States is negligible, "less than 200,000." Those eager to read such materials cannot find them or, if they are lucky, must wait for them to come by mail. It is remarkable that *Letters to a Friend* was published a mere year after migration in 1976 by the Iowa-based Ban Nguoi Viet (in essence, a small operation run out of an apartment), yet Võ Phiến asserts that a general dearth of publishers and readers makes the future of the Vietnamese language in America uncertain. He predicts it will not thrive overseas but merely stay afloat, so to speak (*Letters*, 21). What would be the purpose, then, of writing letters to anonymous Vietnamese readers?

While empires and international organizations tend to frame refugees in finite terms of crisis and emergency, Vietnamese-language letters provide a chronotopically open portrayal of refugeeness. In form, letters offer an open spatial and temporal structure—they connote circulation and invite responses in future time—and when combined with Vietnamese language, they create a venue through which a Vietnamese-literate public can express and consider refugeeness and conditions of refugee production as ongoing. Võ Phiến suggests that letters are the most appropriate form for considering these issues in the particular context of Southeast Asian refugees. Refugees face the difficulty of not being able to speak Vietnamese daily, not simply because refugees have been displaced and dispersed, but also because postwar America adamantly seeks to forget Vietnam. Consider that President Gerald Ford announced in a commencement speech at Tulane University on April 23, 1975, that the war was "finished, as far as America is concerned."[78]

The value of Steinbeck to Võ Phiến's argument for a Vietnamese literary refugee aesthetics becomes clearer as he ruminates on the politics of language; while Steinbeck aestheticizes different languages into a pleasing aural, salad-bowl whole, Võ Phiến points out, English, by definition, dominates and marginalizes other linguistic practices. Viet Thanh Nguyen qualifies the uneven dynamics of language in literary production and criticism, arguing that Vietnamese American literature has come to share certain predictable formal qualities across genres. In addition to being written by the community's most educated class, it is primarily "a literature of translation and affirmation," taking care to "explain some feature of the ethnic community" and criticizing the United States only within understood boundaries to maintain an overarching expectation of "reconciliation and closure."[79] Indeed, Võ Phiến is part of the Vietnamese diaspora's educated class, suggesting how Nguyen's observation may cut across English- and Vietnamese-language works. But in some contrast, in Võ Phiến's work writing in Vietnamese becomes a way to ritualize linguistic practice and maintain a space of critique outside the parameters Nguyen describes.

The specificity of letters in Võ Phiến's texts compels understanding of the epistolary as an early post–Vietnam War form of Vietnamese diasporic culture. Given how various organizations, institutions, and governments interpellated Vietnam War refugees as silent, desperate bodies, letters' formal premise of directly linking the first and second person, the sender and receiver, constructs Vietnamese diasporic conversations outside hegemonic English-language structures of address. They work relationally—or, as Mikhail Bakhtin writes, are interactive and dialogic because of their reciprocal formal structure.[80] In Martin Joseph Ponce's words, letters are a mode through which postcolonial diasporics "join up'" with others in "distant locales."[81]

Hence, Võ Phiến writes about refugees, "We want to hear each other in the same situation." Letters create a common "frame" for Vietnamese diasporics, establishing a familiar linguistic, emotional, and historical milieu. To be sure, no literary milieu is without power dynamics, and Vietnamese language cultures in the diaspora can reproduce forms of cultural nationalism—a topic that is rich for future investigation. Yet in Võ Phiến's epistolary writings, the act of writing letters in Vietnamese becomes creative-critical work—what Peter Hitchcock might call a "genre of postcoloniality" whose serial structure invites continued representation over time and across space[82]—and encourages animated cultural and political discourse in diaspora. "Sending" the letter is consequently a conceptual and material act that forges connections after widespread post-camp dispersal across the globe, calling refugee diasporics into being and conversation. Võ Phiến reimagines Vietnamese refugees through Vietnamese-language letters.

We might think of epistles in terms of Caroline Levine's notion of networks, which she describes as "patterns of interconnection and exchange" that locate the many forces and actors mediating cultural, social, and economic life.[83] Networks comprise varied rhythms, and they allow for multiple constellations without reduction to one self-sufficient narrative. Interpreted through this model, Võ Phiến's letters multiply narratives of America's Vietnam by inserting Vietnamese-language literature into the American literary landscape, intervening in the legalistic, militarized, and pedagogical production of refugees. Enlisting the apostrophic quality of letters—what Barbara Johnson describes as the potential for apostrophe to vivify a relation[84]—his epistolary structures map diasporic geographies across Southeast Asia, the Pacific Ocean, off- and on-the-mainland refugee camps, and multiple sites of post-camp dispersal, calling them into conversation. Yet for Võ Phiến, letters not only become a way to document the upheavals that refugees continue to face as America's Vietnam War book is deemed closed; they also script various versions of the past, present, and future that are not reducible to state-of-emergency narratives that cast refugees as "speechless emissaries," "good refugees," or anticommunist subjects and nothing else. As an *epistolary network* examined through a critical refugee studies lens, Võ Phiến's letters constitute a refugee dwelling in diaspora; they help make possible an emerging body politic and become a place where Vietnamese language, storytelling, and dynamic critique can live.

Letters are complex, constitutive forms in refugee and Asian American literature more broadly. In the late 1970s–1980s, a prominent means through which dispersed Vietnam War refugees reconnected with one another was by placing entries in Vietnamese-language journals. A quick gloss of any of these texts reveals scores of Vietnamese trying to reunite with one another by using what I would describe as the epistolary structure of the classified ad. Here are a few examples from the section "Overseas Searching for Each Other" published in a 1981 issue of *Overseas Vietnamese* (*Việt Nam Hải Ngoại*), which was based in San Diego.

> Looking for Ly Chi, formerly of the army medical corps. . . . [L]eft by boat, arrived in Indonesia[. W]here are you know [*sic*][? P]lease contact Lieu Quang . . . Kaneohe HI.

> Looking for Lê Thị Quyên (the biological sister of Lê thị Kiếm) who used to live in Các Lở (Vũng Tầu). I would like to know where you are now?? Please contact Nguyễn Thị Kim Linh.

> Nguyễn Anh Tuấn, arrived in America in 1980, attended Võ Tánh School (Đàlat) and Cường-Để School (Qui Nhơn). Would like to get in touch with old friends and two close friends: Phạm Đỗ Nam . . . and . . . Trần Đình Tòng.

> Sergeant Major Nguyen Dinh Huong, . . . would like to get in touch with Sergeant CK Dao Van Lac. . . . [P]lease write to Mr. Nguyen Dinh Huong, Boat Number DN 1558 CA, Barrack 80 Zone 4, Polau Galang Refugee Camp Riau, Indonesia.

These entries are hybrid forms—personal letters, classified ads, missing persons notices, and historical documents. Illustrating the varied transnational journeys of refugee migration and resettlement, they record how refugees used an extremely limited space to sketch a geography and history that was brief yet informative enough to identify authors and addressees. They also give a glimpse of the long wait some had to endure, as many of these pieces were written during extended stays in refugee camps, evidenced by some of the return addresses; we might amend Bhabha's notion of the state of emergency as also a state of emergence by understanding refugee status as one of protracted temporality. While American public conversations anticipated the eventual end of the camps, many remained in place for a long time; one of the last groups of Vietnam War refugees to be resettled was a group of Hmong from Laos who were in a Thai camp for thirty years, finally leaving in December 2003, anticipating "the lifetime of waiting"—refugeeness as the norm—that many refugees experience today.[85]

Yet the epistolary conversation I have sketched also qualifies the chiasmic ideal that is often associated with letters. Paul Ricoeur points out that the epistolary form "*presupposes* . . . that it is possible to transfer through writing, with no loss of persuasive power, the force of representation attached to the living voice or theatrical action."[86] That actual transference of a "living voice" is only a possibility and not a guarantee becomes clear when we consider how the chiasmic possibilities of epistles—that the addressee will write back—are not assured. Võ Phiến says as much, drawing attention to how the trajectory of South Vietnam's dissolution, refugee migration, and refugee camp life and dispersal circumscribes senders and receivers: "you are a friend on the same path, of the same time, in the same boat, of the same land, of the same country, an empty friend" (*Letters*, 9). Despite the familiarity and intimacy of Võ Phiến's imagined conversations, it is not actually likely that the friends who are conjured will ever encounter one another: "[D]ear friends, even though you are far, even though we have never met" (*Letters*, 9). Võ Phiến and the classified ads enlist literary strategy to generate hope for refugee dialogues, an intertextual exchange when a direct, intersubjective one may not be possible. But the sense of transience and irrevocable loss—loss of loved ones and of a country that no longer exists—cannot be compensated for, contrary to the ideal of a refugee ending that naturalized citizenship is supposed to realize. In the case of Vietnamese refugees' letters, the addressed may no longer be living, as many died during their journeys, nullifying their hoped-for responses. In this way, the letter also functions epitaphically; refugees' letters demarcate the dead as well as the living.[87]

Expanding the Vietnamese American Archive

In her graphic memoir *One! Hundred! Demons!* Lynda Barry describes her childhood fascination with classified ads: "Like most writers, I loved to read when I was little, but until recently, I never really thought about some of the things I enjoyed reading the most. The classified ads fascinated me. . . . They gave me so many weird blanks to fill in."[88] On the one hand, the classified ad is not the preferred genre of the typical educated reader, speaking instead to what Barry perceives as her "low" tastes, which she associates with her up-bringing as a poor, part-Filipina mixed-race girl. As such, Barry emphasizes genres' class-based hierarchies: at best, classified ads might be considered a subgenre; at worst, they do not constitute a genre at all. On the other hand, the classified ad is more than an example of power dynamics in the literary world. It is inevitably a structure of potential loss, for the object being given up may remain unwanted; what is "lost" may not be "found," and it is always possible that no one will respond to the entreaty posed. But the genre allows Barry to insert herself creatively into real-life stories. The classified ad not only is integral to her imagination; it also inspires Barry's authorship.

Resonating with the value that epistolary structures of address have for Barry, attention to Vietnamese American letters clarifies the national and international political conditions under which one can write and whether, when, and how writings reach their audiences—illuminating what Johnson describes as epistles' "economies of justice" and "effects of power" that especially characterize refugees' letters.[89] Epistles articulate intimate correspondences, diasporic formations, and refugees' histories, and they address displaced people who may have passed. But letters are also entangled in power relations—tied to voting rights, taxes, bills, and other state apparatuses that determine citizenship and selfhood.[90] Consider the fruit and vegetables that Filipino migrant laborers send to one another without return addresses in Carlos Bulosan's mid-century short story "Be American" (first published in 1977), or Japanese American internment notices placed throughout the West Coast during World War II. Epistolary forms have served both to connect and to sever marginalized communities.

Võ Phiến's letters complement Southeast Asian American literary archives that are altering cultural horizons in generative ways, and they compel consideration of how epistles recur not only across Vietnamese American works but also in Asian American and refugee literature more broadly. At once private and public, individual and collective, archived and dialogic, his letters mark the beginnings of postwar Vietnamese American authorship.[91] These texts demonstrate the value of incorporating Vietnamese-language materials in our elaboration of what Dana A. Williams and Marissa K. Lopez call the "ethnic archive," an effort that involves engaging and questioning canons and their prevailing genres and literary histories.[92] Võ Phiến would proceed to write a magisterial overview of South Vietnamese literature based on the archival materials he culled that was published in 1999, followed by a number of books of poetry and plays. But his letters in particular reveal details of camp and post-camp life that have been largely forgotten today, and they show how, in private spaces and in unspoken ways, he theorized the value of writing in Vietnamese in America. Vietnamese-language literature becomes an important, distinct space for refracting the pressures of dominant English to consider how American hegemony works across the century. In his hands, the epistle becomes a foundation for the emergence of Vietnamese American letters.

CONCLUSION

Vietnam's America in a Time of Smoke and Fire

Extending the spirit of this book's interest in genre and longer, transnational literary histories, I conclude by recovering another little-known but important Vietnamese-American encounter from the past: South Vietnamese critics' rearticulation of American literature during the conflict in the form of the literary magazine. Attention to this cultural milieu destabilizes the dominance of English in American literary studies and offers insight into Vietnamese perspectives on U.S. hegemony across the century, as well as on conceptions of the role of literature in a time of war—or, in the words of one journal issue's title, "written in smoke and fire."

Although the Vietnam War was a period of violence and devastation, it was also an era of vibrant literary engagement. The literary scene in 1960s–1970s South Vietnam was dynamic, with hundreds of thousands of newspaper copies disseminated every day and more than one hundred literary publications in circulation.[1] Literary magazines were a significant part of this cultural and political conversation—characteristically, short-lived serial publications often operating on tight budgets, whose selection of different authors, forms, and contents reflect an editor's particular literary vision.[2] An individual issue might have been organized around a theme—for instance, the literature of war—or a Vietnamese or foreign author. Issues were generically diverse, as one could find in them a range of critical essays, musical scores, philosophical pieces, translations, and canonical as well as new nonfiction, fiction, and poetry. Translations of a range of writers were regularly included, often accompanied by critical essays. Covers of individual issues were rich examples of a journal's aesthetic sensibility.

These Vietnamese-language journals regularly engage American cultural and historical contexts and offer a glimpse of *Vietnam's* America. Such cultural crossover marks a shift in literary influence in Vietnam more generally dating from around the 1960s onward, when the South Vietnamese literary community exhibited increased curiosity about reading and studying American works. In many ways, these periodicals continued conversations from an earlier era—the colonial period, when impassioned debates about identity, culture, and politics also took place in an exciting literary sphere. But the mid-century was different, given America's mounting presence in Southeast Asia. The United States was providing South Vietnam with $270 million annually by 1956,[3] and by 1969 the American military presence in Saigon numbered more than 540,000—one American for every fifteen local Vietnamese and thirty times the American population of just four years earlier.[4] In seeming fulfillment of the promises of President Harry Truman's Four Point Speech of 1949, which announced that U.S.-led industrialization and technologizing would lead the globe to freedom, rapid urbanization was taking place in South Vietnam, as was the dissemination of American culture. Increased use of radios and televisions brought shows such as *Batman* and *Gunsmoke* to both Americans and urban Vietnamese living in the Republic of Vietnam (RVN).[5] South Vietnamese journals' interest in American literature often revolved around questions of social and political transition and thus bore a thematic relationship to an RVN in the throes of reconstructing a culture, society, and economy. Vietnamese writers engaged the forms and contents of social change evident in other literary cultures, not necessarily as precedents to mimic but as points of comparison through which to consider the status of literature and criticism in a country experiencing profound transformation.

These publications are rich and abundant and cannot be fully treated here, but my discussion is aimed at generating further conversation about them and about the politics of the genre of the literary journal itself. By offering some thoughts on South Vietnamese literary serials and then pivoting to the similar prominence of anthological forms in contemporary Vietnamese American literature and criticism, I suggest that mixed-genre compilations have been vital for formalizing emergent literary cultures in Vietnam and its diaspora. Focusing on three issues published by two prominent South Vietnamese publications based in Saigon from the 1960s and 1970s—one focused on Carson McCullers, published by *Văn* (Literature); another on William Faulkner, also published by *Văn*; and one on black struggles, published by *Văn Học* (Literature)—I offer thoughts on the range of topics and geographies these issues treated to paint a working picture of writers' efforts to define the role of literature and the critic through the form of the literary magazine.

Evaluated together, these publications constitute complex sites of South Vietnamese nation building, decolonization, and U.S. hegemony. They are hybrid spaces of complicity with and critique of American imperial culture—documentations of the possibilities and limits of South Vietnamese writing within the deepened, globalizing reach of American empire as it was exercised specifically through Cold War culture at the time. If, historically, anthological texts—which I understand in terms of both stand-alone and serial forms—have been cultural projects of racialized, gendered nation making, I focus on how they simultaneously create and disrupt literary canons.[6] The conversation I stage shows how categories such as "Vietnam," "Vietnamese," and "Vietnamese American" depend on the act of not only curating a literary canon, however provisional and changing, but also cultivating a readership for it. Mediating American literature through Vietnamese and other international authors results in a transnational map of literature that asserts the importance of the South Vietnamese literary critic and decenters the singularity of any one paradigm of "world literature."[7]

By foregrounding mid-century South Vietnamese literary journals and linking them to contemporary anthological Vietnamese American works, I suggest a recontextualization of some of the prevailing conceptual frames of Southeast Asian American literary studies. While post-1975 refugee voices in English tend to dominate the field, looking toward 1960s–1970s works in Vietnamese further opens opportunities for parsing the multidimensionality of "Vietnam" that has been a central concern of this project—the varied histories and cultural hybridities that serve as prologue to and context for current Vietnamese American literature and criticism, particularly given the latter's strong ties to South Vietnam as a geography and idea. The texts I investigate index how writers considered the relationship between literature and American empire through South Vietnamese cultural critique, culminating this book's interest in America's Vietnam as necessitating formal, transnational, and *longue durée* engagement.

Văn and *Văn Học*: Transnationalizing American Literature

The journal *Văn* was published between 1964 and 1975 and was founded by the writer Nguyễn Đình Vượng.[8] It emerged in a state of deep historical transition—just over a month after South Vietnam's first head of state, Ngô Đình Diệm, discussed in Chapter 3, was assassinated by a U.S.-backed coup. The magazine's target audience was a young generation of readers, who could devour each issue's one-hundred-plus pages twice a month. In addition to publishing new and established Vietnamese writers, *Văn* was known for its commitment to nurturing and defining South Vietnamese literature. It also had an international vision, evident in its regular inclusion of writers from around the world, including a range of African, American, French, Japanese, Latin American, and Russian authors. In total, *Văn* produced 267 issues at approximately four thousand copies per title. After South Vietnam's dissolution, those who were affiliated with the journal variously migrated abroad or stayed in South Vietnam, where some were imprisoned and died in reeducation camps.[9]

An issue of *Văn* published on July 1, 1965, focuses on William Faulkner, around the third anniversary of his death. At the beginning of the volume is a letter addressed to readers identifying Faulkner as one of America's most representative writers. The letter notes that despite this legacy, Faulkner is still relatively unknown in South Vietnam, a lack that *Văn* expresses it hopes to correct: "Now on the anniversary of Faulkner's death, we would like to reserve this issue to introduce his life and work, thoughts, and representative short stories."[10] In addition to critical essays on Faulkner, the issue includes translations of "A Rose for Emily" (1930), an excerpt from *Go Down, Moses* (1942), and Faulkner's Nobel Prize acceptance speech (1949).

One essay titled "William Faulkner: The Man and His Work," written by Trần Phong Giao, proves particularly intriguing because of its preoccupation with Faulkner's treatment of temporality in relation to rapid modernization in the post–Civil War U.S. South, which is then connected to the multivalence of time and history in South Vietnam. Trần Phong Giao was secretary of *Văn* and a literary critic and translator of Jean-Paul Sartre and Albert Camus, and he was known for being perhaps the strongest advocate of emergent South Vietnamese voices.[11] In the essay, he introduces what he views as Faulkner's defining thematic and formal qualities: characters' complex interiorities, nonlinear time, knotty familial genealogies and historical chronologies, haunting figures and decaying mansions, and the prominence of oral narratives in urgent need of intergenerational transmission. Particular heed is paid to the density of Faulkner's atmospheres: environmental motifs of heat and humidity register the palpable weight of unresolved political conflicts as the region undergoes accelerated New South capitalist development: "The details of a story unfold in an atmosphere submerged with heavy nightmares, the memories of the past, and insinuations that never get resolved—this is the cruel atmosphere of Faulkner."[12] Trần Phong Giao's turn to the persistent life of Faulknerian pasts underscores that the end of the Civil War may have reestablished formal national unity, but deep splinters in national time and space remained. Forging a connection between Faulkner's American South and South Vietnam, Trần Phong Giao then expands Yoknapatawpha County's imagined borders to circle the globe and, hence, implicitly encompass South Vietnam and its resonant history of national division and reconstruction: "The more we dig into Faulkner, the more we'll see that the borders of Yoknapatawpha County go beyond the state of Mississippi, even the nation, to wrap around all those parts of the world that are currently being threatened by modern man."[13] By analogizing the situation of two different "Souths," Trần Phong Giao crafts a common frame through which to understand how developmental forces of capitalism—often occurring under the aegis of American modernization—sweep up disparate humans across the globe.

In the midst of such economic and social upheaval, Faulkner's characters have an inextinguishable fortitude, and Trần Phong Giao notes that it is specifically Faulkner's marginalized figures—African Americans and the disabled, especially—who are the enduring characters of his narratives.[14] Their human spirit prevails, an idea that lies at the core of Faulkner's Nobel Prize speech, parts of which Trần Phong Giao quotes for readers: "I believe that man will not merely endure: he will prevail. He is immortal, not because he alone among creatures has an inexhaustible voice, but because he has a soul, a spirit capable of compassion and sacrifice and endurance."[15] Given that the South Vietnamese population at the time contained large numbers of refugees from North Vietnam in addition to the existing population—bearing a heterogeneity of histories evocative of Faulkner's composite temporalities—Trần Phong Giao's evocation of Faulknerian perseverance encourages the spirit and means to build and rebuild after national division and mass deaths, even as indefinite warfare and human loss continue to loom on Southeast Asia's horizon. Minority voices from the American South find kinship with a Vietnamese South, where a postcolonial accumulation of histories is also waiting to be told.

Trần Phong Giao's emphasis on the tactility of Faulknerian chronotopes reflects an interest in how marginalized histories nevertheless exert a palpable, material, and irrepressible force, while his examination of the human grit that laces Faulkner's narratives seeks a kind of immaterial agency that is stronger than the constraints of material circumstances. Interrupting without warning, figures from the past work against assumptions that the passing of time equals progress, and Trần Phong Giao suggests that the ecological qualities of Faulkner's unresolved histories productively naturalize time and space as multilayered rather than unified beneath a singular nationalist, patriotic identity. However, at the same time that his interpretation of Faulkner decries the inhuman drive of capitalist development, a direct, sustained critique of modernization's capitalist foundations remains muted, moderated by Trần Phong Giao's turn to a liberal, universalizing discourse of human resilience that is at odds with the structural critique that also organizes the essay.

While *Văn*'s issue on Faulkner demonstrates how South Vietnamese engagement with American literature acts as a springboard for linking South Vietnam's particular challenges of nation-building within a longer, transnational history of displacements and reconstructions, a different issue of *Văn* focusing on Carson McCullers suggests that the literary critic plays a crucial role in maintaining a rigorous critique of capitalist development. On April 1, 1968, *Văn* published its issue on McCullers, right after the first phase of the Tết Offensive had ended and a few months after McCullers had passed. Among the primary texts included in the issue are the author's short stories "A Domestic Dilemma" and "The Aliens." A Vietnamese translation of Tennessee Williams's "Afterword" to McCullers's novel *Reflections in a Golden Eye* (1941) is also incorporated, contextualizing her career within a broader terrain of American literature.

In the issue's opening pages, the editors iterate to readers that their mission is to bring literature to the people—particularly to students—so that those who "do not have the good fortune to speak foreign languages may know a few typical features of the rich field of foreign literature." As part of this goal of expanding literary consciousness, *Văn* includes a brief biography and critical assessment of McCullers's work by Hoàng Ngọc Nguyên, sketching how some South Vietnamese critics understood and connected to her body of work. In particular, attention to her portrayal of the grotesque reveals an interest in her depiction of non-normative forms. One of McCullers's defining literary traits, according to Hoàng Ngọc Nguyên, is her rendering of desire as an uncontainable physical and emotional force. It is expansive and takes repugnant, inhuman turns—a desire that exists "between subject and object, between the surreal, intricate developments of interiority and timeless myth, without restraint, enlivened by motives that lie beyond the human sphere."[16] The reading of the materiality of McCullers's aberrant figures and feelings suggests her break from epistemologies that reproduce prevailing norms and remain limited in their imaginative capacity. The outcasts who recur in McCullers's stories could easily be treated simply as such, but Hoàng Ngọc Nguyên's McCullers gives them primacy; they push the edges of convention and challenge the boundaries of the imagination and thus of what is possible within existing circumstances.

Hoàng Ngọc Nguyên's reading of McCullers's recurring representations of disfigurement moves beyond a thematic interest to relate the broader economic and political implications of her works. He makes a fascinating com-

tưởng-niệm

CARSON McCULLERS

Cover of the April 1, 1968, special issue of *Văn* on Carson McCullers. (Photograph by the author.)

ment that contrasts McCullers's forms of monstrosity to those of the market, arguing that in South Vietnam of the 1960s, readers are trained to "value novels with sensational details but which contain nothing that is challenging to understand."[17] He elaborates that capitalist forms of sensationalist representation target audiences who would rather consume literature without questioning how they are being conditioned to read. Those who produce this kind of literature, in turn, should be censured: "These writings [are] victims of advertising that is increasingly monstrous and vulgar." Consequently, Hoàng Ngọc Nguyên frames his introduction of McCullers as "an attempt to bring into memory circumstances that have been forgotten"—a reminder to audiences that part of the power of the literary imagination is to distort, question, and contest rather than advance the commodification of culture.[18] If the homogenizing drive of capitalism is to blame for the literary sacrifice of complex themes and characters, for Hoàng Ngọc Nguyên, Mc-Cullers's works act as a counterweight to market-driven literary production. By introducing McCullers and foregrounding her portrayal of the grotesque as a form of literary agency that pushes against consumptive habits, the essay positions McCullers as an illustrative touchstone for actively considering the conditions and consequences of capitalist enculturation.

By investigating an admired American writer to query how literature negotiates the effects of American-led modernization on the culture of a society, Hoàng Ngọc Nguyên achieves something else of vital significance in his essay: he defines and legitimates the role and agency of the South Vietnamese literary critic. First, by performing expertise in McCullers's career, he establishes authority as a literary historian. Clarifying that McCullers may be unknown to many *Văn* readers, he states that she had great early success in America and has cemented her stature in cultural history, assuming her place alongside an intriguing, male-dominated list of American greats such as "Tennessee Williams, Robert Penn Warren, Truman Capote, Nelson Algren."[19] But Nguyên explains that, in fact, McCullers's reputation in Europe is actually greater than in the United States—a gap, Hoàng Ngọc Nguyên clarifies, that Williams has tried to correct in his "Afterword" to *Reflections in a Golden Eye*: "In Europe the name of Carson McCullers is where it belongs, among the four or five preeminent figures in contemporary American writing."[20] Incorporating literary criticism to detail McCullers's transnational relevance confirms Hoàng Ngọc Nguyên's position of knowledge and expertise in both American and "world" literature.

Hoàng Ngọc Nguyên's treatment of McCullers delineates the stakes of literary criticism in a young, emerging South Vietnam. Situating himself as part of a cultural collective—a trait characteristic of literary magazines' hybrid authorship—he argues that if many authors regrettably produce literature that serves the sensationalist, profit-driven impulses of capitalism, "literary critics must regularly escape the influence of readers' trends and illuminate" the broader structures determining literary production. He explicitly calls on South Vietnamese writers and critics to assume a proactive role and tap in to their potential as influential interpreters in a country that must manage a web of social, economic, and political pressures as a highly contested geopolitical site. His essay is quite methodical in its use of literature as exposition for sociopolitical understanding; asserting McCullers's relevance as an author of cross-scalar renown legitimates her inclusion within the journal, which validates *Văn* as a relevant publication attuned to cultural and political currents on national and transnational levels.

Literary Periodicals in Geopolitical Context

The South Vietnamese special issues on Faulkner and McCullers are just two examples that demonstrate the density of the literary journal as a cultural object and as a popular genre in South Vietnam. Literary magazines help to parse the complexity of both the Vietnam War and the long historical, multidirectional flows of Vietnamese-American cultural encounters. They suggest that the South Vietnamese literary community valued American literature's capacity to help its members imagine yet again how a new society and culture might be constructed, as well as critiqued, and the diverse forms collated within them suggest that generic variety was conducive to cultivating an evolving South Vietnamese literature and literary criticism. Analyzed from a contemporary lens, these materials are also telling documents of culture's relationship to changing forms of empire. The journals' particular interest in young readers indicates not only an awareness of nurturing an audience for the long term but also an anxious concern about the future of the country and how to foster a historicized consciousness, particularly at a time of grave human and material loss and when historical memory is contentious and precarious, fought over regionally and internationally. The anthology format offers a means by which to engage in active intellectual life in diverse forms, while the competing visions within the magazines—from liberal humanist idealization to anti-capitalist critique—demonstrate the varied ideologies that jostle in these literary worlds. Although the United States wanted to determine South Vietnam's present and future through gradually increased "advising," economic policies, and military occupation—efforts that many South Vietnamese supported—contributors to journals such as *Văn* often enlisted American literature to question these happenings. They convened a lively space through which to investigate and potentially intercede in the social, political, and economic dynamics that were shifting the world map.

At the same time, South Vietnamese literary journals cannot be separated from the workings of American Cold War culture. In the mid-century context, the genre of the literary journal was a prominent instrument of U.S. hegemony. As Andrew Rubin notes, the transition from French and British imperialisms to U.S. global power entailed a cultural remobilization, an "entire reconfiguration of cultural relationships . . . that had vast consequences for the position of the writer in society, the conditions of humanistic practice, the ideology of world literature."[21] Mid-twentieth-century America aggressively developed a range of new cultural programs, often affiliating with parallel European efforts, to deter leftist thinking and Americanize—globalize—attitudes about culture and politics around the world. The Paris-based Congress for Cultural Freedom (CCF), established in 1950, was one example. Through publication and translation in one of the CCF's many literary arms—for instance, *Perspectives USA*, *Encounter*, even the *Paris Review*[22]—certain writers found increased international circulation and renown that they might not have had otherwise. T.S. Eliot, Léopold Sédar Senghor, Lionel Trilling, Wole Soyinka, Aimé Césaire, Chinua Achebe, and Tennessee Williams were among them, a notably male, multicultural coterie of writers that suggests the CCF's masculinist proclivities.[23] However, the CCF was funded as well as run by the U.S. Central Intelligence Agency. Its state sponsorship remained a secret until exposed by a *New York Times* article in 1966. Many influential contributors to publications backed by the CCF, such as Hannah Arendt, W. H. Auden, Leslie Fiedler, and many more, were not aware that they were inadvertently contributing to American imperialist objectives.[24]

The CCF had offices and affiliates worldwide and sponsored international readings, conferences, publications, and research to push leftist thinkers and leaders away from communism and toward American political ideology.[25] An important cultural counterpart to increasing U.S. political and military might, the CCF and organizations like it redefined imperial culture by molding Cold War contexts of "world literature" from an Americanist point of view, by coupling military hegemony with strengthened soft weapons of empire.[26] Yet the goals of the CCF were not always reached in the ways envisioned and often produced revealing tensions that expose the impossibility of complete political alignment. The journal *Encounter* assigned Richard Wright the task of reporting on the Bandung Conference, but given his communist affiliations, he had a less linear relationship to the CCF's anticommunist agenda. Robert Lowell veered off-script in Latin America and had to be pulled, while Faulkner's association was eventually deemed bad for the American brand, perhaps explaining why he became more visible in South Vietnam after his death.[27]

Overall, however, American soft imperialism became an extensive and committed Cold War enterprise that turned to literary projects to solicit leftist thinkers while actively working to demonstrate the inferiority of their political leanings. At a time of changing American exceptionalist discourse, the United States attempted to manage cultural production and intellectual thought by assimilating voices around the world into a single American sound.[28] Evocative of French colonial culinary standardization discussed in Chapter 2, U.S. programs of cultural hegemony were efforts of political standardization clothed as literary multiculturalism. Their reach demonstrates that the archive of foreign authors and model of text collation found in South Vietnam's literary publications must be situated within the context of literary imperialism. These works were implicated in literary journals' role in adapting U.S. ideology for the late twentieth century—for instance, by affirming that American-style cultural, economic, and political programs were not hegemonic projects but correctives to the damage wrought by European colonialism.[29] Indeed, some writers featured in special issues of South Vietnamese journals, such as Wright and Camus, were favored by the CCF.[30] This places South Vietnamese literary journals in a contradictory place, situated between complicity with and critique of empire.

Provocative examples of South Vietnamese journals' simultaneous distance from and enmeshment in America's drive toward cultural and economic dominance appear in two special issues of *Văn Học* from 1966 devoted to black culture. *Văn Học* ran from 1962 to 1975 and was approved for publication under President Ngô Đình Diệm's regime. Phan Kim Thịnh founded the publication, and he, like the editor of *Văn*, was committed to building a core generation of young readers. The journal published numerous previously unpublished essays and authors who, even today, are no longer published in Vietnam, and its print numbers varied, ranging from 2,500 to 10,000 copies.[31] On March 15, 1966, *Văn Học* produced "Black Voices," which featured translations of works and excerpts that included Senghor's "On African Socialism," the Ghanaian Matei Markwei's poem "Life in Our Village," the Senegalese poet Birago Diop's "Spirit," Martin Luther King Jr.'s Nobel Prize speech on nonviolence, Langston Hughes's "Puerto-Ricans," and an excerpt from James Baldwin's *Blues for Mister Charlie*. The texts gathered thus ranged from prominent to little-known works and authors, although no Vietnamese interpretations of the works themselves are included.

One piece, by Trần Triệu Luật, explores postcolonial reconstruction in Africa as an example through which to consider global decolonization as a pressing, ongoing struggle. Trần Triệu Luật posits that, because decolonization is a tenuous, contingent process, the youth occupy important roles as "pioneers and activists" who symbolize the "spirit of revolution, social reform and nation building." Yet this combination of terms alone reveals the conflicting position of youth in postcolonial contexts in which social and ideological struggles persist after formal independence has been gained. Consequently, perhaps to caution readers or bring attention to student movements at the time, Trần Triệu Luật stresses that there is some risk to placing so many hopes on not only black youth but also youth elsewhere, including Asia and South America: "The image of the youth brings forth an image of the nation. . . . This brings pride for the youth but at the same time puts the burden of responsibility on their shoulders." Trần Triệu Luật argues that young populations, though central to post-independence projects, are disproportionately tasked with carrying out postcolonial projects across the political spectrum: "holding guns in the jungle and among the hills . . . waving high the flag of progress amid poverty, hunger, illness, ignorance, and racism."[32]

Trần Triệu Luật's interest in the promise and plight of black youth to think through postcolonial conditions in broad terms eventually cuts to the central contradiction of American hegemony: "Blacks have suffered because of euphemistic independence and democracy."[33] The essay's implicit comparativism raises a point often neglected in understandings of Vietnamese-American relations: that in South Vietnam, desires for decolonization were not extinguished with U.S. occupation but were continuing issues with which thinkers wrestled and about which they thought in transnational terms. By focusing on and then enlarging the dilemma of black youth, Trần Triệu Luật offers sobering commentary that different forms of decolonization can take uncertain nationalist turns—whether tilting toward the right or the left, toward capitalism or communism—and are vulnerable to abuses of power. The article takes readers past the negative critiques that ideological factions launch against one another—and complicates the many solidarities that activists around the world claimed with the "Vietnamese"—to anticipate that no clear victor will emerge from the conflict in Vietnam.

Incomplete decolonization in South Vietnam is the topic of another essay, titled "A Historical Scandal," which brings attention to antiblackness in the United States to direct a critical lens on South Vietnamese racism. The title of the article signals the urgency of these issues and thus the need to engage what its author, Nguyễn Hữu Dung, states is a global concern: "The issue of racism against blacks in America is a scandal of history." Perhaps to soften potentially negative responses to the article, the essay takes time to lead up to the thesis of the implications of South Vietnamese discrimination, presenting a series of rhetorical questions concerning why the world has only recently recognized black struggles: "Is it because the conscience of the world has awakened? Is it because blacks and people in the world in general have matured politically?" Like Trần Triệu Luật, Nguyễn Hữu Dung does not posit that the struggle is over and emphasizes that, regardless of the reasons recognition of these grievances is being given now, "black issues are still a reality and an important issue in the twentieth century."[34]

Having established the necessity of recognizing civil rights on a global, long historical scale, the essay then presents a key claim: "I still find that Vietnamese people are afraid to interact with blacks." Nguyễn Hữu Dung notes that only Vietnamese sex workers seem to socialize with blacks, directly linking racialized, gendered, and classed labor in South Vietnam with U.S. militarism. The piece then asks: if Vietnam had "discovered" America, would it have brutally enslaved African Americans? The implicit answer is yes.[35] The gradual, deliberate logic and organization of the essay's anti-racist message suggest the difficulty of raising social inequality in intersectional terms in a South Vietnam that claims to envision a more equitable postcolonial nation. By connecting the promise of the emergent country to the persistence of antiblackness within it, Nguyễn Hữu Dung, echoing Trần Triệu Luật's observation of the gap in postcolonies between formal and actual freedom, submits that the new nation's replication of racism, sexism, and classism prevents true justice from being achieved.

Realities of intersectional inequalities in the postcolony perhaps become most prominent in the thread of capitalism that flickers in and out of *Văn Học*'s issues on black writers. While revolutionary impulses reverberate across the issue, it is also contradicted by variously ambivalent and affirming treatments of capitalism, revealing a hybrid postcolonial discourse attempting to determine the country's future cultural-economic directions. The introduction to the issue is a case in point. It marries the question of Black Nationalism to the political-economic model of capitalist democracy, suggesting that combining the two may accelerate the advancement of black rights; the letter notes that communism, by contrast, is the new colonialism. But perhaps most interesting, a second issue on black culture that appeared two weeks later contains an opening essay that diverts from the issue's ostensible theme. Instead, it concentrates on "the problem of creating capital in underdeveloped areas" and details the reasons why foreign investment has been integral to both developing and developed countries. The essay's author, Lê Linh, argues that "the issue of resource extraction depends largely on the external capitalist," elaborating that Vietnam "has raw materials but lacks capital. . . . [W]ith [a] lack of capital to exploit, foreign contributions into this area are necessary and reasonable."[36] Lê Linh identifies a key challenge facing the RVN, which is how to establish independent economic foundations, given the power and influence of U.S. presence in the country.

In attempting to diagnose South Vietnam's infrastructural challenges, Lê Linh cites resource extraction as a vital seedbed for rebuilding and figures foreign money in primarily economic terms removed from social and political consequences, revealing an incorporation of capitalist teleology. This is further apparent in the gratitude expressed alongside the piece's justification for foreign funding, which is depicted as a beneficent "contribution," and in the essay's foreclosing of alternatives to and even legitimation of foreign profiteering. In Lê Linh's view, capitalist development may be undesirable, but it is unavoidable, giving rise to the article's implicit logic of debt. Although current scholarship typically associates indebtedness with post–Vietnam War refugees, who are expected to perform gratitude in exchange for foreign asylum, as I discussed in Chapter 4, Lê Linh's piece emphasizes how various forms of material and conceptual indebtedness—a sense of economic and emotional liability—have been central to U.S. hegemony's workings across the *longue durée*, severely constraining postcolonial options. Placing Nguyễn Hữu Dung's and Trần Triệu Luật's focus on the problems of African and African American freedom in conversation with Lê Linh's explanation for American occupation and development, a debate concerning the relationship between race and capital emerges. While Lê Linh argues that South Vietnam needs capitalism and foreign support, Nguyễn Hữu Dung and Trần Triệu Luật suggest that capitalism systematically keeps oppression in place for the long term.

Here we arrive at a defining conundrum of South Vietnamese literary journals. As an index of evolving thought, opinion, and imagination, they show how South Vietnamese thinkers attempt to parse possibilities for cultural, political, and economic autonomy in light of North Vietnam's complicated and contentious internal situation and political objectives in the RVN and within the presence of American cultural, military, and economic power.[37] One of the primary forms organizing this conversation—the genre of the literary journal—is itself an instrument of that hegemony. Yet while South Vietnamese literary magazines are imbricated in U.S. cultural imperialism, they also redirect it toward their own concerns, drawing from American literary and social contexts to consider Americans' own critiques of passive consumerism, economic dependence, and social inequality and to relate these issues to South Vietnam's predicament of negotiating U.S. military occupation and neocolonial policies. While the RVN was installed as a client state, as Daniel Kim and Viet Thanh Nguyen remind us,[38] it was not simply a "puppet" state, a claim often made that circumvents nuanced historical inquiry. What emerges in these journals are often nonsynchronous visions of South Vietnam's past, present, and future that cannot be confined to Cold War dichotomies; no consolidated "South Vietnam," and thus "Vietnam," emerges. South Vietnamese critical writings evidence a complicated, transnationally minded intellectual milieu—a space of sometimes competing voices concerned with concrete and intellectual questions that South Vietnamese faced before, during, and after the short-lived, twenty-year existence of the nation.

Certain qualities of South Vietnamese literary journals reveal conceptual and material constraints and thus urge attention to the gaps and fissures that need to be recognized in order to understand these texts as part of a transnational literary map and as themselves precarious objects. The introductory issue of *Văn* (1964) makes clear its doubtful future and legacy, describing how the office's excitement at receiving official approval for publication was tinged with a feeling of dejection, as authorization was granted for only two months.[39] In the piece on Faulkner, Trần Phong Giao admits to the limits of the Afro-Asian analogy drawn, cautious about certain interpretations, particularly those concerning Faulkner's black characters: "In truth, we Vietnamese don't know much about African Americans. We're not clear on their way of life, their habits, their beliefs, their social organizations."[40] Some journal issues also lay bare the role of the state in literary production; censorship marks occasionally manifest in plain view of readers' eyes, with fragments of text or entire paragraphs redacted. The visibility of these censored fragments exposes the state's surveillance of culture, and at the same time, the published censorship marks alter the original text and create a new kind of narrative that is also a story of state oversight. In such cases, censorship not only becomes part of the form and content of the work. It also acts meta-narratively to make the institutional politics of the literary journal genre explicit. Observing these textual particulars reveals important material details that transnational approaches to literature must consider.

A final example illustrates how South Vietnamese literary journals mark both the reach and boundaries of American cultural power. As noted, U.S. cultural imperialism during the Cold War dispersed American literary journals to peripheries as part of a putatively apolitical effort to connect—and correct—the world through literature. However, while some of the foreign authors favored by the United States appear in South Vietnamese periodicals, such as Wright and Camus,[41] writers not endorsed by the CCF also found a place in RVN publications. Camus was given the U.S. seal of approval while Jean-Paul Sartre was not, yet Sartre was the topic of two special issues of *Văn*. (Camus appeared in the issue 2 [1964], and Sartre appeared twice—in issue 17 [1964] and 152 [1970]). Moreover, Lê Linh's essay on the merits of foreign capitalist development was followed by a translation of Sartre's essay "Black Orpheus," which outlines the linkage between capital and whiteness and engages Négritude as a vehicle through which blacks reconstitute blackness and develop the proletariat.[42] In addition, Vietnamese translators for the journals worked from both French and American texts. In one of *Văn Học*'s issues on black writers, an excerpt from Charles Wright's *The Messenger* (1963), a novel about queer black life in New York City,[43] was translated into Vietnamese from a French translation of the English-language version. There are many examples like this one that outline the multiple linguistic, cultural, and political mediations underpinning the conversations that take place within South Vietnamese literary journals. European and American imperialist aims may have overlapped in Vietnam, sometimes aligned in their overarching imperial interests, but this confluence was situated within and diffused by a hybridity of South Vietnamese priorities. These translations and cross-cultural dialogues bring greater attention to the complexities of the magazines' transnationalism—the multiple literary cultures they engage expose a spectrum of concerns rather than exemplify complete standardization.

South Vietnamese journals exercised some control over the shaping of "world literature" in various ways, from exposing state surveillance to recontextualizing different thinkers by juxtaposing them with varied, sometimes opposing viewpoints. These tensions compel us to reconsider current premises of world literature models that presuppose literature's movement from the center to peripheries. Joseph Slaughter takes particular issue with this assumption, deploring critics' tendency to recognize only those literary systems and genres that fit dominant views of what constitutes the literary.[44] It is undeniable that U.S. literary dissemination is part of the South Vietnamese historical picture; one of the first photos I saw as a child was of my mother working in an American library set up at the Củ Hành Air Base in Pleiku, complete with a "Read" poster in the background that was part of the American Library Association's popular campaign. But to Slaughter's point, the details I have presented show that literary routes and genres do not simply move from center to periphery or assume dominant forms, such as the novel, but in fact take refracted, circuitous routes and varied generic shapes. South Vietnamese literary magazines illustrate that U.S.-endorsed authors are topics of interest but also sidelined to Vietnamese and writers from other countries deemed equally important. When subject to a specifying lens, the universalizing claims of American literature as a Cold War enterprise emerge as disrupted, fractured by South Vietnamese interpretations, translations, intellectual concerns, and institutional contingencies.

Rather than posit that a specific kind of South Vietnamese literature or identity was the central focus of South Vietnamese literary journals, I suggest that perhaps most important to these publications was asserting the relevance of the literary milieu. The cachet given to South Vietnamese literary critics, for example, pivots on their ability to shape transnational maps of literature while also maintaining distance from prevailing ideologies to develop alternative frames of interpretation and being through literary engagement. Critics were presented as uniquely positioned to track and assess long and expansive confluences of regional, national, and international cultures and politics and register what it was like to be at the crossroads of these developments. While notions of South Vietnamese identity and culture were certainly at stake in these exchanges—Võ Phiến, discussed in Chapter 4, was heavily involved in these explorations—also at issue was the creation of South Vietnamese literary criticism in periodical form as an energetic, meaningful mission.[45] The dialogic and formally diverse structure of the journals facilitated the curation of diverse texts and contexts to imagine South Vietnamese literary critique as a legitimate, complex project. At times, incorporating American voices served as a basis from which to consider the role of South Vietnamese writers and thinkers as attuned critics with a transnational vision, able to particularize and abstract from their cultural-political conditions and affirm the importance of the literary vocation in a time of war.

Vietnamese American Literary Studies and Anthological Forms

Analyzing the form of the literary magazine in South Vietnam contributes to our understanding of Vietnamese American literature and literary criticism in the present. Yen Le Espiritu has studied the importance of venues such as Internet memorials and street names as Vietnamese-language sources for South Vietnamese memory and mourning after the conflict.[46] In the spirit of Espiritu's argument, I suggest that the history of literary periodicals in South Vietnam serves as context for Vietnamese-language culture in the diaspora. For instance, several figures who worked for those publications were instrumental in cultivating different venues for postwar diasporic literary production and criticism.[47] Võ Phiến was a contributor to journals in South Vietnam, as well as in the diaspora, while Nguyễn Xuân Hoàng worked for *Văn* and blogged for the Vietnamese-language Voice of America and ran the *Viet Tribune* in San Jose, California. Their experiences with periodicals in uncertain times in the RVN perhaps aided their efforts to create and sustain Vietnamese-language literary production and criticism overseas.

In the English-language Vietnamese American milieu, as Isabelle Thuy Pelaud compellingly shows, anthological works such as *Once upon a Dream* (1995) and *Watermark* (1997) and special issues of *Manoa Journal* (2002) and *Michigan Quarterly Review* (2004) have aimed to educate audiences about Vietnamese diasporic struggles and losses and establish Vietnamese American writers as a recognized group. Most of these publications have been one-offs, without the continuity and seriality of *Văn* and *Văn Học*, and, as Pelaud notes, some of their editors used vague selection criteria and problematically reified certain categories of literature, such as what constituted "Vietnamese" or "Vietnamese American," thus arbitrarily determining what was worthy of inclusion. Nevertheless, what many of them shared was a desire to forge "a collective bound by shared history and culture."[48] Given the recent fortieth anniversary of Vietnam's reunification, we can add a number of other anthological texts to this list, such as *Looking Back on the Vietnam War* (2016) and special issues of journals such as "(Re)Collecting the Vietnam War" (*Asian American Literary Review*, 2015) and "Refugee Cultures: Forty Years after the Vietnam War" (*MELUS*, 2016). These publications question the category of "Southeast Asia" in the global imaginary by highlighting alternative genealogies and geographies and outlining new conceptual directions. Rather than focusing on Vietnamese American literature and perspectives, for example, they begin to foreground other contexts, such as Hmong American and Cambodian American aesthetics, and aim to highlight works in different media. Such efforts commit to elaborating the variations and specificities of disparate Vietnam War histories rather than presupposing a common, universal Vietnam War experience and narrative.

Speaking to what Ma Vang might describe as Southeast Asian American anthological texts' reterritorializing power—their potential to write against and reconstitute dominant forces[49]—one might say that these publications disrupt canons at the same time that they create them, offering not infinitely open-ended groupings but varied configurations of historically situated Southeast Asian American texts. The present progressive of titular terms such as "looking back" and "recollecting" suggests those critical actions as ongoing and positions "Vietnam" as a shifting construction. These writings share with South Vietnamese literary journals a self-reflective, rhizomatic engagement with the literary categories that they also help bring into being.

The field of Vietnamese American literary studies, in turn, sheds light on the politics of South Vietnamese culture, particularly when we consider recent observations regarding the problem of literary exclusions. For instance, one current critique is that a severe internal asymmetry exists within Vietnamese American literature. As Viet Thanh Nguyen asserts, this body of work is overwhelmingly written by "an urban, educated class," whose writing relates to a primarily rural country.[50] This fact would seem to affirm Nguyen's argument that the literary marketplace values ethnic literature as long as it affirms multiculturalism without delving too deeply into issues of social inequality.[51] The fact of many of these texts' "elite" origins compels us to reconsider South Vietnamese literary journals as a socially uneven practice, as they were arguably the work of a culturally elite group of authors and marginalized some important topics, such as the region's ethnic minorities. What I have discussed is thereby not representative but introductory and part of a broader, multilayered picture. Critically rereading South Vietnamese and Vietnamese

American literature through each other adds texture to our understanding of both contexts, bringing visibility to a host of issues related to various market-places of "Vietnam" literature that warrant further investigation.

In the Internet age, a different kind of literary magazine has emerged online. The Diasporic Vietnamese Artists Network's *diaCRITICS* blog is a prominent example whose digital seriality underscores how the field of Vietnamese American studies is about not only collating a canon and collective of critics but also convening an audience. Currently edited by Nguyen, *diaCRITICS* delineates its genesis by acknowledging "the first diacritic" (the artist Richard Streitmatter-Tran, whose website is diacritic.org) and casts a wide, accessible net. As the multilingual home page states, the site's "diaCRITICS write about anything and everything related to the arts and culture of the Vietnamese in their homeland or in the diaspora. Music, film, literature, fashion, food, visual arts, you name it. Oh yeah, maybe politics too. And history. And any good story that comes our way. Have we forgotten something? Let us know. diaCRITICS also write about the ways that other people write about the Vietnamese."[52] The *diaCRITICS* blog publishes established and new writers while crediting those behind the scenes. The contributors reflect a spectrum of cultural and social interests and self-identify with a range of genders and sexualities, while the site as a whole addresses a transnational audience through geographically diverse coverage. Still, one might argue that what Nguyen describes as non-elite demographics and issues, such as the interests or writings of agrarian or poor populations, remain minimally represented. Nevertheless, blogs such as *diaCRITICS*, which I would characterize as a new kind of literary magazine, reach beyond the academic sphere and the boundaries of the university. By soliciting feedback from readers and inviting them to become diaCRITICS themselves, the online publication highlights the participatory role of the audience in creating, sustaining, and defining literary classifications and communities.

American depictions and interpretations of others' literatures and histories through simplistic, monolithic, and consumable tropes ultimately blind us to the motivations, consequences, and long histories of not only U.S. militarism and cultural hegemony but also other imperialisms and hegemonies.[53] They also obscure regional dynamics and conflicts, complicated responses to those histories, and the aesthetic and historical nuances of the literary works themselves. The literary texts I have gathered help to foster a more complex, multidimensional approach that the familiar, often dichotomizing language of public discourse associated with "Vietnam" forecloses. They offer an alternate archive through which we can grapple with the intricate context of South Vietnamese cultural, social, military, and economic life and recognize South Vietnamese thought as viable, variable, and fraught.

It then becomes imperative to practice Southeast Asian American literary studies—many of whose works are strongly but not solely tied to histories of South Vietnam—as similarly heterogeneous and consisting of different groupings of historically specific writings that shape and are shaped by critics', authors', and editors' particular visions.

South Vietnamese Journals as Archives for Literary History

When I began exploring South Vietnamese literary journals at the General Sciences Library in Hồ Chí Minh City, my mind kept returning to the tumultuous year of 1968, which ushered in the Tết Offensive, as well as war-related movements around the globe, including in South Vietnam. I could not help but wonder what it was like to sit down and plan pieces for publication and continue to conceptualize the role of literature and literary critics during a time of intense warfare and grief on all sides. How were editors and writers shaped by the uncertainty of the RVN's fate? The issue of *Văn* dated March 1, 1968, offers some insights, having appeared a month before the one on Mc-Cullers and helping to bookend a painful month by mobilizing two different cover illustrations of unidealized femininity, as if to express these magazines' transnational vision as well as the precariousness of literary production.

The issue's editorial note acknowledges the turbulent times that readers are facing and expresses gratitude for the outpouring of support the journal has received. As letters of concern pour into *Văn*'s office throughout 1968 and after, the note affirms the special relationship the journal has with readers and reiterates its commitment to building it with future issues: "We will keep trying, we will never cease trying so that we do not betray your respect and trust." During a Lunar New Year season in which greeting the new became a time of searching for the dead—in the words of the editor, when the sounds of firecrackers welcoming the new year merged with the sounds of bombs—*Văn* updates readers on the fate of Vietnamese writers caught in the fray of the fighting and appeals to specific individuals to help find those who are missing. In addition to asserting the journal's service as a means of communication and even a lifeline, the editor expresses hope that *Văn* can help create a community that will exceed the dire circumstances at hand: "Our hope is that each interaction we have with you will be dear and lasting."[54] The comment reminds us that literature can serve needs that are quite immediate and tangible. In this case, periodicals' apostrophic structure of address enables the literary journal to function as a vehicle for finding material support, as documentation of survivors and the missing, as elegy for those who may have passed.

VIẾT TRONG KHÓI LỬA

Cover of the March 1, 1968, issue of *Văn,* titled "Written in Smoke and Fire."
(Photograph by the author.)

South Vietnamese found themselves engaging in literary practice through the anthological form as both a conceptual project and a material practice—indeed, in many ways, a way to survive. For them, literature and the genre of the literary journal were politically tense spaces but also forms of imaginative and critical possibility. However uncertain the future might be, *Văn* pledged to continue publishing new pieces in a context of ongoing warfare, pieces necessarily "written in smoke and fire" (the issue's title). Even as the republic was in jeopardy and "Vietnam" was drastically shifting geopolitically, the journals' editors perhaps aimed to do what they often claimed was their duty: establish a venue for regular expression and commentary and try to leave behind a paper trail, an archive for literary history.[55]

NOTES

INTRODUCTION

1. See https://history.state.gov/countries/vietnam, accessed January 15, 2015.

2. The different names identifying Vietnam are the subject of a monograph by the Southeast Asia historian Christopher Goscha, who shows how "Vietnam" is just one option out of many that have been used from the tenth century onward to reference what we today call Vietnam. For instance, Đại Việt was the name of the independent state that was formed in the tenth century, after centuries of Chinese rule: see Christopher E. Goscha, *Going Indochinese: Contesting Concepts of Space and Place in French Indochina*, Nordic Institute of Asian Studies Classics Series (Copenhagen: Nordic Institute of Asian Studies Press, 2012), 14.

3. As Viet Thanh Nguyen writes, "Even if the name [Vietnam War] is abbreviated to Vietnam, as it so often is, many people still understand it to mean the war": Viet Thanh Nguyen, *Nothing Ever Dies: Vietnam and the Memory of War* (Cambridge, MA: Harvard University Press, 2016), 6.

4. Viet Thanh Nguyen, "Refugee Memories and Asian American Critique," *Positions: East Asia Cultures Critique* 20, no. 3 (2012): 913.

5. This genealogy is often neglected because, as Espiritu notes, American memory and history of the war are predicated on "organized forgetting": Yen Le Espiritu, *Body Counts: The Vietnam War and Militarized Refugees* (Berkeley: University of California Press, 2014), 81.

6. Aamir R. Mufti, *Forget English! Orientalisms and World Literatures* (Cambridge, MA: Harvard University Press, 2016).

7. Fiona I. B. Ngo, Mimi Thi Nguyen, and Mariam B. Lam, "Southeast Asian American Studies Special Issue: Guest Editors' Introduction," *Positions: East Asia Cultures Critique* 20, no. 3 (2012): 673.

8. Yunte Huang, Hua Hsu, Lisa Lowe, Colleen Lye, and Min Hyoung Song have offered important periodizations of Asian American literature in terms of shifting im-

migration policies, Pacific-oriented geopolitical imaginaries, and the influence of these contexts on formal practices: see Yunte Huang, *Transpacific Imaginations: History, Literature, Counterpoetics* (Cambridge, MA: Harvard University Press, 2008); Hua Hsu, *A Floating Chinaman: Fantasy and Failure across the Pacific* (Cambridge, MA: Harvard University Press, 2016); Lisa Lowe, *Immigrant Acts: On Asian American Cultural Politics* (Durham, NC: Duke University Press, 1996); Lisa Lowe, *The Intimacies of Four Continents* (Durham, NC: Duke University Press, 2015); Colleen Lye, *America's Asia: Racial Form and American Literature, 1893–1945* (Princeton, NJ: Princeton University Press, 2005). Min Hyoung Song, *The Children of 1965: On Writing, and Not Writing, as an Asian American* (Durham, NC: Duke University Press, 2013). Denise Cruz and Martin Joseph Ponce have traced novel Southeast Asian American literary genealogies through examination of expansive archives and temporal frames, paying particular attention to cultural and historical formations of gender and sexuality: see Denise Cruz, *Transpacific Femininities: The Making of the Modern Filipina* (Durham, NC: Duke University Press, 2012); Martin Joseph Ponce, *Beyond the Nation: Diasporic Filipino Literature and Queer Reading*, Sexual Cultures (New York: New York University Press, 2012).

9. Fernand Braudel and Immanuel Wallerstein, "History and the Social Sciences: The Longue Durée," *Review (Fernand Braudel Center)* 32, no. 2 (2009): 173–174.

10. Fernand Braudel, *On History* (Chicago: University of Chicago Press, 1980), 39.

11. Braudel and Wallerstein, "History and the Social Sciences," 182.

12. In his reading of *The Book of Salt*, David Eng importantly identifies Braudel's model as a generative one for analyzing race. My focus is on a long historical understanding of literary encounters between Vietnam and America as refracted through generic dynamics. See David Eng, "The End(s) of Race," *PMLA* 123, no. 5 (2008): 1480. I am also in line with Sahar Amer and Laura Doyle's suggestion that a longer historical approach can "reframe historical and geographic dynamics": see Sahar Amer and Laura Doyle, "Theories and Methodologies: Reframing Postcolonial and Global Studies in the Longer Durée [Special Section]," *PMLA* 130, no. 2 (2015): 331.

13. The goals of this book are akin to Wai Chee Dimock's mapping of American literature through "deep time"—an approach oriented around extended time and that attends to texts' many "loops of relations" that bring into view the world's variety of "historical phenomena": Wai Chee Dimock, *Through Other Continents: American Literature across Deep Time* (Princeton, NJ: Princeton University Press, 2006), 3, 5. For Franklin and Jefferson, see, e.g., Benjamin Franklin, "From Benjamin Franklin to John Bartram, 7 October 1772," Franklin Papers, *Founders Online*, National Archives, available at https://founders.archives.gov/?q=cochin%20china&s=1111311111&r=1; Thomas Jefferson, "From Thomas Jefferson to William Drayton, 30 July 1787," Jefferson Papers, *Founders Online*, National Archives, available at https://founders.archives.gov/documents/Jefferson/01-11-02-0568.

14. Fredric Jameson, *Postmodernism, or, The Cultural Logic of Late Capitalism*, Post-contemporary Interventions (Durham, NC: Duke University Press, 1991), 44–45.

15. Fredric Jameson, *The Political Unconscious: Narrative as a Socially Symbolic Act* (Ithaca, NY: Cornell University Press, 1981).

16. Wai Chee Dimock, "Introduction: Genres as Fields of Knowledge," *PMLA* 122, no. 5 (2007): 1379. Dimock elaborates on regenreing as "cumulative reuse, an alluvial process, sedimentary as well as migratory."

17. Betsy Huang, *Contesting Genres in Contemporary Asian American Fiction* (New York: Palgrave Macmillan, 2010), 6.

18. Monique T. D. Truong, "The Reception of Robert Olen Butler's *A Good Scent from a Strange Mountain*: Ventriloquism and the Pulitzer Prize," *Viet Nam Forum* 16 (Fall 1997): 81.

19. Recent formalist approaches to Asian American culture include Rocio G. Davis and Sue Im-Lee's broad call for aesthetic-oriented studies; Colleen Lye's understanding of race in terms of "racial form," the literary or stylistic contours of Asian American character; Christopher Lee's notion of identity as a project not of reflective representation but of aesthetic mediation; Josephine Park's and Timothy Yu's investigations of Asian American poetics; and Joseph Jonghyun Jeon's focus on the formal qualities of Asian American things. Huang's *Contesting Genres in Contemporary Asian American Fiction* stands out as explicitly invested in genre, examining popular fiction to show how Asian American authors' experimentations with genre constitute "a troubling act"—a disruption of generic expectations of assimilation and conciliation that correspond with American national imperatives of immigration and identity: see ibid. Lye also notes the contingency of form on the historical: "Formalist desires of Asian American criticism are also deeply at heart formalist desires": see Colleen Lye, "Racial Form," *Representations* 104, no. 1 (2008): 99.

20. In Dimock's words, genres are continuously unstable and intertextual and can act as a "heuristic map" for interpretation: Dimock, *Through Other Continents*, 73.

21. As Derrida writes, "There are no arch-genres that can totally escape historicity while preserving a generic definition": Jacques Derrida and Avital Ronell, trans., "The Law of Genre," *Critical Inquiry* 7, no. 1 (1980): 62.

22. Raymond Williams, *Marxism and Literature, Marxist Introductions* (Oxford: Oxford University Press, 1977), 185.

23. John Frow echoes Williams's approach, writing, "Genre must be defined in terms of particular constellations of thematic, rhetorical, and formal features": see John Frow, *Genre*, 2nd ed., New Critical Idiom (London: Routledge, Taylor and Francis, 2015), 71.

24. The field of Asian American literary studies often concentrates on the Asian American subject rather than object as the primary node of investigation (although the two often bleed into each other). For instance, Lye's concept of "racial form" (the literary or stylistic contours of Asian American character) and Kandice Chuh's "subjectless" discourse (deconstructing "Asian America" as a subject for critique) are two influential examples that reflect the centrality of Asian American subjectivity in literary critique, whether to observe its surfacing or its dissolution: see Lye, "Racial Form"; Kandice Chuh, *Imagine Otherwise: On Asian Americanist Critique* (Durham, NC: Duke University Press, 2003).

25. Woloch defines the character-system as "the arrangement of multiple and differentiated character-spaces—differentiated configurations of the human figure—into a unified narrative structure": Alex Woloch, *The One versus the Many: Minor Characters and the Space of the Protagonist in the Novel* (Princeton, NJ: Princeton University Press, 2003), 14.

26. Alex Woloch, "Partial Representation," in *The Work of Genre: Selected Essays from the English Institute*, ed. Robyn Warhol-Down (Cambridge, MA: English Institute in collaboration with the American Council of Learned Societies, 2013).

27. Gilles Deleuze and Félix Guattari, *A Thousand Plateaus: Capitalism and Schizophrenia* (Minneapolis: University of Minnesota Press, 1987), 5–25.

28. Act of March 3, 1819, chap. 77, 4 (1819) available at https://www.loc.gov/law/help/statutes-at-large/15th-congress/c15.pdf.

29. The case, famously prosecuted by Daniel Webster, inspired Edgar Allan Poe's "The Tell-Tale Heart" (1843) and Nathaniel Hawthorne's *The House of Seven Gables* (1851).

30. John White, *History of a Voyage to the China Sea* (Boston: Wells and Lilly, 1823), vi. Hereafter, page numbers are cited in parentheses in the text.

31. White hoped to find a translator in Manila to take with him to Vietnam.

32. At least three editions of White's text were published: the American version published by Wells and Lilly of Boston in 1823 and British versions titled *A Voyage to Cochin China* published in 1824: John White, *A Voyage to Cochin China* (London: A. and R. Spottiswoode, 1824); John White, *A Voyage to Cochin China* (London: Longman, Hurst, Rees, Orme, Brown, and Green, 1824). The British editions do not include the appendix on Vietnamese language. I have not been able to locate the logbook of the *Franklin*'s journey; it is not housed at the Peabody Essex Museum, which has materials from the East India Marine Society to which White belonged and donated items from his trip. Reference librarians and archivists I have spoken to there do not know what happened to the logbook.

33. Jean Louis, "Note on the Geography of Cochin China," *Journal of the Asiatic Society of Bengal* 6, no. 2 (1837): 737.

34. Margaret Cohen, *The Novel and the Sea*, Translation/Transnation (Princeton, NJ: Princeton University Press, 2010), 69. For instance, White's depictions of Vietnam's post-civil war "ravages" (337) quote from other sources.

35. Cohen, *The Novel and the Sea*, 75–76.

36. This is not to romanticize Vietnamese resistance but to iterate the uncertainties of both sides of the interaction.

37. Hester Blum, *The View from the Masthead: Maritime Imagination and Antebellum American Sea Narratives* (Chapel Hill: University of North Carolina Press, 2008), 3. Blum focuses on antebellum sea stories from the ground up—that is, from the perspective of the "common laboring sailor." I adapt her term here because, even though White captains the Franklin, I read his depictions as informed by others' observations "from below."

38. Tana Li, "The Water Frontier: An Introduction," in *Water Frontier: Commerce and the Chinese in the Lower Mekong Region, 1750–1880*, ed. Nola Cooke and Tana Li (Singapore: Rowman and Littlefield, 2004). See also Tana Li, "The Late-Eighteenth and Early-Nineteenth-Century Mekong Delta in the Regional Trade System," in Cooke and Li, *Water Frontier*.

39. Alexander Woodside, cited in Nhung Tuyet Tran and Anthony Reid, "Introduction," in *Việt Nam: Borderless Histories*, ed. Nhung Tuyet Tran and Anthony Reid, New Perspectives in Southeast Asian Studies (Madison: University of Wisconsin Press, 2006), 12.

40. Li, "The Water Frontier," 2.

41. Ibid., 7.

42. Ibid., 5–6.

43. Ibid., 1.

44. Ibid., 3.

45. Tana Li, "The Eighteenth-Century Mekong Delta and Its World of Water Frontier," in Tran and Reid, *Việt Nam*, 158; Li, "The Water Frontier," 3.

46. Anthony Reid, cited in Li, "The Late-Eighteenth and Early-Nineteenth-Century Mekong Delta in the Regional Trade System," 158. The early decades of Singapore trade were dominated by independent states such as "Siam, Việt Nam, Aceh, Siak, Trengganu, and the Balinese states."

47. For instance, in the sixteenth and seventeenth centuries, the ceramics trade in Hội An involved Persia, India, Spain, Portugal, and Holland.

48. Gia Long was the only surviving family member of the Nguyễn lords who had ruled the south.

49. Christopher E. Goscha, *Vietnam: A New History* (New York: Basic, 2016), 10.

50. Ibid., 42.

51. Ibid., 44.

52. White does reference the devastations and challenges that Vietnam faces after the civil war, noting strained resources, national insecurity, and other overall "ravages" (337). He bypasses Vietnamese efforts at reconstruction, instead opting to give special credit to Bishop Pigneau de Behaine, a French missionary, for acting as "oracle and guide of the king" (93). His death, White argues, brought an end to "the wholesome laws, institutions, and regulations" he initiated (94). Pigneau de Behaine helped to arrange a treaty between a younger Gia Long and Louis XVI that provided French military aid for Gia Long's attempt to defeat the Tây Sơn brothers, although the treaty's terms were never fulfilled. The French would later refer to the unfulfilled treaty to justify its colonization of what would become French Indochina. According to White, Pigneau de Behaine, rather than any Vietnamese figures, was Vietnam's ultimate modernizer, leading projects to clear roads, canals, and land, developing a Vietnamese dictionary of European military strategies, opening schools, and reforming the legal system.

53. Lê Quang Định, "Vietnamese Geographical Expansion," trans. George Dutton, in *Sources of Vietnamese Tradition*, ed. George Dutton, Jayne Susan Werner, and John K. Whitmore, Introduction to Asian Civilizations (New York: Columbia University Press, 2012), 262.

54. Dutton, Werner, and Whitmore, *Sources of Vietnamese Tradition*, 257.

55. Li, "The Water Frontier," 5.

56. Kale Bantigue Fajardo, *Filipino Crosscurrents: Oceanographies of Seafaring, Masculinities, and Globalization* (Minneapolis: University of Minnesota Press, 2011), 19.

57. Nguyễn Văn Nhơn (1753–1822, also Nguyễn Văn Nhân) was the first governor of what White calls Saigon. (Saigon at the time included only Cholon, the Chinese area of present-day Saigon city.) Perhaps the only figure depicted with admiration in *History of a Voyage*, the governor is described as having a "military and dignified" appearance, "the air of an experienced courtier, blended with the frankness of a soldier. He was a man of mind, and is no doubt destined, in the event of future wars, or domestic commotions, to fill an important page in the history of his country" (305). Complementing his dignified bearing are his equally dignified interiors, decorated with "handsome porcelain vases, . . . beautiful exotic and native plants[,] . . . a garden, laid out with considerable taste" (305). Again, the currency of Vietnamese subjects is bound up with space, which is here as tastefully contained as the figures's comportment.

58. David Brewster, *A Treatise on the Kaleidoscope* (Edinburgh: A. Constable [etc.], 1819), 6.

59. For instance, much thought went into deciding which metals worked best, how smooth their surfaces should be, and what eye position would maximize color and symmetry: ibid., 4–8.

60. Ibid., 2.

61. Helen Groth, "Kaleidoscopic Vision and Literary Invention in an 'Age of Things: David Brewster, Don Juan, and 'a Lady's Kaleidoscope,'" *ELH* 74, no. 1 (2007):

217. By 1819, 200,000 kaleidoscopes had been sold in London and Paris: Brewster, *A Treatise on the Kaleidoscope*, 7.

62. Toni Morrison, *Playing in the Dark: Whiteness and the Literary Imagination*, William E. Massey Sr. Lectures in the History of American Civilization (Cambridge, MA: Harvard University Press, 1992), 33.

63. Cohen, *The Novel and the Sea*, 24, 66–74.

64. Williams, *Marxism and Literature*, 185.

65. To my knowledge, no American literary scholar has studied White's narrative while several Southeast Asia scholars have, dissecting its ambiguities to shed light on the region's intricate maritime networks. See Byung Wook Choi, "The Nguyen Dynasty's Policy toward Chinese on the Water Frontier in the First Half of the Nineteenth Century," in Cooke and Li, *Water Frontier*. Tana Li, "Ships and Shipbuilding in the Mekong Delta, c. 1750–1840," in Cooke and Li, *Water Frontier*.

66. Robert Hopkins Miller, *The United States and Vietnam, 1787–1941* (Washington, DC: National Defense University Press, 1990), 287–288.

67. Lye, *America's Asia*.

68. Any attempt to capture a definitive interpretation of Vietnam would be betrayed by the term's own etymological complexity, for Vietnam itself is a polysemous term that comprises a "multitude of Vietnams," as Christopher Goscha puts it, that were consolidated by different national leaders in 1945: see Goscha, *Vietnam*, xi. See also Goscha, *Going Indochinese*.

69. In other words, this book is by no means exhaustive but encourages us to "imagine" Vietnam "otherwise," to second Chuh's call for continued critical reconfigurations of Asian America: see Chuh, *Imagine Otherwise*. For instance, such a project might include the use of more bilingual primary and secondary sources. Such an approach does not inherently result in more nuanced scholarship, but it does require an intellectual rationale that would advance detailed understanding of Asian American cultural networks in a transnational frame. In the story I recover—which, in drawing from mostly English-language secondary sources, has its limits—America has had a long-standing presence in Vietnam, and American imperialism as well as responses to it continually rethink and revise themselves across that duration. While I do not dispute the position of the United States as a global power, this book also attends to moments of American and Vietnamese political ambivalence and uncertainty that we need to recognize in order to parse the complex relations between the two regions.

CHAPTER 1

1. Harry Hervey, *Congaï* (New York: Cosmopolitan, 1927), 307. Hereafter, page numbers are cited in parentheses in the text. I first came across Hervey's works in 1999 when I began compiling a bibliography of American works published on Vietnam before 1954. Since then, there has been some increased interest in him and his career. *Congaï* has also recently been reprinted by the small, independent press DatAsia, with a foreword by Pico Iyer: Harry Hervey, *Congaï*, ed. Kent Davis (Holmes Beach, FL: DatAsia, 2014).

2. I draw from Sedgwick's model of homosociality in English literature, which argues that in a context of imperialism, women are often rendered inconsequential to the immediate sphere of colonial homosocial desire and competition: see Eve Kosofsky Sedgwick, *Between Men: English Literature and Male Homosocial Desire*, Gender and Culture (New York: Columbia University Press, 1985).

3. *Congaï* finally closed on March 23, 1929. For comparison, here are the runs of some plays that were contemporaneous with *Congaï.* Among *The New York Times Book of Broadway*'s list of "Twenty-five Productions That Defined the Century" are *The Hairy Ape*, by Eugene O'Neill, opening night March 9, 1922, 108 performances; *Show Boat*, by Oscar Hammerstein and Jerome Kern, opening night December 27, 1927, 572 performances; and *Waiting for Lefty*, by Clifford Odets, opening night February 10, 1935, 96 performances. Under "The Unforgettable Productions of the Century" appear *Funny Face*, opening night November 22, 1927, 244 performances; *The Front Page*, opening night August 14, 1928, 276 performances; and *Animal Crackers*, opening night October 23, 1928, 191 performances: see Ben Brantley, ed., *The New York Times Book of Broadway* (New York: St. Martin's Press, 2001), xi.

4. The historian Mark Bradley provides an important study of American-Vietnamese cultural relations during the first half of the twentieth century. Bradley examines a temporally and linguistically diverse selection of American representations of Vietnam and Vietnamese representations of America. He asserts that during the interwar period, "Vietnam held only marginal significance for American diplomats and businesspeople," but he provides an interesting discussion of the writings of journalists, scholars, travelers, missionaries, and hunters that are set in Vietnam but did not circulate widely. For Bradley, this corpus offers "the first sustained body of American commentary on Vietnamese society, French colonialism in Indochina, and Vietnamese nationalism." Yet "[had] it not been for the outbreak of the Pacific war in 1941, interwar American perceptions of Vietnam might best be viewed as little more than a historical curiosity": Mark Bradley, *Imagining Vietnam and America: The Making of Postcolonial Vietnam, 1919–1850*, The New Cold War History (Chapel Hill: University of North Carolina Press, 2000), 45–47. Scott Laderman argues that Hollywood films about Vietnam before 1965 relied on stereotypical portrayals that conveyed an area "in need of U.S. tutelage and instruction": Scott Laderman, "Hollywood's Vietnam, 1929–1964: Scripting Intervention, Spotlighting Injustice," *Pacific Historical Review* 78, no. 4 (2009): 579.

5. The film *Prestige*, based on a story by Hervey, was released by RKO-Pathé in 1932 and portrayed French brutality at Lao Bảo, a historical colonial prison in Indochina. A thorough analysis of the film is not within the purview of this chapter, but I would surmise that it escaped censorship because it dealt squarely with French imperial evils rather than commenting on evolving American empire, as *Congaï* does.

6. Harlan Greene, "The Multi-talented Harry Hervey," *Gay and Lesbian Review* (May–June 2017): 24.

7. See, e.g., Harry Hervey, "The Young Men Go Down," *The Nation* 118, no. 3056 (January 24, 1924): 112–114. This story was selected in 1924 for inclusion in a volume of best short stories for 1924. See Edward J. O'Brien, ed. *The Best Short Stories of 1924 and the Yearbook of the American Short Story* (Boston: Small, Maynard, 1925).

8. Greene, "The Multi-talented Harry Hervey," 26.

9. For critical treatments of "congai's" history and cultural usages, see Marie-Paule Ha, "'La Femme Française aux Colonies': Promoting Colonial Female Emigration at the Turn of the Century," *French Colonial History* 6 (2005): 205–224. Frank Proschan, "Eunuch Mandarins, Soldats Mamzelles, Effeminate Boys, and Graceless Women," *GLQ* 8, no. 4 (2002), 435–467; Frank Proschan, "'Syphilis, Opiomania, and Pederasty': Colonial Constructions of Vietnamese (and French) Social Diseases," *Journal of the History of Sexuality* 11, no. 4 (2002): 610–636. Ann Laura Stoler, *Car-*

nal Knowledge and Imperial Power: Race and the Intimate in Colonial Rule (Berkeley: University of California Press, 2002), 48.

10. Stung Treng (also Steung Treng) had been a part of Laos until it was transferred to Cambodia in 1904. Annam often stood in for all three Vietnamese units of Indochina. It was both a pejorative term and not, used by colonials and Vietnamese nationalists prior to 1945: Christopher E. Goscha, *Going Indochinese: Contesting Concepts of Space and Place in French Indochina*. Nordic Institute of Asian Studies Classics Series (Copenhagen: Nordic Institute of Asian Studies, 2012), 10.

11. Peter Brooks, *The Melodramatic Imagination: Balzac, Henry James, Melodrama, and the Mode of Excess* (New Haven, CT: Yale University Press, 1976), 19.

12. For an excellent discussion on the distinctions between French and American melodrama, see Elisabeth R. Anker, *Orgies of Feeling: Melodrama and the Politics of Freedom* (Durham, NC: Duke University Press, 2014), 65–109.

13. Brooks, *The Melodramatic Imagination*, 34.

14. Linda Williams, *Playing the Race Card: Melodramas of Black and White from Uncle Tom to O. J. Simpson* (Princeton, NJ: Princeton University Press, 2001), 35.

15. Brooks, *The Melodramatic Imagination*, 4, emphasis added.

16. Anker, *Orgies of Feeling*, 15.

17. Laura Wexler, *Tender Violence: Domestic Visions in an Age of U.S. Imperialism*, Cultural Studies of the United States (Chapel Hill: University of North Carolina Press, 2000), 101.

18. Lauren Berlant, "Thinking about Feeling Historical," *Emotion, Space and Society* 1, no. 1 (2008): 4–9. See also Dana Luciano, "Conversation: Lauren Berlant with Dana Luciano," January 13, 2013, available at http://socialtextjournal.org/periscope_article/conversation-lauren-berlant-with-dana-luciano.

19. Lauren Berlant, "The Subject of True Feeling: Pain, Privacy, and Politics," in *Cultural Pluralism, Identity Politics, and the Law*, ed. Austin Sarat and Thomas R. Kearns (Ann Arbor: University of Michigan Press, 1999), 44.

20. Williams, *Playing the Race Card*, 5. The term "racial legibility" in Williams's book is credited to Misa Oyama, whose doctoral dissertation offers an invaluable analysis of melodrama as a mode through which Asian bodies become simultaneously legible and erased. According to Oyama, racial legibility is "the belief that race is inherent in the individual and can be recognized, usually by association with specific physical, behavioral, or cultural signs": Misa Oyama, "The Asian Look of Melodrama, Moral and Racial Legibility in the Films of Sessue Hayakawa, Anna May Wong, Winnifred Eaton, and James Wong Howe" (Ph.D. diss., University of California, Berkeley, 2007), 7. I am indebted to conversations with Oyama for advancing this book's understanding of how the depictions and performances of Asiatic bodies in American melodrama illuminate the mode's intertwining of morality, emotion, and race.

21. For example, Joshua Takano Chambers-Letson analyzes how David Belasco's 1900 stage production of *Madame Butterfly* communicated U.S.-Asian temporal disjuncture through decorative innovations made possible by technological advances in the theater. The performance opened with a set of curtains that gave rise to another set of curtains painted with Japanese motifs, followed by "lushly painted screens" after which Cho-Cho San and her cottage finally appeared. By postponing Cho-Cho San's appearance, the layers of curtains and screens stylized Asian emergence as stalled. See Joshua Takano Chambers-Letson, *A Race So Different: Performance and Law in Asian America*, Postmillennial Pop Series (New York: New York University Press,

2013), 34. Also see Josephine D. Lee, *The Japan of Pure Invention: Gilbert and Sullivan's "The Mikado"* (Minneapolis: University of Minnesota Press, 2010). For a treatment of melodrama in the Vietnamese context, see Khai Thu Nguyen, "Sensing Vietnam: Melodramas of Nation from Colonialism to Market Reform" (Ph.D. diss., University of California, Berkeley, 2010).

22. Joseph Jonghyun Jeon, *Racial Things, Racial Forms: Objecthood in Avant-Garde Asian American Poetry*, Contemporary North American Poetry Series (Iowa City: University of Iowa Press, 2012).

23. A rich body of scholarship exists on the relationship between melodrama and Asian American culture, and my focus on melodramas' objects is indebted to this work. Depictions of Asian-American relations have often been rooted in the melodramatic tradition and mixed-race themes—as Susan Koshy writes, melodramas of miscegenation re-narrate Asian-American geopolitical conflict as "romantic plots about the possibility of love between individuals from different races": see Susan Koshy, *Sexual Naturalization: Asian Americans and Miscegenation*, Asian America (Stanford, CA: Stanford University Press, 2004), 20. Similarly, Gina Marchetti demonstrates that, organized around a variable fear of and desire for cross-racial contact, melodramas of white-Asian desire replace direct depictions of expanding U.S. power and Asian-American political conflict with romanticized narratives of interracial love: Gina Marchetti, *Romance and the "Yellow Peril": Race, Sex, and Discursive Strategies in Hollywood Fiction* (Berkeley: University of California Press, 1993), 219. Christina Klein does not focus on melodrama, but her study *Cold War Orientalism* does address examples of interracial romance in American culture to illustrate how the popularity of such portrayals helped to promote integration as U.S. ideology during the Cold War: see Christina Klein, *Cold War Orientalism: Asia in the Middlebrow Imagination, 1945–1961* (Berkeley: University of California Press, 2003). It is worth noting that analyzing objects is perhaps even more revelatory in Asian American contexts, given what Oyama describes as American melodramas' historical denial of deep feeling to Asiatic characters. In Asian American–themed melodramas, Asians typically "withhold rather than express"; their feelings do not count. Asians' denied expression and withheld dramatic agency render them inscrutable and narratively destabilizing, continually frustrating the aim of moral clarity toward which melodrama strives. Oyama shows that whatever resolution melodramas' practitioners devise to culminate their narratives, the "justice" that results typically must not overthrow the moral system of a narrative's white characters: see Oyama, "The Asian Look of Melodrama," 9.

24. Anne Cheng, "Shine: On Race, Glamour, and the Modern," *PMLA* 126, no. 4 (2011): 1022–1041.

25. Pham's conception of fashion as racialized virtual ideology in the early twentieth century demonstrates how imaginings of dystopia during this time often took the form of sartorialized Orientalism: see Minh-Ha T. Pham, "Paul Poiret's Magical Techno-Oriental Fashions (1911): Race, Clothing, and Virtuality in the Machine Age," *Configurations* 21, no. 1 (Winter 2013): 1.

26. Camille Robcis, *The Law of Kinship: Anthropology, Psychoanalysis, and the Family in France* (Ithaca, NY: Cornell University Press, 2013), 2, 19, 262.

27. *Métis* born out of wedlock did not fit initial legal classifications and forced revisions to the law. They became divided into three subcategories: those "recognized" by the French father and eligible for French citizenship; those "non-recognized" by the French parent; and the "abandoned," or those not recognized by either parent,

whether those parents were interracial or both were Asian: Christina E. Firpo, "Lost Boys: 'Abandoned' Eurasian Children and the'Management of the Racial Topography in Colonial Indochina, 1938–1945," *French Colonial History* 8 (2007): 205–206. In 1889, France declared that the state could acquire custody of *métis* children whose French fathers had abandoned them and whose mothers were deemed incompetent. *Métis* generally meant those who were both abandoned and illegitimate: Emmanuelle Saada, *Empire's Children: Race, Filiation, and Citizenship in the French Colonies*, trans. Arthur Goldhammer (Chicago: University of Chicago Press, 2012), 20. See also Julia Clancy-Smith and Frances Gouda, "Introduction," in *Domesticating the Empire: Race, Gender, and Family Life in French and Dutch Colonialism*, ed. Julia Clancy-Smith and Frances Gouda (Charlottesville: University of Virginia Press, 1998), 18–19.

28. Ann Laura Stoler, "Sexual Affronts and Racial Frontiers: European Identities and the Cultural Politics of Exclusion in Colonial Southeast Asia," in *Tensions of Empire: Colonial Cultures in a Bourgeois World*, ed. Frederick Cooper and Ann Laura Stoler (Berkeley: University of California Press, 1997), 199. In the early years of French rule, authorities turned a blind eye toward relations of *métissage* because they could not or did not want to disrupt existing structures of *métissage* that wealthy Europeans maintained and because of the low population of white women. Ideologies of the danger of racial mixing manifested in hygiene manuals published throughout the 1920s and 1930s. These publications often called for racial segregation between whites, blacks, and "yellows" to "prevent the spread of disease in the short time and the dilution of superior white stock through miscegenation in the long term": see Alice L. Conklin, *A Mission to Civilize: The Republican Idea of Empire in France and West Africa, 1895–1930* (Stanford, CA: Stanford University Press, 2000), 72.

29. Stoler, "Sexual Affronts and Racial Frontiers," 199.

30. Ibid., 61, 82.

31. As quoted in ibid., 207.

32. In Cheng's words, the Euro-American "equation between the Asian woman and decoration" has circulated since the eighteenth century: see Cheng, "Modernism," 316. Lisa Lowe's analysis of William Makepeace Thackeray's *Vanity Fair* (1848) discusses similar connotations of chinoiserie in the novel: see Lisa Lowe, *The Intimacies of Four Continents* (Durham, NC: Duke University Press, 2015), 74–100.

33. As quoted in Stoler, "Sexual Affronts and Racial Frontiers," 207.

34. The 1928 decree also exhibits the historically gendered terms of the law. While French colonial administrators were threatened with dismissal if they were found in miscegenous relationships during periods of close surveillance of *métissage*, other colonials did not come under close scrutiny, even when murder was involved: see Penny Edwards, "Womanizing Indochina: Fiction, Nation and Cohabitation in Colonial Cambodia, 1890–1930," in Clancy-Smith and Gouda, *Domesticating the Empire*, 117–118. Since recognition of *métis* subjects depended on the father's recognition of the child, citizenship was *patrilineal*, something also undergirding French law in the metropole, as French women were denied the full spectrum of citizenship rights until 1944: see Saada, *Empire's Children*, 1–3.

35. Saada, *Empire's Children*, 3. The 1928 policy also illustrates how French colonial law, under the banner of post–French Revolution principles, explicitly went against them by negating the liberal ideal that individual "will" rather than "origin" determined civic and political participation: ibid., 1.

36. Ibid., 185. Saada explains that "possession of status" is rooted in Roman law, and in the Napoleonic Code it is determinable by an individual's "bearing the father's name (*nomen*), parental and filial behavior (*tractatus*), and reputation in the social milieu (*fama*)."

37. Saada, *Empire's Children*, 1, emphasis added. Between 1914 and 1922 in Indo-china, the courts granted citizenship to only seventy people. The years 1926–1930 did not fare much better, with 160 successfully applying for citizenship; these numbers include foreigners, not just mixed-race individuals, and Saada notes that rejections of *métis* requests were quite high, even though many candidates fulfilled all legal requirements, as the administration itself admitted: ibid., 113.

38. As Karen E. Fields and Barbara Jeanne Fields write, "The categories imposed by racism . . . are too restrictive to fit anyone" at all: Karen E. Fields and Barbara Jeanne Fields, *Racecraft: The Soul of Inequality in American Life* (London: Verso, 2012), 109.

39. Vũ Trọng Phụng, *Kỹ Nghệ Lấy Tây and Cơm Thầy Cơm Cô* (Hanoi: Nhà Xuất Bản Văn Học, 2004). The translations are mine, unless noted otherwise. For an English translation of *Kỹ Nghệ Lấy Tây*, see Vũ Trọng Phụng, *The Industry of Marrying Europeans*, trans. Thuy Tranviet, Southeast Asia Program Series, vol. 22 (Ithaca, NY: Cornell University, Southeast Asia Program Publications, 2006). For an informative and incisive examination of Vũ Trọng Phụng and Vietnamese modernism, see Peter Zinoman, "Vũ Trọng Phụng's *Dumb Luck* and the Nature of Vietnamese Modernism," in *Dumb Luck, a Novel by Vũ Trọng Phụng*, ed. Zinoman, Southeast Asia: Politics, Meaning, Memory (Ann Arbor: University of Michigan Press, 2002), 1–30. Vũ Trọng Phụng was known for his anticolonial, noncommunist left leanings and, in the words of Peter Zinoman, was a "lower-class, untraveled, half-educated, opium-addicted, colonized subject from a remote outpost of France's second-rate empire." He was prolific, publishing twelve book-length works and hundreds of texts in other genres. Vũ Trọng Phụng's works left a strong, controversial legacy and demonstrate the shifting dynamic of literary criticism and history; the author's writings were banned in communist Vietnam from 1960 through the early 1980s, but today he is taught in schools as a writer whose texts aimed to "undermine the bourgeois colonial order and to advance the revolution": see ibid., 1–4.

40. For Vũ Trọng Phụng, literature was "an instrument of struggle" that could help eradicate "injustice from society," while reportage afforded the portrayal of concrete realities to address specific contexts of exploitation and potential reform (as opposed to depicting a broad vision of revolutionary change): quoted in Peter Zinoman, *Vietnamese Colonial Republican: The Political Vision of Vũ Trong Phụng* (Berkeley: University of California Press, 2014), 41.

41. Phụng, *Kỹ Nghệ Lấy Tây*, 11.

42. Ibid., 26.

43. Matt K. Matsuda, *Empire of Love: Histories of France and the Pacific* (New York: Oxford University Press, 2005). Elizabeth Povinelli offers a useful but slightly different conceptualization of "empire of love," focusing on the dynamics of social intimacy in liberal settler contexts: Elizabeth A. Povinelli, *The Empire of Love: Toward a Theory of Intimacy, Genealogy, and Carnality*, Public Planet Books (Durham, NC: Duke University Press, 2006). Vũ Trọng Phụng's area of focus was Thị Cầu, Bắc Ninh Province, outside Hanoi.

44. Phụng, *Kỹ Nghệ Lấy Tây*, 101.

45. Ibid., 101. During the Depression, the Indochinese economy was volatile and controlled by a few French conglomerates: Zinoman, *Vietnamese Colonial Republican*, 57–58.

46. Phụng, *Kỹ Nghệ Lấy Tây*, 63.

47. Ibid., 67.

48. Phụng, *The Industry of Marrying Europeans*, 57.

49. Phụng, *Kỹ Nghệ Lấy Tây*, 63.

50. Ibid., 52.

51. Ibid., 24.

52. Ibid., 92.

53. Ibid., 52–54.

54. Conceptions of imperial melodrama tend to focus on the British empire and, in particular, the late Victorian period, whereas I trace its American manifestations and its explicitly "anti-imperial" rhetoric: see, e.g., Heidi Holder, "Melodrama, Realism, and Empire on the British Stage," in *Acts of Supremacy: The British Empire and the Stage, 1790–1930*, ed. J. S. Bratton (Manchester, UK: Manchester University Press, 1991), 129–149.

55. As Edwards reminds us, managing colonial social relations and mores in colonial Indochina often hinged on preventing colonized subjects from noticing the construction of race, particularly when similarities of class or sexuality emerged: "The spectacle of poor-whitism was feared and condemned across the global colonial map as a serious detriment to imperial prestige. White women who violated bourgeois ideals were considered dangerous threats to the racial and moral hierarchy of colonial rule. . . . Colonial horrors of degeneration and hybridity led to an obsession with constructing and maintaining bipolar native and European milieus as bridgeheads of national, racial, and cultural purity": see Edwards, "Womanizing Indochina," 113. Tyler Stovall also identifies how colonial authorities conjured race to explain away racial similarity and inscribe racial difference during World War I in the metropole. See Tyler Stovall, "The Color Line behind the Lines: Racial Violence in France during the Great War," *American Historical Review* 103, no. 3 (June 1998): 737–769.

56. This number was second only to Algerians. Of these, 30,425 were stationed in France, other parts of the eastern front, or North Africa: Eric Thomas Jennings, "Remembering 'Other' Losses: The Temple du Souvenir Indochinois of Nogent-sur-Marne," *History and Memory* 15, no. 1 (2003): 10.

57. Firpo, "Lost Boys," 207. See also Kimloan Vu-Hill, "Strangers in a Foreign Land: Vietnamese Soldiers and Workers in France during World War I," in *Việt Nam: Borderless Histories*, ed. Nhung Tuyet Tran and Anthony Reid, New Perspectives in Southeast Asian Studies (Madison: University of Wisconsin Press, 2006), 256. While Hervey does not explicitly mention these developments, they may have informed the sense of social and political unease he registers.

58. Kimloan Vu-Hill, *Coolies into Rebels: Impact of World War I on French Indochina* (Paris: Les Indes Savantes, 2011), 17–30.

59. Fueling heightened racial tensions during and after the Great War was the fact that anticolonial Vietnamese were attending schools in France, Russia, and China: see Peter Zinoman, *The Colonial Bastille: A History of Imprisonment in Vietnam, 1862–1940* (Berkeley: University of California Press, 2001), 221–222. Anticolonials were also clandestinely taking political literature back to Vietnam: see David G. Marr, *Vietnamese Tradition on Trial, 1920–1945* (Berkeley: University of California Press, 1981), 40.

60. Marr, *Vietnamese Tradition on Trial*, 8. Vietnamese nationalism had been building in momentum with the first generation of intellectuals prior to the war. One important historical event was the 1925 public trial of Phan Bội Châu, who was tried for "eight criminal charges dealing with assassinations and conspiracy plots" in 1913. The trial drew large crowds of supporters: see ibid., 15–16.

61. Fredrik Logevall, *Embers of War: The Fall of an Empire and the Making of America's Vietnam* (New York: Random House, 2012), 9; Marr, *Vietnamese Tradition on Trial*, 5–6; Saada, *Empire's Children*, 118.

62. For a discussion of pop psychology's notion of inner primitivism, see Joel Pfister, "Glamorizing the Psychological: The Politics of the Performances of Modern Psychological Identities," in *Inventing the Psychological: Toward a Cultural History of Emotional Life in America*, ed. Joel Pfister and Nancy Schnog (New Haven, CT: Yale University Press, 1997). Anne Cheng also provides a provocative discussion of the primitive within clean, streamlined modernist surfaces and architectures in Anne Anlin Cheng, *Second Skin: Josephine Baker and the Modern Surface* (Oxford: Oxford University Press, 2011).

63. Cheng, "Modernism," 324.

64. For an important study of the relationship between melodramatic romance and U.S.-Asian geopolitics, see Marchetti, *Romance and the "Yellow Peril."* In chapters 5 and 9, Marchetti provides a useful overview of different retellings of the Butterfly story that revise justifications of American hegemony. For instance, she traces how the centrality of the sacrificial Butterfly figure in these tales begins to diminish across the twentieth century and across the Vietnam War era, as the Pinkerton figure from Long's tale assumes center stage: "No longer is the tragic Cho-Cho-San at the heart of the story; rather, Pinkerton is now the protagonist, elevated from a cad to the morally troubled but genuinely righteous champion of American hegemony": ibid., 103.

65. Jane Caplan, "Introduction," in *Written on the Body: The Tattoo in European and American History*, ed. Jane Caplan (Princeton, NJ: Princeton University Press, 2000), xi.

66. As Bradley notes regarding interwar nonfiction about Vietnam, "Observers offered a withering critique of the failures of French colonialism in Vietnam that implicitly reflected the contemporary celebratory discourse surrounding America's state-building efforts at home and its colonial project in the Philippines": Bradley, *Imagining Vietnam and America*, 22.

67. David Palumbo-Liu, *Asian/American: Historical Crossings of a Racial Frontier* (Stanford, CA: Stanford University Press, 1999), 89.

68. Wilson, "President Woodrow Wilson's Fourteen Points."

69. Horace Remillard, "Departure of Governor-General Sarraut—His Colonial Policy, June 6, 1919," ed. Department of State, Record Group (RG) 59, Records of the Department of State Relating to Internal Affairs of France, 1910–1929, U.S. National Archives, Washington, DC, 1919.

70. Oscar P. Austin, *Colonial Administration, 1800–1900. Methods of Government and Development Adopted by the Principal Colonizing Nations in Their Control of Tropical and Other Colonies and Dependencies. With Statistical Statements of the Area, Population, Commerce, Revenue, Etc., of Each of the World's Colonies. Including Bibliography of Colonies and Colonization Prepared by the Library of Congress. From the Summary of Commerce and Finance for October, 1901* (Washington, DC: U.S. Government Printing Office, 1901), 1409–1410. These discussions reveal a tactic of

American empire premised on the notion of what William V. Spanos calls the "interregnum"—imagining an interim period through which to situate the United States as a savior of territories imagined as in between governing regimes: William V. Spanos, *Redeemer Nation in the Interregnum: An Untimely Meditation on the American Vocation* (New York: Fordham University Press, 2016), 86–87.

71. Mae M. Ngai, *Impossible Subjects: Illegal Aliens and the Making of Modern America*, Politics and Society in Twentieth-Century America (Princeton, NJ: Princeton University Press, 2004), 98.

72. William McKinley, "First Annual Message," December 6, 1897, Miller Center, University of Virginia, Charlottesville, available at https://millercenter.org/the-presidency/presidential-speeches/december-6-1897-first-annual-message. McKinley's "benevolent assimilation proclamation" of 1898 crystallized the American imperial ideology of mutual will and desire between colonizer and colonized. In McKinley's words, the United States would "[substitute] the mild sway of justice and right . . . for the greater good of the governed": William McKinley, "Executive Order," December 21, 1898, American Presidency Project, comp. Gerhard Peters and John T. Woolley, available at http://www.presidency.ucsb.edu/ws/?pid=69309.

73. Woodrow Wilson, "President Woodrow Wilson's Fourteen Points," January 8, 1918, Lillian Goldman Law Library, available at http://avalon.law.yale.edu/20th_cen tury/wilson14.asp, emphasis added.

74. Gaston Giraud, "Trade with French Indo-China," in *Official Report of the Seventh National Foreign Trade Convention* (New York: O. K. Davis, Secretary, National Foreign Trade Convention, 1920), 407–409.

75. Leland L. Smith, "Department's Instruction No. 623: Monthly Report on Commerce and Industries for November, 1921," ed. U.S. Department of State, RG 59, Records of the Department of State Relating to Internal Affairs of France, 1910–1929, U.S. National Archives, Washington, DC, 1921, 1. It is worth noting that these documents are incomplete and in fact can muddy material realities—for example, goods traded between the United States and Indochina were often undocumented if they traveled indirectly through multiple ports, such as Manila or Singapore.

76. William H. Taft, *William Howard Taft: Essential Writings and Addresses* (Madison, NJ: Fairleigh Dickinson University Press, 2009), 226.

77. Susan Kay Gillman argues that melodramas often remain unsolved, revealing social quandaries that persist and indicate "the provisional outcome" of American race relations: see Susan Kay Gillman, *Blood Talk: American Race Melodrama and the Culture of the Occult* (Chicago: University of Chicago Press, 2003), 22. Gillman's examination of the "tragic mulatto" shows how the mixed-race figure in Pauline Hopkins's works uncovers a "hidden self" that centers America's history of interracial rape—"a permeating but unacknowledged presence behind the veil of American identity": ibid., 75. Many of Hervey's works seek to invert what melodrama makes visible and invisible to bring unacknowledged social structures and materialities into the foreground.

78. I follow Kadji Amin's suggestion to understand "queer" in historicist terms—its meanings in spatially and temporally specific contexts. In Amin's words, in the early twentieth century moment in which Hervey writes, "queer longings for affiliation had no obvious terminus; rather, they carried with them a sense of openness and potentiality." This aptly describes queer segments in *Congaï*, which express desires for affiliations that exist outside the social norms prescribed by imperial culture and law: Kadji Amin,

Disturbing Attachments: Genet, Modern Pederasty, and Queer History (Durham, NC: Duke University Press, 2017), 122.

79. Celine Parreñas Shimizu, *The Hypersexuality of Race: Performing Asian/American Women on Screen and Scene* (Durham, NC: Duke University Press, 2007), 15–16.

80. Gillman, *Blood Talk*.

81. Anker, *Orgies of Feeling*, 81.

82. Amin, *Disturbing Attachments*, 80.

83. Hervey, *Travels in French Indo-China*, 277–279.

84. Proschan, "Syphilis, Opiomania, and Pederasty," 612, 617–620. Proschan shows that French physicians and anthropologists in the late nineteenth and early twentieth centuries often described Annamese males—regardless of age—as effeminate and solicitous and male prostitution in Indochina as endemic. Travelers who succumbed to putative Indochinese lasciviousness endangered the empire by developing dangerous illnesses.

85. Ibid., 636.

86. Amin, *Disturbing Attachments,* 110, 121.

87. Ibid., 42.

88. Richard Berrong argues that little to no emotion exists between the two lovers, Pierre and Okané San, in Pierre Loti's *Madame Chrysanthème*. Instead, desire emerges in the queer relationship between Pierre and Yves Kermadec, Pierre's male friend who accompanies him to Japan. Yves vets Okané San for Pierre, has a room in Pierre and Okané San's home, and in one scene shares their bed. Berrong suggests that because Loti's other works—namely, *My Brother Yves* and *Iceland Fisherman*—are explicit about homoerotic passion, we can situate *Madame Chrysanthème* within a series of his works that are very much about a queer desire that remains in the background: Richard M. Berrong, *In Love with a Handsome Sailor: The Emergence of Gay Identity and the Novels of Pierre Loti* (Toronto: University of Toronto Press, 2003), 121–122. For a study of homosocial anxieties in Rudyard Kipling's works, see Anjali Arondekar, "Lingering Pleasures, Perverted Texts: Colonial Desire in Kipling's Anglo-India," in *Imperial Desire: Dissident Sexualities and Colonial Literature*, ed. Philip Holden and Richard J. Ruppel (Minneapolis: University of Minnesota Press, 2003).

89. Greene, "The Multi-talented Harry Hervey," 25.

90. Ibid.

91. Hervey, *Travels in French Indo-China*, 54.

92. Harlan Greene and James M. Hutchisson, "Introduction: The Charleston Renaissance Considered," in *Renaissance in Charleston: Art and Life in the Carolina Low Country, 1900–1940*, ed. James M. Hutchisson and Harlan Greene (Athens: University of Georgia Press, 2003), 1–18.

93. Hervey, *Travels in French Indo-China* 272.

94. Ibid., 54.

95. Mamoulian, who was known for maximizing technological innovations to handle crowd scenes, rhythm, color, and emotion, noted, "The use of color and colored lights was one of my main joys and excitement in the theatre. Surely, the effectiveness of productions like *Porgy, Marco's Millions*, and *Congai* . . . would have been sadly decreased if I were forced not to use color in sets, costumes, and lights on the stage": Rouben Mamoulian, "Will Talking Pictures Become 'Talking Paintings'?," in *Celebrity Articles from the Screen Guild Magazine*, ed. Anna Kate Sterling (Metuchen, NJ: Scarecrow Press, 1987), 73.

96. Quoted in David Luhrssen, *Mamoulian: Life on Stage and Screen* (Lexington: University of Kentucky Press, 2013), 39.

97. See, e.g., ibid., 38.

98. Edwin Schallert, "George White of 'Scandals' Fame Signs as Fox Producer; Studio and Theater News," *Los Angeles Times*, September 22, 1933.

99. Percy Hammond, "New York Theaters," *Los Angeles Times*, January 27, 1929, C28.

100. "'Congai' Falls Short of Its Dramatic Goal," *New York Times*, November 28, 1928, 33.

101. Harry Hervey, "Congaï," ms. 1695, Harry Hervey Papers, Georgia Historical Society, Savannah, box 3, folder 7.

102. Wilfred J. Riley, "The New Plays on Broadway: Sam H. Harris," *Billboard*, December 8, 1928.

103. The racial and geopolitical dimensions of conversations about aesthetic "taste" of course have not gone away. These responses evoke Amiri Baraka's assessment that the "aesthetic" argument is often used to discount artistic works' potential radicalism. He writes, "The liberal white man's objection to the theatre of revolution . . . will be on aesthetic grounds": Amiri Baraka, *Home: Social Essays* (New York: William Morrow, 1966), 214. I am grateful to Joel Pfister for guiding me to this quote.

104. *The Captive* was performed in front of full houses and was well reviewed: Michael Abernethy, "Edouard Bourdet's Lesbian Play, 'The Captive,' Was Certainly Captive of Its Time," available at http://www.popmatters.com/column/edouard-bourdets-lesbian-play-the-captive-was-certainly-captive-of-its-time.

105. As quoted in Richard Meyer, *Outlaw Representation: Censorship and Homosexuality in Twentieth-Century American Art* (Oxford: Oxford University Press, 2002), 227–228.

106. Harlan Greene, *The Damned Don't Cry—They Just Disappear: The Life and Works of Harry Hervey* (Columbia: University of South Carolina Press, 2017), 168.

107. Chapin Hall, "Notes from Hollywood's Studios," *New York Times*, July 24, 1932, X3. According to Hall, Paramount's apparent stalling prompted MGM to express interest in purchasing the story of *Congaï*, but this also fell through.

108. Susan Courtney, *Hollywood Fantasies of Miscegenation: Spectacular Narratives of Gender and Race, 1903–1967* (Princeton, NJ: Princeton University Press, 2005), 113. The clause identifies miscegenation as "sex relations between the white and black races," but as Courtney notes, efforts to identify miscegenation in screenplays for censorship purposes reveal an attempt to "identify . . . a range of 'race and color' that is considerably more diverse than the Code's 'white and black.'" The clause would reappear in the more enforceable Production Code of 1934.

109. Ibid., 330, 76n, 120.

110. Ibid., 330, 76n, emphasis added.

111. "The Gossip Shop," *Bookman* 44 (February 1922): 762.

112. Austin, *Colonial Administration*, 1245.

113. Ibid., 1462.

114. Daniel B. Schirmer and Stephen Rosskamm Shalom, *The Philippines Reader: A History of Colonialism, Neocolonialism, Dictatorship, and Resistance* (Boston: South End, 1987), 43.

115. Harry Hervey, "Indo-China," ms. 1695, Harry Hervey Papers, Georgia Historical Society, Savannah, 1934, box 5, folder 2; Hervey, "Saigon," ms. 1695, Harry

Hervey Papers, box 5, folders 7–8, box 6, folder 1. *Saigon* became the title for a different film released by Paramount in 1948.

116. Marion won Oscars for *The Big House* (1930) and *The Champ* (1931) and is often referred to as one of the most talented screenwriters of the twentieth century. *Prestige*, as mentioned earlier, takes place in a French penal colony and was produced by RKO-Pathé. Apparently, it encountered no censorship issues, likely because it ends with clear white victory over natives: see Ruth Vasey, *The World According to Hollywood, 1918–1939* (Madison: University of Wisconsin Press, 1997), 262–263. Both *Indo-China* and *Saigon* went through "the treatment" in Hollywood. *Saigon* underwent the treatment at least until August 1943. Hervey wrote in a letter, "SAIGON is greatly improved. Frances [Marion] says it is eighty percent better than most of the properties that MGM owns." He was delighted that *Saigon* was a "feather in Frances's cap": Harry Hervey, "Letter to Carleton Hildreth," July 21, 1943, Carleton Hildreth Papers, Georgia Historical Society, Savannah.

117. Melodrama's persuasive political force endures. In Anker's words, "Melodrama shapes the legitimation strategies of national politics, and the very operations of state power": Anker. *Orgies of Feeling*, 2.

CHAPTER 2

1. Monique T. D. Truong, *The Book of Salt* (Boston: Houghton Mifflin, 2003).

2. Alice B. Toklas, *The Alice B. Toklas Cook Book* (New York: Harper, 1954). Hereafter, page numbers are cited in parentheses in the text.

3. This standard was set by Fannie Farmer's *The Boston Cooking-School Cook Book* (1896): see Doris Witt, *Black Hunger: Soul Food and America* (Minneapolis: University of Minnesota Press, 2004), 55.

4. Pamela Thoma refers to a recipe's finished product as the culinary "consumable at the close": Pamela S. Thoma, *Asian American Women's Popular Literature: Feminizing Genres and Neoliberal Belonging* (Philadelphia: Temple University Press, 2014), 153.

5. Witt, *Black Hunger*, 11–12.

6. Robert Ji-Song Ku, Martin F. Manalansan, and Anita Mannur, "An Alimentary Introduction," in *Eating Asian America: A Food Studies Reader,* ed. Robert Ji-Song Ku, Martin F. Manalansan, and Anita Mannur (New York: New York University Press, 2013).

7. For Kyla Wazana Tompkins, the text is "perhaps the seminal text in the modern literary history of food culture, consistently [interrupting] the narrative flow of recollection with a recipe": Kyla Wazana Tompkins, "Consider the Recipe," *J19: The Journal of Nineteenth-Century Americanists* 1, no. 2 (Fall 2013): 442. Rafia Zafar interprets the *Cook Book* in terms of elegy: Rafia Zafar, "Elegy and Remembrance in the Cookbooks of Alice B. Toklas and Edna Lewis," *MELUS* 38, no. 4 (Winter 2013): 33.

8. Anne L. Bower views cookbooks as injecting a sense of romance into everyday life: see Anne L. Bower, "Romanced by Cookbooks," *Gastronomica* 4, no. 2 (2004): 35–42.

9. Tompkins, "Consider the Recipe," 439.

10. In Bruce Robbins's words, the servant as laborer is also the "servant as narrator": Bruce Robbins, *The Servant's Hand: English Fiction from Below* (New York: Columbia University Press, 1986), 91–96.

11. For Alex Woloch, minor characters threaten to "disrupt the narrative if we pay them the attention they deserve": Alex Woloch, *The One versus the Many: Minor Characters and the Space of the Protagonist in the Novel* (Princeton, NJ: Princeton University Press, 2003), 13.

12. Janet Malcolm, *Two Lives: Gertrude and Alice* (New Haven, CT: Yale University Press, 2007), 4.

13. Witt, *Black Hunger*, 11.

14. Michel Serres's term "multitemporality" is useful in thinking about cookbooks' heterogeneous times. It describes objects' embodiment of temporal diversity, "a time that is gathered together": Michel Serres and Bruno Latour, *Conversations on Science, Culture, and Time,* Studies in Literature and Science (Ann Arbor: University of Michigan Press, 1995), 60.

15. The historian Mark Bradley argues that the works of journalists, "missionaries, hunters, and travelers" constitute "the first sustained body of American commentary on Vietnamese society," but the previous chapter's analysis of Harry Hervey's fiction about Vietnam amends this timeline: see Mark Bradley, *Imagining Vietnam and America: The Making of Postcolonial Vietnam, 1919–1950,* New Cold War History (Chapel Hill: University of North Carolina Press, 2000), 46.

16. Virginia Thompson, *French Indo-China* (New York: Macmillan, 1937), 43, 48–49, 143. Thompson became the first Distinguished Scholar in Residence at the Institute of International Studies, University of California, Berkeley, in 1978–1979. *French Indo-China* was published for the American Council, Institute of Pacific Relations.

17. Mona Gardner, *The Menacing Sun* (New York: Harcourt, 1939), 57–58.

18. James Clifford, "On Ethnographic Surrealism," *Comparative Studies in Society and History* 23, no. 4 (October 1981): 542.

19. Catharine R. Stimpson, "'Gertrice/Altrude': Stein, Toklas, and the Paradox of the Happy Marriage," in *Mothering the Mind,* ed. Ruth Perry and M. W. Brownley (New York: Holmes and Meier, 1984), 130. Stimpson writes that "to oversimplify the Stein/Toklas marriage and ménage is stupid" and clarifies that Toklas was "also a willful woman whom Stein sought to please." While Toklas is increasingly viewed as having been central to Stein's success, the question of her influence remains unsettled. Malcolm discusses the stylistic affinities between *The Alice B. Toklas Cook Book* and Stein's *The Autobiography of Alice B. Toklas* (New York: Vintage, 1990), noting, "The similarity of tone of the two books only deepens the mystery of who influenced whom": Malcolm, *Two Lives,* 4.

20. Repetition for Stein was both a playful, aesthetic endeavor and a politicized move—a turn toward possible recombinations of language that run against the teleological and structured patterns of the "language of the Father": see Marianne DeKoven, *Rich and Strange: Gender, History, Modernism* (Princeton, NJ: Princeton University Press, 1991), 101. Scholars variously refer to Stein's literary repetitions as "reduced vocabulary" or "repetition with a difference." See DeKoven, *Rich and Strange,* 184. Stein herself referred to this literary experimentation as "insistence": see Gertrude Stein, *Lectures in America* (Boston: Beacon, 1985), 166. Stein's practices of linguistic repetition did not remain static over time, as DeKoven points out in her thorough periodization of Stein's work: see Marianne DeKoven, *A Different Language: Gertrude Stein's Experimental Writing* (Madison: University of Wisconsin Press, 1983).

21. Stimpson, "Gertrice/Altrude," 131–132.

22. Shari Benstock, *Women of the Left Bank* (Austin: University of Texas Press, 1986), 77, 157–158.

23. Natalia Cecire, "Ways of Not Reading Gertrude Stein," *ELH* 82, no. 1 (2015).

24. In Benstock's words, Stein was marginalized in many ways—discriminated against, as a woman and as a lesbian. It was not until the publication of *The Autobiography of Alice B. Toklas* (1933) that Stein gained wider acceptance and fame: see

Benstock, *Women of the Left Bank*, 77, 157–158, 200. At the same time, DeKoven and Stimpson identify the tension between her radical poesis and her conservative politics: see DeKoven, *Rich and Strange*, 200; Stimpson, "Gertrice/Altrude," 131. For a provocative discussion of modern Steins and postmodern Steins, see Nicola Pitchford, "Modernism, Unlikely Postmodernism: Stein's *Tender Buttons*," *American Literary History* 11 (1999): 642–667. Jessica Rabin also provides a discussion of Stein's and Toklas's outsiderism alongside other prominent American female writers in Jessica G. Rabin, *Surviving the Crossing: (Im)Migration, Ethnicity, and Gender in Willa Cather, Gertrude Stein, and Nella Larsen* (New York: Routledge, 2004). Yunte Huang offers a brief and interesting discussion of Stein's continued "undervalued" place in the American canon vis-à-vis Maxine Hong Kingston's canonization in American literary studies in Yunte Huang, *Transpacific Displacement: Ethnography, Translation, and Intertextual Travel in Twentieth-Century American Literature* (Berkeley: University of California Press, 2002), 156–160.

25. Gertrude Stein, letter postmarked July 13, 1934, in Edward Burns, ed., *The Letters of Gertrude Stein and Carl Van Vechten 1913–1946* (New York: Columbia University Press, 1986). Stein's letters to Van Vechten offer affectionate depictions of Trac through Stein's eyes, as well as through Van Vechten's: see Stein's letters postmarked June 15, 1934, June 26, 1934, July 28, 1934, August 3, 1934, September 1, 1934, and October 1, 1934, in ibid.

26. Truong, *The Book of Salt*, 31. Hereafter, page numbers are cited in parentheses in the text.

27. Y-Dang Troeung, "'A Gift or a Theft Depends on Who Is Holding the Pen': Postcolonial Collaborative Autobiography and Monique Truong's *The Book of Salt*," *Modern Fiction Studies* 56, no. 1 (2010): 129–130; Catherine Fung, "A History of Absences: The Problem of Reference in Monique Truong's *The Book of Salt*," *Novel* 45, no. 1 (2012): 96.

28. Troeung's and Fung's insights echo David Eng's reading of *The Book of Salt* as relating the possibility that inheres in unknowability and situated in an "alternative time and space" that exists "outside the authorized terms of dominant representation": see David Eng, "The End(s) of Race," *PMLA* 123, no. 5 (2008): 1491.

29. Eng, "The End(s) of Race," 1488.

30. In Fung's compelling argument, Binh is "textually inaccessible" and thus demonstrates the novel's refusal to place the "burden of authenticity on the subaltern": Fung, "A History of Absences," 97–98.

31. Crystal Parikh, *Writing Human Rights: The Political Imaginaries of Writers of Color* (Minneapolis: University of Minnesota Press, 2017), 22.

32. As quoted in Fung, "A History of Absences," 96.

33. In this way, I agree wholeheartedly with Eng's argument that *The Book of Salt* compels interpretation through the *longue durée*: Eng, "The End(s) of Race," 1480.

34. Tompkins provocatively argues that cooking actions consist of "a choreographed series of discrete and uneven temporal movements and gestures" that also serve as a recipe's "historical remains": Tompkins, "Consider the Recipe," 445, fn9.

35. Amy J. Elias, *Sublime Desire: History and Post-1960s Fiction*, Parallax: Re-Visions of Culture and Society (Baltimore: Johns Hopkins University Press, 2001), 34.

36. Denise Cruz similarly argues that the Vietnamese cooks in *The Book of Salt* mark "the hitherto unacknowledged presence of Vietnamese laborers in the overlapping global and domestic spaces" that thwart these spaces' normative structures of

power. I delve more into the material circuits of this labor and its foodways. See Denise Cruz, "'Love Is Not a Bowl of Quinces': Food, Desire, and the Queer Asian Body in Monique Truong's *The Book of Salt*," in Ku, Manalansan, and Mannur, *Eating Asian America*, 355.

37. Gary Y. Okihiro, *Pineapple Culture: A History of the Tropical and Temperate Zones*, California World History Library (Berkeley: University of California Press, 2009), 3.

38. Ibid., 2–3.

39. Cristoforo Borri and S. Baron, *Views of Seventeenth-Century Vietnam: Christoforo Borri on Cochinchina and Samuel Baron on Tonkin*, Studies on Southeast Asia (Ithaca, NY: Southeast Asia Program Publications, Cornell University, 2006), 102.

40. Erica Peters notes that even today, "The Vietnamese are especially particular about peeling their pineapples, carefully removing all the skin and the eyes, without allowing any of the fruit to go to waste": see Erica J. Peters, *Appetites and Aspirations in Vietnam: Food and Drink in the Long Nineteenth Century* (Lanham, MD: Altamira, 2012), 203–204.

41. Commissariat General de l'Indo-Chine, *L'Indo-Chine a l'exposition coloniale de Marseille, 1906* (Marseille: Imprimerie Marseillaise, 1906), 73. See also Paul Hubert, *Ananas*, Bibliotheque Pratique du Colon (Paris: H. Dunod et E. Pinat, 1908), 36.

42. Peters, *Appetites and Aspirations in Vietnam*, 174.

43. Ibid., 176.

44. Ibid., 49.

45. Salt producers were required to keep records in French and sell their product to the administration at a price the French determined, effectively wiping out many salt producers. For a detailed examination of the alcohol monopoly in French Indochina, see Gerard Sasges, "State, Enterprise and the Alcohol Monopoly in Colonial Vietnam, *Journal of Southeast Asian Studies* 43, no. 1 (2012): 133–157.

46. Peters, *Appetites and Aspirations in Vietnam*, 98–99. In both the metropole and the colony, the French "used food to make themselves feel French," even if this meant regular consumption in the colonies of imported, unhealthy canned versions of French foods. Bread made in Indochina was sometimes considered French only when made by a French baker, even if the flour came from elsewhere, such as Australia or the United States: ibid., 57–58, 150–151.

47. For an astute reading of the epistemological implications of Binh's complex understanding of salt, see Michelle Peek, "A Subject of Sea and Salty Sediment: Diasporic Labor and Queer (Be)Longing in Monique Truong's *The Book of Salt*," *Journal of Transnational American Studies* 4, no. 1 (2012), available at https://eschoarship.org/uc/item/5kr4j4z1.

48. Peters, *Appetites and Aspirations in Vietnam*, 83–84. Less salt meant less well preserved and fermented foods, which had a direct impact on people's health.

49. Scott McConnell, *Leftward Journey: The Education of Vietnamese Students in France, 1919–1939* (New Brunswick, NJ: Transaction, 1989), 49.

50. Students would find ways around these restrictions, with some finding sponsors that supported their travel to the empire to study at *lycées* and others stowing away on ships: David G. Marr, *Vietnamese Tradition on Trial, 1920–1945*, (Berkeley: University of California Press, 1981), 33–36.

51. Sarah Sharma, *In the Meantime: Temporality and Cultural Politics* (Durham, NC: Duke University Press, 2014), 14.

52. Margo Natalie Crawford offers an insightful reading of the politics of modernist "interracial parties" during the Harlem Renaissance, which the Black Arts Movement would later critique: Margo Natalie Crawford, "The Interracial Party of Modernist Primitivism and the Black 'After-Party,'" in *The Modernist Party*, ed. Catherine Mary McLoughlin (Edinburgh: Edinburgh University Press, 2013).

53. David L. Eng and Alice Y. Hom, *Q & A: Queer in Asian America*, Asian American History and Culture (Philadelphia: Temple University Press, 1998), xi.

54. Eng, "The End(s) of Race," 1483. Eng further specifies that *The Book of Salt* establishes a relationship between a mixed-race southerner and a Vietnamese laborer in a way that "[queers] the black Atlantic": ibid., 1489. Other scholars have noted that, although *The Book of Salt*'s main characters have displacement and queerness in common, they are differentiated by varied positions within structures of class, race, and colonialism. For example, Michelle Peek points out the "profound differences in racialized histories" that distinguish the characters: Peek, "A Subject of Sea and Salty Sediment," 5. Rei Magosaki demonstrates how the novel's "colonial-imperial registers" differentiate varied forms of "abjection and identification": Rei Magosaki, *Tricksters and Cosmopolitans: Cross-Cultural Collaborations in Asian American Literary Production* (New York: Fordham University Press, 2016), 107.

55. Sophie Quinn-Judge, *Hồ Chí Minh: The Missing Years, 1919–1941* (Berkeley: University of California Press, 2002), 23.

56. Ibid., 11–28.

57. Erez Manela, *The Wilsonian Moment: Self-Determination and the International Origins of Anticolonial Nationalism* (Oxford: Oxford University Press, 2007), 3–4.

58. Quinn-Judge, *Hồ Chí Minh*, 11–28.

59. Hồ Chí Minh began attracting international attention in 1919, when he sent out a petition entitled "The Demands of the Vietnamese People" at the Paris Peace Conference. The French Sûreté made concerted efforts to gather information about him thereafter: see Quinn-Judge, *Hồ Chí Minh*, 11. While much has been made of his ability to "marry" nationalism and communism, the picture is much more complex. David Marr argues that "it would be wrong to characterize Ho Chi Minh or any other major Vietnamese Communist leader as a nationalist," as he had publicly warned that nationalism could violently trump communist movements—witness the Kuomintang-Chinese Communist Party split in 1927 and his imprisonment by the Chinese Nationalists: see Marr, *Vietnamese Tradition on Trial*, 320. William Duiker describes him as a committed Marxist who also gave equal and sometimes greater importance to the issue of nationalism: see William J. Duiker, *Ho Chi Minh: A Life* (New York: Hyperion, 2000), 122. Quinn-Judge and Christopher Goscha give attention to his vulnerability within the international communist movement. Goscha notes Stalin's concern over his commitment as a Marxist after Hồ dissolved the Indochinese Communist Party in 1945: see Christopher E. Goscha, "Courting Diplomatic Disaster? The Difficult Integration of Vietnam into the Internationalist Communist Movement (1945–1950)," *Journal of Vietnamese Studies* 1, nos. 1–2 (2006): 59–103.

60. The French Sûreté was France's national police force.

61. Tyler Stovall, "The Color Line behind the Lines: Racial Violence in France during the Great War," *American Historical Review* 103, no. 3 (June 1998): 741.

62. Erica J. Peters, "Resistance, Rivalries, and Restaurants: Vietnamese Workers in Interwar France," *Journal of Vietnamese Studies* 2, no. 1 (2007): 109.

63. Authorities identified Vietnamese restaurants and cafés as sites of Euro-Afro-Asian militancy that threatened to expand from local to global scales, and they consis-

tently targeted eateries frequented by Vietnamese as sites of alleged crime, anticolonial plotting, social transgressions, and miscegenation: ibid.

64. Vietnamese students participated in leftist and Marxist organizations and famously smuggled political literature back to Vietnam, often while they labored to support their radical projects: Marr, *Vietnamese Tradition on Trial*, 40. Revolutionary organizations sprang up throughout colonial Vietnam during this year, with Thanh Niên, the revolutionary youth association Hồ Chí Minh helped found in 1925, emerging as the strongest: Quinn-Judge, *Hồ Chí Minh*, 103. Thanh Niên based most of its activities and training in Canton before sending promising recruits elsewhere. See also Kim Khánh Huỳnh, *Vietnamese Communism, 1925–1945* (Ithaca, NY: Cornell University Press, 1982), 63–88; Hue-Tam Ho Tai, *Radicalism and the Origins of the Vietnamese Revolution* (Cambridge, MA: Harvard University Press, 1992).

65. In an interview with her publisher, Mariner Books, Truong discusses the decision to include the character Nguyễn Ái Quốc in her novel: "I think of the character in *The Book of Salt* as a fictional Nguyen Ai Quoc as opposed to a fictional Ho Chi Minh. As Nguyen Ai Quoc, he was a young man living in Paris who read Shakespeare and Dickens in the original English, who wrote plays and newspaper articles, who earned money as a painter of fake Chinese souvenirs, a photographer's assistant." See http://houghtonmifflinbooks.com/booksellers/press_release, accessed November 24, 2010.

66. Empire also emerges in Toklas's portrayal of her experiences with food shortages in addition to rationing in German-occupied France, another instance of the *Cook Book's* accommodation of a history of "conquests and occupations" in Europe: Toklas, *The Alice B. Toklas Cook Book*, 43, 203–223.

67. For examinations of Toklas's and Stein's relationship to the Vichy regime, particularly Stein's close friendship with Bernard Faÿ and her pro-Nazi sentiments and translations, see Barbara Will, *Unlikely Collaboration: Gertrude Stein, Bernard Faÿ, and the Vichy Dilemma*, Gender and Culture (New York: Columbia University Press, 2011). See also Malcolm, *Two Lives*.

68. Zafar, "Elegy and Remembrance in the Cookbooks of Alice B. Toklas and Edna Lewis."

69. Quoted in Allison Carruth, *Global Appetites: American Power and the Literature of Food* (New York: Cambridge University Press, 2013), 59.

70. Ibid., 80.

71. Allison Carruth, "War Rations and the Food Politics of Late Modernism," *Modernism/Modernity* 16, no. 4 (2009): 783.

72. Ibid., 791.

73. Mark Padoongpatt, "'Oriental Cookery': Devouring Asian and Pacific Cuisine during the Cold War," in Ku, Manalansan, and Mannur, *Eating Asian America*, 187–188.

74. "Interview with Monique Truong," Writerswrite.com, May 2003, available at https://www.writerswrite.com/books/moniquetruong.htm.

75. Viet Thanh Nguyen, *Nothing Ever Dies: Vietnam and the Memory of War* (Cambridge, MA: Harvard University Press, 2016), 212.

76. John Carlos Rowe, "US Novels and US Wars," in *Cambridge History of the American Novel*, ed. Leonard Cassuto (New York: Cambridge University Press, 2011), 827–828.

77. Susan Koshy, "The Rise of the Asian American Novel," in *The Cambridge History of the American Novel*, ed. Leonard Cassuto (New York: Cambridge University Press, 2011), 1059.

CHAPTER 3

1. Michael Herr, *Dispatches* (New York: Alfred A. Knopf, 1977). Hereafter, page numbers are cited in parentheses in the text.

2. Carl Sessions Stepp, "The Golden Era of a Magazine with Attitude," *American Journalism Review* (October 1995), available at http://ajrarchive.org/article.asp?id=1856.

3. Raymond Sokolov, "Heart of Darkness," *Newsweek*, November 14, 1977.

4. Portions of *Dispatches* that were previously printed in other publications are noted on the text's copyright page.

5. See, e.g., John Leonard, "Books of the Times," *New York Times*, October 28, 1977, C27.

6. Susan Jeffords, *The Remasculinization of America: Gender and the Vietnam War*, Theories of Contemporary Culture (Bloomington: Indiana University Press, 1989).

7. Joyce Wadler, "*Dispatches:* Michael Herr's Stark Account of Terror," *Washington Post*, November 4, 1977, 3.

8. Tom Wolfe and E. W. Johnson, eds., *The New Journalism* (New York: Harper and Row, 1973).

9. For instance, scholars admire Herr's "displacements and deferrals," which allow "soldiers [to] speak for themselves" and immerse the reader in the disturbing and disorienting power of American war and media technologies: Thomas Carmichael, "Postmodernism and American Cultural Difference: *Dispatches, Mystery Train*, and *The Art of Japanese Management*," *boundary 2* 21, no. 1 (1994): 232; Bill Kovach and Tom Rosenstiel, *The Elements of Journalism: What News People Should Know and the Public Should Expect* (New York: Three Rivers, 2001), 158; Michael P. Clark, "The Work of War after the Age of Mechanical Reproduction," in *The Vietnam War and Postmodernity*, ed. Michael Bibby (Amherst: University of Massachusetts Press, 1999), 25.

10. Fredric Jameson, *Postmodernism, or, The Cultural Logic of Late Capitalism*, Post-contemporary Interventions (Durham, NC: Duke University Press, 1991), 44.

11. Ibid., 45.

12. Ibid., 44.

13. Peter Brantlinger, *Rule of Darkness: British Literature and Imperialism, 1830–1914* (Ithaca, NY: Cornell University Press, 1990).

14. Alexandra Warwick, "Imperial Gothic," in *The Encyclopedia of the Gothic*, ed. William Hughes, David Punter, and Andrew Smith (Chichester, UK: Wiley Blackwell, 2016), 340.

15. William Hughes, "Imperial Gothic," in *Historical Dictionary of Gothic Literature*, ed. William Hughes (Lanham, MD: Rowman and Littlefield, 2013), 142.

16. Ibid.

17. As Colleen Lye notes, "A 'gothic narrative of race'" tends to result in transhistorical readings that diminish the "potential, and potentially radical, variability of racial forms" in relation to their historical texts: see Colleen Lye, "Introduction: In Dialogue with Asian American Studies," *Representations* 99, no. 1 (2007), 2–3.

18. Even the Hollywood icon Errol Flynn leaves a mark in Herr's Vietnam through the presence of his son, Sean Flynn, in *Dispatches*. Flynn was a reporter and photojournalist whose work Herr greatly admired.

19. John Carlos Rowe, *The Cultural Politics of American Studies* (Ann Arbor: Open Humanities, 2012), chap. 1, available at http://dx.doi.org/10.3998/ohp.10945585.0001.001.

20. Sidonie Smith and Julia Watson, *Reading Autobiography: A Guide for Interpreting Life Narratives* (Minneapolis: University of Minnesota Press, 2010), 3-4.

21. As Chantelle Warner argues, for a life narrative "to *feel authentic* to the reader, the gap between the act of narrating and the embodied experience of that which is being narrated must somehow be eroded": Chantelle Warner, "Speaking from Experience: Narrative Schemas, Deixis, and Authenticity Effects in Verena Stefan's Feminist Confession Shedding," *Language and Literature* 18, no. 1 (2009): 20.

22. Mark Heberle, "Michael Herr's Traumatic New Journalism: *Dispatches*," in *The Vietnam War: Topics in Contemporary North American Literature*, ed. Brenda M. Boyle (New York: Bloomsbury Academic, 2015), 36.

23. Rowe, *The Cultural Politics of American Studies*, chap. 1.

24. Guy Debord, *The Society of the Spectacle*, trans. Donald Nicholson-Smith (New York: Zone, 1995), 145–146.

25. Viet Thanh Nguyen, *Nothing Ever Dies: Vietnam and the Memory of War* (Cambridge, MA: Harvard University Press, 2016), 229.

26. Roland Barthes, *Camera Lucida: Reflections on Photography* (New York: Hill and Wang, 1981), 70.

27. Achille Mbembe, "Necropolitics," *Public Culture* 15, no. 1 (2003): 39.

28. Ibid., 35.

29. Linda Nochlin, *The Body in Pieces: The Fragment as a Metaphor of Modernity*, Walter Neurath Memorial Lectures (New York: Thames and Hudson, 1995).

30. Viet Thanh Nguyen, "On True War Stories," *Asian American Literary Review* 6, no. 2 (2015): 140–145. Rachel Lee reminds us that depictions of Asian American human fragments contain neither positive nor negative values in and of themselves; their implications depend on the politics of their portrayals: Rachel C. Lee, *The Exquisite Corpse of Asian America: Biopolitics, Biosociality, and Posthuman Ecologies*, Sexual Cultures (New York: New York University Press, 2014), 20.

31. Michael G. Vann, "Of Pirates, Postcards, and Public Beheadings: The Pedagogic Execution in French Colonial Indochina," *Historical Reflections/Réflexions Historiques* 36, no. 2 (2010): 49–51. Vann elaborates that the display of heads did have a history in Vietnamese law, as it did in Europe. But under French rule, these displays became "a form of state terror by the colonial authorities."

32. Ibid.

33. Vietnamese dismemberment in *Dispatches* also evokes what Sylvia Chong terms the "oriental obscene," or moments of representational stall in which portrayals of Vietnamese as especially violating or violated figures act as figurative vehicles through which Americans can resolve conflicting feelings and ethical dilemmas related to the conflict: Sylvia Shin Huey Chong, *The Oriental Obscene: Violence and Racial Fantasies in the Vietnam Era* (Durham, NC: Duke University Press, 2012), 79.

34. Võ An Ninh died in 2009, at age 103.

35. Geoffrey C. Gunn, *Rice Wars in Colonial Vietnam: The Great Famine and the Viet Minh Road to Power*, Asia/Pacific/Perspectives (Lanham, MD: Rowman and Littlefield, 2014), 16. Some note the numbers might have been higher.

36. Hồ Chí Minh, "Vietnam Declaration of Independence (September 2, 1945)," in *Vietnam and America: A Documented History*, ed. Marvin E. Gettleman, Jane Franklin, Marilyn B. Young, and H. Bruce Franklin (New York: Grove, 1995), 27. During

this speech, Hồ Chí Minh proclaimed the Provisional Government of the Democratic Republic of Vietnam.

37. Lien-Hang T. Nguyen, *Hanoi's War: An International History of the War for Peace in Vietnam*, New Cold War History (Chapel Hill: University of North Carolina Press, 2012), 34–35. See also de Warren, "Hopes of a Generation," 264.

38. Nochlin, *The Body in Pieces*, 17–18.

39. Alan Liu, *Local Transcendence: Essays on Postmodern Historicism and the Database* (Chicago: University of Chicago Press, 2008), 188.

40. Frantz Fanon, *The Wretched of the Earth*, trans. Richard Philcox (New York: Grove, 2004), 1.

41. Jean-François Lyotard and Paul Ricoeur deemed the text "remarkable," while Roland Barthes called it "brilliant": see Nicolas de Warren, "Hopes of a Generation: The Life, Work, and Legacy of Trần Duc Thao," *Graduate Faculty Philosophy Journal* 30, no. 2 (2009): 267.

42. Some scholars argue that Trần Đức Thảo shaped Derrida's formulation of concepts such as the "trace" and *différance* and, potentially, his deconstructive methodology." Ibid., 278–279. De Warren provides an important and illuminating sketch of Trần Đức Thảo's biography and still marginalized legacies.

43. The three articles by Trần Đức Thảo in *Les Temps Modernes* are "Sur l'Indochine" (1946), "Les relations Franco-Vietnamiennes" (1947), and "Sur l'interpretation trotzkyste des evenements d'Indochine" (1947). According to de Warren, these pieces may have informed the thinking of not only Fanon but also Albert Memmi: see de Warren, "Hopes of a Generation," 264.

44. As quoted in Jérôme Melançon, "Anticolonialisme et dissidence: Tran Duc Thao et *Les Temps modernes*," in *L'itinéraire de Tran Duc Thao: Phénoménologie et transferts culturels*, ed. Jocelyn Benoist and Michel Espagne (Paris: Armand Colin, 2013), 201.

45. Louis Althusser, *The Future Lasts Forever: A Memoir*, trans. Richard Veasey (New York: New Press, 1993), 178. Althusser notes that Trần Đức Thảo gave private lessons at the École Normale Supérieure: ibid., 328.

46. De Warren, "Hopes of a Generation," 264–271.

47. Trần Đức Thảo, "Sur L'Indochine," *Les Temps Modernes* 5 (1946): 898.

48. Ibid. My readings of Trần Đức Thảo's articles in *Les Temps Modernes* have greatly benefited from analyses in de Warren, "Hopes of a Generation"; Melançon, "Anticolonialisme et dissidence"; and Perrine Simon-Nahum, "L'évolution de la pensée de Tran Duc Thao, de Sartre à Fanon," in Benoist and Espagne, *L'itinéraire de Tran Duc Thao*, 216–229.

49. Ibid., 899.

50. Quoted in de Warren, "Hopes of a Generation," 264.

51. Trần Đức Thảo, "Le conflit franco-vietnamien," *La Pensée* 22 (January–February 1949): 17.

52. Ibid., 19.

53. De Warren, "Hopes of a Generation," 264–65. Interestingly, the Vietnamese state awarded Trần Đức Thảo a high honor posthumously in 2001, eliminating from his biography past conflicts with the government: see Shawn McHale, "Vietnamese Marxism, Dissent, and the Politics of Postcolonial Memory: Tran Duc Thao, 1946–1993," *Journal of Asian Studies* 61, no. 1 (2002): 24.

54. Quoted in de Warren, "Hopes of a Generation," 266.

55. Thierry Marchaisse, quoted in ibid., 265–266.

56. Tri Vũ-Phan Ngọc Khuê, *Trần Đức Thảo: Những Lời Trăng Trối* (Arlington, VA: Tổ Hợp Xuất Bản Miền Đông Hoa Kỳ, 2014), 376–385, 414–422.

57. Douglas Martin, "Henry A. Prunier, 91, Dies," *New York Times*, April 17, 2013.

58. British-Indian troops occupied southern Vietnam until France's return. Britain occupied southern Vietnam from September 1945 to March 1946 in what was called Operation Masterdom. For a helpful discussion of this period, see Geraint Hughes, "A 'Post-War' War: The British Occupation of French-Indochina, September 1945–March 1946," *Small Wars and Insurgencies* 17, no. 3 (2006): 263–286. To complicate matters more, Britain found itself needing the defeated Japanese soldiers to maintain "order" and unexpectedly became embroiled in a fight against the Việt Minh, whom the United States had just helped train. French troops returned to Indochina in late 1945. Yet another example of shifting structures of cooperation in Indochina is China's oversight of Japan's surrender in northern Vietnam.

59. Those who supported developing the north and peaceful reunification were called "north-firsters," while those favoring militant struggle in the south were referred to as "south-firsters": see Nguyen, *Hanoi's War*, chap. 1.

60. Post–Stalin Moscow advocated peaceful reunification and Beijing called for militant reunification through protracted guerrilla warfare and no negotiation: ibid.

61. Trường Chinh was also a part of this old guard. Hồ Chí Minh was even publicly silenced through blackmail and shamed by Lê Duẩn: ibid., 63.

62. Nguyen, *Hanoi's War*, 56.

63. For instance, Ngô Đình Diệm founded several anticolonial groups and tried to convince France to grant Vietnam independence: see Edward Garvey Miller, *Misalliance: Ngo Dinh Diem, the United States, and the Fate of South Vietnam* (Cambridge, MA: Harvard University Press, 2013), 32–34. Ngô Đình Diệm also attempted to unify Vietnamese nationalist forces in the 1940s through underground means, veiling his involvement by not taking leadership positions within the organizations he founded or supported. He periodically communicated with the Việt Minh, putatively hoping to persuade some of them to join his ranks. He was even summoned for a meeting with Hồ Chí Minh in 1946 to discuss possibilities for collaboration. Ngô Đình Diệm's rhetoric of decolonization at times sounded no less revolutionary than the north's, expressing his vision for the south "a total revolution . . . implemented in every facet of the organization and life of the nation": quoted in ibid., 5.

64. Ngô Đình Diệm, "Statement of June 18, 1954," in *Major Policy Speeches* (Saigon: Press Office, Presidency of the Republic of Viet Nam, 1956), 6.

65. Miller, *Misalliance*, 31–32.

66. Ngô Đình Diệm noted that under post–World War II French occupation, the notion of Vietnam as an entity within a French Union was absurd. He said, "Why complicate matters by having Vietnam in the French Union?": quoted in ibid., 34.

67. Ibid., 230.

68. Miller provides an excellent discussion of Ngô Đình Diệm's regime's relationship to American community development ideology: see ibid., 54–84.

69. Quoted in Nguyen, *Hanoi's War*, 284.

70. Ibid.

71. Lê Đức Thọ would become the only recipient to refuse the prize.

72. Ernst Bloch, "Nonsynchronism and the Obligation to Its Dialectics," *New German Critique* 11 (Spring 1977): 22–38.

73. Jean-François Lyotard, *The Postmodern Condition: A Report on Knowledge*, Theory and History of Literature (Minneapolis: University of Minnesota Press, 1984), 15.

74. As Sean McCann and Michael Szalay suggest about mid-century New Left critiques, the magic of language and personal self-awareness become elevated to "revolutionary importance"—a commitment to the unspeakable and unrepresentable becomes the only ethical position, indicating awareness of the state's mystification of our relationship to it: Sean McCann and Michael Szalay, "Do You Believe in Magic? Literary Thinking after the New Left," *Yale Journal of Criticism* 18, no. 2 (2006): 460.

75. Mark Bowden, "Introduction," in Robert Pisor, *Siege of Khe Sanh: The Story of the Vietnam War's Largest Battle* (New York: W. W. Norton, 2018), 1.

76. Peter Braestrup, *Big Story: How the American Press and Television Reported and Interpreted the Crisis of Tet 1968 in Vietnam and Washington* (New Haven, CT: Yale University Press, 1983), 258.

77. What was called the Tết Offensive struck the majority of central and southern Vietnam's capitals and major cities, including the U.S. Embassy, the Saigon airport, the presidential palace, and the Citadel in Huế: Nguyen, Hanoi's War, 228–229; George C. Herring, America's Longest War: The United States and Vietnam, 1950–1975, 4th ed. (New York: McGraw-Hill, 2002), 226–227.

78. Mark Heberle, "Michael Herr's Traumatic New Journalism: *Dispatches*," in *Vietnam War: Topics in Contemporary North American Literature*, ed. Brenda M. Boyle (New York: Bloomsbury Academic, 2015), 33–34.

79. Braestrup, *Big Story*, 9–41.

80. John Carlos Rowe, "US Novels and US Wars,: in *Cambridge History of the American Novel*, ed. Leonard Cassuto (New York: Cambridge University Press, 2011), 827.

81. Braestrup, *Big Story*, 20.

82. Ibid.

83. Frank Lentricchia, "How to Do Things with Wallace Stevens," in *Close Reading: The Reader*, ed. Frank Lentricchia and Andrew DuBois (Durham, NC: Duke University Press, 2003), 152.

84. For a discussion of pyrotechnics in military contexts, see Liu, *Local Transcendence*, 2.

85. As film critic Andrew Britton suggests, "There is no more characteristic feature of the 1970s Hollywood cinema than the invitation to purchase the bankruptcy of American capitalism as the ultimate spectacle: the end of the world is realized as an exchange value." Britton proceeds to analyze various Vietnam War films as exemplifying this dynamic: see Andrew Britton, "Sideshows: Hollywood in Vietnam," in *Britton on Film: The Complete Film Criticism of Andrew Britton*, ed. Barry Keith Grant (Detroit: Wayne State University Press, 2009), 85.

86. Nhã Ca, *Mourning Headband for Hue: An Account of the Battle for Hue, Vietnam 1968*, trans. Olga Dror (Bloomington: Indiana University Press, 2014).

87. Ibid., 7, 285.

88. Fax Bahr, Eleanor Coppola, and George Hickenlooper, *Hearts of Darkness: A Filmmaker's Apocalypse* (San Francisco: Zoetrope Studios, 1991).

89. Ocean Vuong, *Night Sky with Exit Wounds* (Port Townsend, WA: Copper Canyon, 2016). Hereafter, page numbers are cited in parentheses in the text.

90. *Oxford English Dictionary*, online ed., s.v. "exit wound, *n.*" https://en.oxford dictionaries.com/definition/exit_wound.

91. Toni Morrison, "The Site of Memory," in *Inventing the Truth: The Art and Craft of Memoir*, ed. William Zinsser (New York: Houghton Mifflin, 1995), 95.

92. Cathy J. Schlund-Vials, "Re-seeing Cambodia and Recollecting *the 'Nam*," in *Looking Back on the Vietnam War*, ed. Brenda M. Boyle and Jeehyun Lim (New Brunswick, NJ: Rutgers University Press, 2016), 162–163.

93. In an interview, Vuong remarks on the continual newness of memory, which provides a way for thinking about how to model the representation and interpretation of war as evolving: "Every time we remember, we create new neurons, which is why memory is so unreliable": Amy Rose Spiegel, "Ocean Vuong on Being Generous in Your Work," interview, Thecreativeindependent.com, May 16, 2017, available at https://thecreativeindependent.com/people/ocean-vuong-on-being-generous-in-your-work.

94. Michiko Kakutani, "Review: 'Night Sky with Exit Wounds,' Verses from Ocean Vuong," *New York Times*, May 9, 2016.

95. Daniel Wenger, "How a Poet Named Ocean Means to Fix the English Language," *New Yorker*, April 7, 2016, available at https://www.newyorker.com/books/page-turner/how-a-poet-named-ocean-means-to-fix-the-english-language.

96. Junot Díaz, "MFA versus POC," *New Yorker*, available at http://www.newyorker.com/books/page-turner/mfa-vs-poc.

97. Wenger, "How a Poet Named Ocean Means to Fix the English Language."

98. Kakutani, "Review."

99. Kate Kellaway, "*Night Sky with Exit Wounds* by Ocean Vuong Review—Violence, Delicacy and Timeless Imagery," Guardian News and Media, available at https://www.theguardian.com/books/2017/may/09/night-sky-with-exit-wounds-ocean-vuong-review.

100. Bruce Weber, "Michael Herr, Author of a Vietnam Classic, Dies at 76," *New York Times*, June 25, 2016.

101. Vuong, "Ocean Vuong on Being Generous in Your Work."

CHAPTER 4

1. Lan P. Duong, *Treacherous Subjects: Gender, Culture, and Trans-Vietnamese Feminism*, Asian American History and Culture (Philadelphia: Temple University Press, 2012); Yen Le Espiritu, *Body Counts: The Vietnam War and Militarized Refuge(es)* (Berkeley: University of California Press, 2014); Viet Thanh Nguyen, "Just Memory: War and the Ethics of Remembrance," *American Literary History* 25, no. 1 (2013): 160.

2. Võ Phiến, *Thư Gửi Bạn* [Letters to a Friend] (Des Moines, IA: Nhà Xuất bản Người Việt, 1976);Võ Phiến, *Lại Thư Gửi Bạn* [Again, Letters to a Friend] (Westminster, CA: Người Việt, 1979). Hereafter, page numbers from these works are cited in parentheses in the text as *Letters* and *Again, Letters*. An excerpt from *Lại Thư Gửi Bạn* is translated by Quí-Phiệt Trần in Võ Phiến, "Vietnamese Americans," trans. Quí-Phiệt Trần, in *Not a War: American Vietnamese Fiction, Poetry and Essays*, ed. Dan Duffy (New Haven, CT: Yale University Council on Southeast Asia Studies, 1997), 68–74.

3. I draw from Brent Hayes Edwards's notion of diaspora as an active practice: Brent Hayes Edwards, *The Practice of Diaspora: Literature, Translation, and the Rise of Black Internationalism* (Cambridge, MA: Harvard University Press, 2003).

4. Lisa Lowe, *Immigrant Acts: On Asian American Cultural Politics* (Durham, NC: Duke University Press, 1996), 67.

5. Sau-ling Cynthia Wong, *Reading Asian American Literature: From Necessity to Extravagance* (Princeton, NJ: Princeton University Press, 1993), 25.

6. Anita Mannur, *Culinary Fictions: Food in South Asian Diasporic Culture* (Philadelphia: Temple University Press, 2010), 7–8.

7. John C. Schafer, *Võ Phiến and the Sadness of Exile*, Monograph Series on Southeast Asia (DeKalb: Northern Illinois University, Southeast Asia Publications, Center for Southeast Asian Studies, 2006), 26–27.

8. Ibid., 28–29

9. Ibid., 31–35.

10. Ibid., 37.

11. Ngô Đình Diệm was the Republic of Vietnam's (South Vietnam's) first president and ruled from 1955 until his assassination on November 2, 1963.

12. Schafer, *Võ Phiến and the Sadness of Exile*, 39.

13. Ibid., 42–44.

14. Anh Do, "The Orange County Writer Who Saved Vietnam's Wartime Literature, Poem by Poem, Dies," *Los Angeles Times*, September 30, 2015.

15. Schafer, *Võ Phiến and the Sadness of Exile*, 41.

16. Homi K. Bhabha, *The Location of Culture* (London: Routledge, 1994), 41.

17. Quí-Phiệt Trần's English translation of this essay omits this passage from the original: see Võ Phiến, "Vietnamese Americans."

18. "Roosevelt Demands Race Fusion Here." *New York Times*, September 9, 1917.

19. Ibid.

20. John Steinbeck, *Travels with Charley: In Search of America* (New York: Penguin, 1980), 154.

21. John Steinbeck, *America and Americans and Selected Nonfiction*, ed. Susan Shillinglaw and Jackson J. Benson (New York: Viking, 2002), 304.

22. Colleen Lye, *America's Asia: Racial Form and American Literature, 1893–1945* (Princeton, NJ: Princeton University Press, 2005), 178.

23. Alfredo G. A Valladão, *The Twenty-First Century Will Be American*, trans. John Howe (New York: Verso, 1996), 65. I am indebted to Joel Pfister for pointing out this concept.

24. Jodi Kim, *Ends of Empire: Asian American Critique and the Cold War*, Critical American Studies Series (Minneapolis: University of Minnesota Press, 2010), 3.

25. Ibid.

26. Espiritu, *Body Counts*, 2.

27. Mimi Thi Nguyen, *The Gift of Freedom: War, Debt, and Other Refugee Passages*, Next Wave: New Directions in Women's Studies (Durham, NC: Duke University Press, 2012).

28. I draw from Espiritu's idea that America as a "nation of refuge" is a fiction that the "trope of the 'good refugee'" in the post–Vietnam War era helps to recuperate and sustain: Espiritu, *Body Counts*, 2. In my reading, this narrative has a distinctly melodramatic framework.

29. Nguyen, *Nothing Ever Dies*, 5.

30. Hannah Arendt, "We Refugees," in *Altogether Elsewhere: Writers on Exile*, ed. Marc Robinson (Winchester, MA: Faber and Faber, 1994), 110.

31. Ibid., 115.

32. Ibid., 117.

33. Ibid.

34. Ibid., 119.

35. Espiritu, *Body Counts*, 121.

36. Schafer, *Võ Phiến and the Sadness of Exile*, 242.

37. Ibid., 245.

38. Camp Pendleton opened on April 29, 1975, and closed on October 31, 1975; Fort Chaffee opened on May 2, 1975, and closed on December 31, 1975; Eglin Air Force Base opened on May 4, 1975, and closed on September 15, 1975; and Fort Indiantown Gap opened on May 28, 1975, and closed on December 15, 1975. Eglin Air Force Base housed at least five thousand refugees, while the three other camps capped at about twenty-six thousand. The military was officially in charge of security and logistics, including providing food service and basic supplies: see Darrel Montero, *Vietnamese Americans: Patterns of Resettlement and Socioeconomic Adaptation in the United States* (Boulder, CO: Westview, 1979), 64–65. This source is dated but contains useful details about the camps.

39. Jana K. Lipman, "A Refugee Camp in America: Fort Chaffee and Vietnamese and Cuban Refugees, 1975–1982," *Journal of American Ethnic History* 33, no. 2 (Winter 2014): 61.

40. The IATF was established quickly on April 18, 1975. The task force's personnel spanned twelve government agencies and were charged with developing cultural programs, executing policy, and overseeing refugee processing and resettlement. More specific duties of the IATF included appointing a civilian coordinator to run each camp following task force guidelines; delineating protocols for Immigration and Naturalization Service (INS) processing; managing security clearance by the INS, Central Intelligence Agency, U.S. Department of Defense, U.S. Department of the Treasury, and the Federal Bureau of Investigation; and overseeing social services. Civilian coordinators, who were typically affiliated with the U.S. State Department, were charged with coordinating and managing relations between the government and private agencies, as well as integrating the duties taken on by these different arms and resolving conflicts: Montero, *Vietnamese Americans*, 64–65.

41. Ibid., 25. See also Gail Paradise Kelly, *From Vietnam to America: A Chronicle of the Vietnamese Immigration to the United States* (Boulder, CO: Westview, 1977), 79–81.

42. Kelly, *From Vietnam to America*, 81.

43. Ibid., 28.

44. Ibid., 130–160.

45. Montero, *Vietnamese Americans*, 26–27.

46. Lipman, "A Refugee Camp in America," 60.

47. Espiritu, *Body Counts*, 17–18.

48. Giorgio Agamben, *Homo Sacer: Sovereign Power and Bare Life*, trans. Daniel Heller-Roazen, Crossing Aesthetics (Stanford, CA: Stanford University Press, 1998), 175–176.

49. Ibid., 25.

50. Ibid., 170.

51. Andrew Norris, "Giorgio Agamben and the Politics of the Living Dead," *Diacritics* 30, no. 4 (2000): 46.

52. David Palumbo-Liu, *Asian/American: Historical Crossings of a Racial Frontier* (Stanford, CA: Stanford University Press, 1999), 239.

53. Lipman, "A Refugee Camp in America," 64.

54. Kelly, *From Vietnam to America*, 76.

55. Achille Mbembe, "Necropolitics," *Public Culture* 15, no. 1 (2003): 34.

56. Jack Nelson, "Refugee Plans Draw Protests by Thousands," *Los Angeles Times*, April 30, 1975.

57. As quoted in Peter Nyers, "Emergency or Emerging Identities? Refugees and Transformations in World Order," *Millennium: Journal of International Studies* 28, no. 1 (1999): 15.

58. Kelly, *From Vietnam to America*, 67.

59. William T. Liu, Maryanne Lamanna, and Alice Murata, *Transition to Nowhere: Vietnamese Refugees in America* (Nashville, TN: Charter House, 1979), 169. See also William T. Liu and Alice Murata, "The Vietnamese in America: Refugees or Immigrants?" *Bridge: An Asian American Perspective* 5, no. 3 (Fall 1997): 32–33.

60. The refugee as a distinct category in America first emerged in the Truman Directive of December 22, 1945, which stated preferences for refugees rather than non-refugees in the context of millions of displaced Europeans. Subsequent refugee legislation defined similar exceptions. Section 212(d)(5) of the Immigration and Nationality Act of 1952 gave the attorney-general the power of parole to admit aliens beyond the quotas under crisis situations: see Edward M. Kennedy, "Refugee Act of 1980," *International Migration Review* 15, nos. 1–2 (1981): 141. See also Edwin B. Silverman, "Indochina Legacy: The Refugee Act of 1980," *Publius* 10, no. 1 (Winter 1980): 28.

61. For a critique of the liberalism of the McCarran-Walter Act (Immigration and Nationality Act of 1952), see Mae M. Ngai, *Impossible Subjects: Illegal Aliens and the Making of Modern America*, Politics and Society in Twentieth-Century America (Princeton, NJ: Princeton University Press, 2004), 239–243.

62. The 1977 act was added to the Indochina Migration and Refugee Assistance Act of 1975 (PL 94–23), which became law on May 25, 1974, and convened the IATF and provided protocols for assessing the needs, concerns, and potential problems arising from the resettlement process at the local, state, and federal levels: see Montero, *Vietnamese Americans*, 4.

63. John T. Woolley, Gerhard Peters, and University of California, Santa Barbara, "Bills Concerning Indochina Refugees and Prisoner Transfers with Mexico and Canada Remarks on Signing H.R. 7769 and S. 1662 Into Law," October 28, 1977, American Presidency Project, comp. Gerhard Peters and John T. Woolley, available at http://www.presidency.ucsb.edu/ws/?pid=6855.

64. Ibid.

65. Randy Lippert, quoted in Espiritu, *Body Counts*, 8.

66. Liisa H. Malkki, "Speechless Emissaries: Refugees, Humanitarianism, and Dehistoricization," *Cultural Anthropology* 11, no. 3 (1997): 377–404.

67. Susan Kneebone and Felicity Rawlings-Sanaei, *New Regionalism and Asylum Seekers: Challenges Ahead*, Studies in Forced Migration (New York: Berghahn, 2007), 12.

68. This deflection also rested on cloaking Cold War agendas of favoring noncommunist refugees: see, e.g., Palumbo-Liu, *Asian/American*, 238.

69. Liu, Lamanna, and Murata, *Transition to Nowhere*, 2. Indeed, the logistical aspects of Southeast Asian American refugee experiences must be linked to the history of U.S. military buildup in Guam and the Philippines, the latter also being the site of America's first concentration camps: see Espiritu, *Body Counts*, 24–35. See also Jonathan Hyslop, "The Invention of the Concentration Camp: Cuba, Southern Africa and the Philippines, 1896–1907," *South African Historical Journal* 63, no. 2 (2011): 251–276.

70. John Carlos Rowe, *The Cultural Politics of the New American Studies* (Ann Arbor: Open Humanities Press, 2012), 31–51, available at http://quod.lib.umich.edu/o/ohp/10945585.0001.001.

71. Espiritu, *Body Counts*, 2.

72. A parolee in this case is a noncitizen who is physically in a country but cannot legally enter.

73. Montero, *Vietnamese Americans*, 7, 37.

74. Court Robinson, *Terms of Refuge: The Indochinese Exodus and the International Response*, Politics in Contemporary Asia (New York: St. Martin's Press, 1998), 127.

75. Liu, Lamanna, and Murata, *Transition to Nowhere*, 153.

76. St. Louis U.S. Army Engineer District, Mandatory Center of Expertise for the Curation and Management of Archaeological Collections, "An Archaeological Collections Summary for Fort Indiantown Gap, Pennsylvania," ed. U.S. Army Corps of Engineers, U.S. Army NAGPRA Compliance Project, Technical Report no. 16, July 1995, 3, available at www.dtic.mil/get-tr-doc/pdf?AD=ADA363686. See also "Indiantown Gap National Cemetery," U.S. Department of Veterans Affairs, National Cemetery Administration, available at https://www.cem.va.gov/cems/nchp/indiantowngap.asp.

77. As cited in Robinson, *Terms of Refuge*, 127.

78. Gerald Ford, "Address at a Tulane University Convocation," April 23, 1975, American Presidency Project, comp. Gerhard Peters and John T. Woolley, available at http://www.presidency.ucsb.edu/ws/?pid=4859.

79. Nguyen, *Nothing Ever Dies* 203–205. Nguyen also emphasizes the importance of developing new literary histories of Vietnam War literature that are not focused solely on American authors, an argument that accords with the spirit of this chapter's focus on Vietnamese-language literature: see Viet Thanh Nguyen, "The Great Vietnam War Novel Was Not Written by an American," *New York Times*, May 2, 2017, available at https://www.nytimes.com/2017/05/02/opinion/vietnam-war-novel-was-not-written-by-an-american.html.

80. Mikhail M. Bakhtin, *Problems of Dostoevsky's Poetics*, Theory and History of Literature (Minneapolis: University of Minnesota Press, 1984), 113, 204–205.

81. Martin Joseph Ponce, *Beyond the Nation: Diasporic Filipino Literature and Queer Reading*, Sexual Cultures (New York: New York University Press, 2012), 56.

82. Peter Hitchcock, *The Long Space: Transnationalism and Postcolonial Form*, Cultural Memory in the Present (Stanford, CA: Stanford University Press, 2010). Hitchcock argues that seriality relates the unfinished project of decolonization by enacting long temporalities: "the *long* in my title refers to future persistence, a mode of engagement more extensive than the exigencies of the present and a level of commitment consonant with the task of facing the enduring facility for exploitation in global integration": ibid., 4.

83. Caroline Levine, *Forms: Whole, Rhythm, Hierarchy, Network* (Princeton, NJ: Princeton University Press, 2015), 113.

84. Barbara Johnson, "Apostrophe, Animation, and Abortion," *Diacritics* 16, no. 1 (1986): 31.

85. United Nations High Commissioner for Refugees, "A Lifetime of Waiting," UNHCR Tracks, available at http://tracks.unhcr.org/2014/08/a-lifetime-of-waiting.

86. Paul Ricoeur, *Time and Narrative*, vol. 2 (Chicago: University of Chicago Press, 1984), 12, emphasis added.

87. My conceptualization of the epitaphic potential of Võ Phiến's letters, and letters more generally, is distinct from Nguyen-Vo Thu-Huong's important model of the epitaphic premise of narratives of the modern Vietnamese nation-state. In her examination of Nguyễn Trọng Quản's *Larazo Phiền* (1887), which she posits has been excluded from northern-based Vietnamese literary histories because of its southern genesis, she writes, "The precolonial nation serves in this context as merely a site of haunting, a space of projection for the modern nation to make itself perceptible in an apparition": Thu-Huong Nguyen-Vo, "Epitaphic Nation: The Problem of the South and Necropolitics in Early Modern Vietnamese National Literature," *PMLA* 126, no. 3 (2011): 690. Nguyen-Vo demonstrates how modern Vietnamese writers *imagine* a precolonial Vietnam to, in turn, conjure a Vietnamese modernity. If Nguyen-Vo's model illustrates writers envisioning an abstract past to bring into being a similarly tentative, apparitional future, my conception of Vietnamese American literature as epitaphic works slightly differently, suggesting that refugee classifieds look back to both living and "dead" material histories to begin constructing a future that is also tentative and apparitional, as in Nguyen-Vo's model.

88. Lynda Barry, *One! Hundred! Demons!* (Seattle: Sasquatch, 2002), 209.

89. Barbara Johnson, "The Frame of Reference: Poe, Lacan, Derrida," *Yale French Studies* 55, nos. 55–56 (1977): 458.

90. William Merrill Decker, *Epistolary Practices: Letter Writing in America before Telecommunications* (Chapel Hill: University of North Carolina Press, 1998), 5.

91. By no means do I suggest that Võ Phiến's works mark the absolute starting point of the emergence of Vietnamese American letters. Rather, I propose that varied genealogies of the field would benefit from incorporating more Vietnamese-language works. Scholars have attended to the body of literature produced before Vietnam's reunification—most notably, Vu H. Pham, "Antedating and Anchoring Vietnamese America: Toward a Vietnamese American Historiography," *Amerasia Journal* 29, no. 1 (2003): 137–152. See also Isabelle Thuy Pelaud, *This Is All I Choose to Tell: History and Hybridity in Vietnamese American Literature*, Asian American History and Culture (Philadelphia: Temple University Press, 2011), 22–23.

92. Dana A. Williams and Marissa K. Lopez, "More than a Fever: Toward a Theory of the Ethnic Archive," *PMLA* 127, no. 2 (2012): 357.

CONCLUSION

1. Olga Dror, "Translator's Introduction," in *Mourning Headband for Hue: An Account of the Battle for Hue, Vietnam 1968*, ed. Olga Dror (Bloomington: Indiana University Press, 2014), xvi–xvii.

2. In their edited collection of essays *The Little Magazine in Contemporary America*, Ian Morris and Joanne Diaz opt for the term "little magazine" over "literary journal" to describe the genre. Morris and Diaz argue that, in addition to the qualities I mention, the little magazine reflects an idiosyncratic editorial perspective, publishes literary and nonliterary materials (hence, the choice of "little" over "literary"), and functions "as a 'front guard' that anticipates the newest movements in literature, politics, and art." In the late twentieth century, universities played a larger role in the production of little magazines: Ian Morris and Joanne Diaz, "Preface," in *The Little Magazine in Contemporary America*, ed. Ian Morris and Joanne Diaz (Chicago: Uni-

versity of Chicago Press, 2015), ix–xv. My discussion differs slightly from their argument by highlighting the transnational, geopolitical dynamics of the genre. Their book uses both "literary journal" and "little magazine," and I adapt that cue by referring to "literary journal" and "literary magazine." I also believe that the typical distinction between journal and magazine—that the former is aimed at a more specialized audience while the latter appeals to a more general one—is difficult to discern in the context of South Vietnamese publications because these works were not only highly literary but also more broadly cultural, social, and political. Lawrence-Minh Bui Davis, co-founder and co-editor of the *Asian American Literary Review*, uses the term "literary journal" to describe his publication, which publishes creative and critical works. For Davis, the literary journal is the "sibling" to the anthology—"the bastard son [usurping] the long-standing monarch"—but differs in its "timeliness," as opposed to aspirations toward "timelessness": see Gerald Maa and Lawrence-Minh Bùi Davis, "The World Doesn't Stop for Derek Walcott, Or: An Exchange between Coeditors," in Morris and Diaz, *The Little Magazine in Contemporary America*, 88.

3. Christopher E. Goscha, *Vietnam: A New History* (New York: Basic, 2016), 290.

4. Neil L. Jamieson, *Understanding Vietnam* (Berkeley: University of California Press, 1993), 292–293, 352.

5. Ibid., 293.

6. As some scholars have noted, Norton anthologies are prime examples of the genre's circulation as projects of nation making: see Joe Lockard and Jillian Sandell, "National Narratives and the Politics of Inclusion: Historicizing American Literature Anthologies," *Pedagogy* 8, no. 2 (2008): 227–254.

7. Current debates on the concept of "world literature" are wide and vast, and it is not my intention to delve into that debate here. In my view, Emily Apter and Joseph Slaughter offer compelling critiques of the topic: see Emily S. Apter, *Against World Literature: On the Politics of Untranslatability* (London: Verso, 2013); Joseph Slaughter, "Form and Informality: An Unliterary Look at World Literature," in *The Work of Genre: Selected Essays from the English Institute*, ed. Robyn Warhol-Down (Cambridge, MA: English Institute in collaboration with the American Council of Learned Societies, 2011), available at http://hdl.handle.net/2027/heb.90055.0001.001. I touch on the merits of Slaughter's argument later in this chapter.

8. *Văn* was renamed *Giai Phẩm* [Literary Works] in 1972.

9. François Guillemot, "Tạp Chí Văn (1964–1975)—Nguyễn Đình Vượng: Un panorama des idées littéraires et philosophiques au Sud Viêt-Nam," *Hypotheses*, available at http://indomemoires.hypotheses.org/24195.

10. Trần Phong Giao, "William Faulkner: Con Người Và Tác Phẩm," *Văn* 2, no. 37 (1965): 3.

11. Trần Hoài Thư, "Trần Phong Giao Và Những Người Viết Trẻ," available at http://damau.org/archives/9351.

12. Trần Phong Giao, "William Faulkner," 8.

13. Ibid., 18.

14. Ibid., 9.

15. I have quoted from Faulkner's original speech: William Faulkner, "William Faulkner—Banquet Speech," Nobel Media AB 2014, available at http://www.nobelprize.org/nobel_prizes/literature/laureates/1949/faulkner-speech.html.

16. Hoàng Ngọc Nguyên, "Carson McCullers, Người Săn Đuổi Cô Đơn," *Văn*, no. 103 (1968): 30.

17. Ibid., 19.

18. Ibid.

19. Ibid.

20. Ibid. I have cited from the English-language version of Williams's "Afterword": see Tennessee Williams, "Afterword," in Carson McCullers, *Reflections in a Golden Eye* (New York: Mariner, 2000), 136.

21. Andrew Rubin, *Archives of Authority: Empire, Culture, and the Cold War*, Translation/Transnation (Princeton, NJ: Princeton University Press, 2012), 17.

22. Ibid., 9; Frances Stonor Saunders, *Who Paid the Piper? The CIA and the Cultural Cold War* (London: Granta, 1999), 246.

23. Rubin, *Archives of Authority*, 58–60.

24. Ibid., 17. The CCF was run by a CIA agent between 1950 and 1967.

25. Saunders, *Who Paid the Piper?*

26. Rubin, *Archives of Authority*, 12.

27. Ibid., 49–69.

28. Consider how R. P. Blackmur, editor of *Perspectives USA*, described this moment of Americanized literary multiculturalism: "'Listening to its Babel all at once, one realizes how many wars—how many journeys and how many forms of pity—cry in the *one* American voice. One sees why America is . . . moved by traditions it does not know how to acknowledge and driven by immediate response, looking to uniformity and acting in diversity'": quoted in ibid., 68.

29. Ibid., 4.

30. Ibid., 54.

31. François Guillemot, "Tạp Chí Văn Học (1962–1975)—Phan Kim Thịnh (Chủ Trương Biên Tập): Aperçu historique et production éditoriale," *Hypotheses*, available at https://halshs.archives-ouvertes.fr/halshs-01398942.

32. TrầnTriệu Luật, "Những Người Trẻ Da Đen Giữa Lồng Giấy Trang," *Văn Học* 56 (1966).

33. Ibid., 18.

34. Nguyễn Hữu Dung, "Một Tai Tiếng Lịch Sử," *Văn Học* 56 (1966): 3.

35. Ibid., 4.

36. Lê Linh, "Lời Giới Thiệu," *Văn Học* 56 (1966): 1.

37. For a thorough and persuasive analysis of the political situation of North Vietnam at the time, see Lien-Hang Nguyen, *Hanoi's War: An International History of the War for Peace in Vietnam*, New Cold War History (Chapel Hill: University of North Carolina Press, 2012).

38. Daniel Y. Kim and Viet Thanh Nguyen, "The Literature of the Korean War and Vietnam War," in *The Cambridge Companion to Asian American Literature*, eds. Crystal Parikh and Daniel Y. Kim (New York: Cambridge University Press, 2015), 60.

39. "Thân Gửi Bạn Đọc," *Văn* no. 1 (1964): 1.

40. Trần Phong Giao, "William Faulkner," 4.

41. The possibility of direct financial or institutional links between South Vietnamese literary journals and the CCF is a topic worthy of further analysis.

42. It is notable that Frantz Fanon, a writer with whom Sartre is closely associated, was not featured as the focus of a special issue. He was also not given the CCF's seal of approval: see Rubin, *Archives of Authority*, 54.

43. According to Fern Marja Eckman, James Baldwin admired Wright's novel

and credited it with helping him imagine a life beyond Harlem: Fern Marja Eckman, *The Furious Passage of James Baldwin* (New York: M. Evans, 1966). Eckman does not provide a source for this detail.

44. Slaughter contextualizes notions of world literary systems through the history of intellectual property ownership and challenges the idea that world literature can be mapped by tracing generic patterns and evolutions. In his view, this replicates center-periphery models in which recognizable genres migrate to the margins and ignore cultural forms that do not fit those genres or patterns: Slaughter, "Form and Informality," 187. However, any serious grappling with literary forms and systems in terms of various kinds of power relations has to engage "recognizable forms," and Slaughter's analysis of Chris Abani's novel *Graceland* to argue his point exemplifies this. In highlighting genres in the making, such as Herr's brand of literary journalism, and overlooked aspects of familiar but nondominant genres, such as the epistolary form's refugee contexts, I suggest that the problem may not be genre per se but our conception of genre as tethered to the dominant.

45. For an insightful analysis of how American presence in Vietnam shaped notions of South Vietnamese identity and culture, see Nu-Anh Tran, "South Vietnamese Identity, American Intervention, and the Newspaper *Chính Luận*," *Journal of Vietnamese Studies* 1, nos. 1–2 (2006): 169–209. Tran briefly discusses Võ Phiến's assessment of South Vietnamese nationalism as partly a response to "American domination": see ibid., 171–172.

46. Yen Le Espiritu, *Body Counts: The Vietnam War and Militarized Refuge(es)* (Berkeley: University of California Press, 2014), 121–155.

47. My sincere thanks to Nguyen Nguyet Cam for this information.

48. Isabelle Thuy Pelaud, *This Is All I Choose to Tell: History and Hybridity in Vietnamese American Literature*, Asian American History and Culture (Philadelphia: Temple University Press, 2011), 33–35. I would add that these editorial visions are also informed by broader Americanist and Asian Americanist editorial perspectives.

49. Ma Vang, "Writing on the Run: Hmong American Literary Formations and the Deterritorialized Subject," *MELUS* 41, no. 3 (2016): 90.

50. Viet Thanh Nguyen, *Nothing Ever Dies: Vietnam and the Memory of War* (Cambridge, MA: Harvard University Press, 2016), 208.

51. For an insightful treatment of Asian American literature's relationship to institutionalized multiculturalism, see Amy Cynthia Tang, *Repetition and Race: Asian American Literature after Multiculturalism* (New York: Oxford University Press, 2016).

52. Diasporic Vietnamese Artists Network, "What Is Diacritics?" available at http://diacritics.org/?page_id=6200.

53. When it comes to the Vietnam War, the global imagination continues to focus on the American side of things, and Nguyen takes the public to task for such willful neglect. Partly in response to a *New York Times* article by Maureen Ryan published in 2017 that defines the "long history of the Vietnam novel" in terms of white male authors writing in English, he notes, "The literature by Vietnamese and Vietnamese Americans is out there for anyone who knows how to use Google. But so many here and abroad would rather not know." The stakes of such elisions are not isolated and abstract but have broad, concrete consequences. Nguyen explains, "This pattern of ignorance arguably continues today, both in terms of what Americans continue to ignore about Vietnam and what Americans refuse to know about the Middle East": see Maureen Ryan, "The Long History of the Vietnam Novel," *New York Times*, March

17, 2017; Viet Thanh Nguyen, "The Great Vietnam War Novel Was Not Written by an American," *New York Times*, May 2, 2017.

54. "Thư Tòa Soạn," *Văn*, nos. 100–101 (March 1, 1968): 1–2.

55. For instance, the editorial note in the March 15, 1968, issue stated its "hope that readers would continue to support the publication in dire times so that *Văn* could speak out, in a continuous way and even if in a minor voice, its truth": see "Thư Tòa Soạn," *Văn*, no. 102 (March 15, 1968): 1.

BIBLIOGRAPHY

Abernethy, Michael. "Edouard Bourdet's Lesbian Play, 'the Captive,' Was Certainly Captive of Its Time." Available at http://www.popmatters.com/column/edouard-bourdets-lesbian-play-the-captive-was-certainly-captive-of-its-time.

Agamben, Giorgio. *Homo Sacer: Sovereign Power and Bare Life*, trans. Daniel Heller-Roazen. Crossing Aesthetics. Stanford, CA: Stanford University Press, 1998.

Althusser, Louis. *The Future Lasts Forever: A Memoir*, trans. Richard Veasey. New York: New Press, 1993.

Amer, Sahar, and Laura Doyle. "Theories and Methodologies: Reframing Postcolonial and Global Studies in the Longer Durée [Special Section]." *PMLA* 130, no. 2 (2015): 331–335.

Amin, Kadji. *Disturbing Attachments: Genet, Modern Pederasty, and Queer History*. Durham, NC: Duke University Press, 2017.

Anker, Elisabeth R. *Orgies of Feeling: Melodrama and the Politics of Freedom*. Durham, NC: Duke University Press, 2014.

Apter, Emily S. *Against World Literature: On the Politics of Untranslatability*. London: Verso, 2013.

———. "Untranslatables: A World System." *New Literary History* 39, no. 3 (Summer 2008): 581–598.

Arendt, Hannah. "We Refugees." In *Altogether Elsewhere: Writers on Exile*, ed. Marc Robinson, 110–119. Winchester, MA: Faber and Faber, 1994.

Arondekar, Anjali. "Lingering Pleasures, Perverted Texts: Colonial Desire in Kipling's Anglo-India." In *Imperial Desire: Dissident Sexualities and Colonial Literature*, ed. Philip Holden and Richard J. Ruppel, 65–89. Minneapolis: University of Minnesota Press, 2003.

Austin, Oscar P. *Colonial Administration, 1800–1900. Methods of Government and Development Adopted by the Principal Colonizing Nations in Their Control of Tropical and Other Colonies and Dependencies. With Statistical Statements of the Area, Population, Commerce, Revenue, Etc., of Each of the World's Colonies. Including Bibliography of Colonies and Colonization Prepared by the Library of Congress.*

From the Summary of Commerce and Finance for October, 1901. Washington, DC: U.S. Government Printing Office, 1901.

Bahr, Fax, Eleanor Coppola, and George Hickenlooper. *Hearts of Darkness: A Filmmaker's Apocalypse.* San Francisco: Zoetrope Studios, 1991.

Bakhtin, Mikhail M. *Problems of Dostoevsky's Poetics.* Theory and History of Literature. Minneapolis: University of Minnesota Press, 1984.

Baraka, Amiri. *Home: Social Essays.* New York: William Morrow, 1966.

Barry, Lynda. *One! Hundred! Demons!* Seattle: Sasquatch, 2002.

Barthes, Roland. *Camera Lucida: Reflections on Photography.* New York: Hill and Wang, 1981.

Benstock, Shari. *Women of the Left Bank.* Austin: University of Texas Press, 1986.

Berlant, Lauren. "The Subject of True Feeling: Pain, Privacy, and Politics." In *Cultural Pluralism, Identity Politics, and the Law,* ed. Austin Sarat and Thomas R. Kearns, 49–84. Ann Arbor: University of Michigan Press, 1999.

———. "Thinking about Feeling Historical." *Emotion, Space and Society* 1, no. 1 (2008): 4–9.

Berrong, Richard M. *In Love with a Handsome Sailor: The Emergence of Gay Identity and the Novels of Pierre Loti.* Toronto: University of Toronto Press, 2003.

Bhabha, Homi K. *The Location of Culture.* London: Routledge, 1994.

Bloch, Ernst. "Nonsynchronism and the Obligation to Its Dialectics." *New German Critique* 11 (Spring 1977): 22–38.

Blum, Hester. *The View from the Masthead: Maritime Imagination and Antebellum American Sea Narratives.* Chapel Hill: University of North Carolina Press, 2008.

Borri, Cristoforo, and S. Baron. *Views of Seventeenth-Century Vietnam: Christoforo Borri on Cochinchina and Samuel Baron on Tonkin.* Studies on Southeast Asia. Ithaca, NY: Southeast Asia Program Publications, Cornell University, 2006.

Bowden, Mark. "Introduction." In Robert Pisor, *Siege of Khe Sanh: The Story of the Vietnam War's Largest Battle.* New York: W. W. Norton, 2018.

Bower, Anne L. "Romanced by Cookbooks." *Gastronomica* 4, no. 2 (2004): 35–42.

Bradley, Mark. *Imagining Vietnam and America: The Making of Postcolonial Vietnam, 1919–1950.* New Cold War History. Chapel Hill: University of North Carolina Press, 2000.

Braestrup, Peter. *Big Story: How the American Press and Television Reported and Interpreted the Crisis of Tet 1968 in Vietnam and Washington.* New Haven, CT: Yale University Press, 1983.

Brantley, Ben, ed. *The New York Times Book of Broadway.* New York: St. Martin's Press, 2001.

Brantlinger, Peter. *Rule of Darkness: British Literature and Imperialism, 1830–1914.* Ithaca, NY: Cornell University Press, 1990.

Braudel, Fernand. *On History.* Chicago: University of Chicago Press, 1980.

Braudel, Fernand, and Immanuel Wallerstein. "History and the Social Sciences: The *Longue Durée.*" *Review (Fernand Braudel Center)* 32, no. 2 (2009): 171–203.

Brewster, David. *A Treatise on the Kaleidoscope.* Edinburgh: A. Constable [etc.], 1819.

Britton, Andrew. "Sideshows: Hollywood in Vietnam." In *Britton on Film: The Complete Film Criticism of Andrew Britton,* ed. Barry Keith Grant, 74–96. Detroit: Wayne State University Press, 2009.

Brooks, Peter. *The Melodramatic Imagination: Balzac, Henry James, Melodrama, and the Mode of Excess.* New Haven, CT: Yale University Press, 1976.

Burns, Edward, ed. *The Letters of Gertrude Stein and Carl Van Vechten 1913–1946.* New York: Columbia University Press, 1986.

Butler, Judith. *Giving an Account of Oneself.* New York: Fordham University Press, 2005.

Ca, Nhã. *Mourning Headband for Hue: An Account of the Battle for Hue, Vietnam 1968*, trans. Olga Dror. Bloomington: Indiana University Press, 2014.

Caplan, Jane. "Introduction." In *Written on the Body: The Tattoo in European and American History*, ed. Jane Caplan, xi–xxiii. Princeton, NJ: Princeton University Press, 2000.

Carmichael, Thomas. "Postmodernism and American Cultural Difference: *Dispatches, Mystery Train*, and *The Art of Japanese Management*." *boundary 2* 21, no. 1 (1994): 220–232.

Carruth, Allison. *Global Appetites: American Power and the Literature of Food*. New York: Cambridge University Press, 2013.

———. "War Rations and the Food Politics of Late Modernism." *Modernism/Modernity* 16, no. 4 (2009): 767–795.

Cecire, Natalia. "Ways of Not Reading Gertrude Stein." *ELH* 82, no. 1 (2015): 281–312.

Chambers-Letson, Joshua Takano. *A Race So Different: Performance and Law in Asian America*. Postmillennial Pop Series. New York: New York University Press, 2013.

Cheng, Anne. "Modernism." In *The Routledge Companion to Asian American and Pacific Islander Literature*, ed. Rachel C. Lee, 315–328. New York: Routledge, 2014.

———. *Second Skin: Josephine Baker and the Modern Surface*. Oxford: Oxford University Press, 2011.

———. "Shine: On Race, Glamour, and the Modern." *PMLA* 126, no. 4 (2011): 1022–1041.

Choi, Byung Wook. "The Nguyen Dynasty's Policy toward Chinese on the Water Frontier in the First Half of the Nineteenth Century." In *Water Frontier: Commerce and the Chinese in the Lower Mekong Region, 1750–1880*, ed. Nora Cooke and Tana Li, 85–99. Singapore: Rowman and Littlefield, 2004.

Chong, Sylvia Shin Huey. *The Oriental Obscene: Violence and Racial Fantasies in the Vietnam Era*. Durham, NC: Duke University Press, 2012.

Chuh, Kandice. *Imagine Otherwise: On Asian Americanist Critique*. Durham, NC: Duke University Press, 2003.

Clancy-Smith, Julia, and Frances Gouda. "Introduction." In *Domesticating the Empire: Race, Gender, and Family Life in French and Dutch Colonialism*, ed. Julia Clancy-Smith and Frances Gouda, 1–20. Charlottesville: University of Virginia Press, 1998.

Clark, Michael P. "The Work of War after the Age of Mechanical Reproduction." In *The Vietnam War and Postmodernity*, ed. Michael Bibby, 17–48. Amherst: University of Massachusetts Press, 1999.

Clifford, James. "On Ethnographic Surrealism." *Comparative Studies in Society and History* 23, no. 4 (October 1981): 539–564.

Cohen, Margaret. *The Novel and the Sea*. Translation/Transnation. Princeton, NJ: Princeton University Press, 2010.

Commissariat General de l'Indo-Chine. *L'Indo-Chine a l'exposition coloniale de Marseille, 1906*. Marseille: Imprimerie Marseillaise, 1906.

Conklin, Alice L. *A Mission to Civilize: The Republican Idea of Empire in France and West Africa, 1895–1930*. Stanford, CA: Stanford University Press, 2000.

Courtney, Susan. *Hollywood Fantasies of Miscegenation: Spectacular Narratives of Gender and Race, 1903–1967*. Princeton, NJ: Princeton University Press, 2005.

Crawford, Margo Natalie. "The Interracial Party of Modernist Primitivism and the Black 'After-Party.'" In *The Modernist Party*, ed. Catherine Mary McLoughlin, 164–177. Edinburgh: Edinburgh University Press, 2013.

Cruz, Denise. "'Love Is Not a Bowl of Quinces': Food, Desire, and the Queer Asian Body in Monique Truong's *The Book of Salt*." In *Eating Asian America: A Food Studies Reader*, ed. Robert Ji-Song Ku, Martin F. Manalansan, and Anita Mannur, 354–370. New York: New York University Press, 2013.

———. *Transpacific Femininities: The Making of the Modern Filipina*. Durham, NC: Duke University Press, 2012.

Debord, Guy. *The Society of the Spectacle*, trans. Donald Nicholson-Smith. New York: Zone, 1995.

Decker, William Merrill. *Epistolary Practices: Letter Writing in America before Telecommunications*. Chapel Hill: University of North Carolina Press, 1998.

DeKoven, Marianne. *A Different Language: Gertrude Stein's Experimental Writing*. Madison: University of Wisconsin Press, 1983.

———. *Rich and Strange: Gender, History, Modernism*. Princeton, NJ: Princeton University Press, 1991.

Deleuze, Gilles, and Félix Guattari. *A Thousand Plateaus: Capitalism and Schizophrenia*. Minneapolis: University of Minnesota Press, 1987.

Derrida, Jacques, and Avital Ronell, trans. "The Law of Genre." *Critical Inquiry* 7, no. 1 (1980): 55–81.

de Warren, Nicolas. "Hopes of a Generation: The Life, Work, and Legacy of Trần Duc Thao." *Graduate Faculty Philosophy Journal* 30, no. 2 (2009): 263–283.

Dimock, Wai Chee. "Introduction: Genres as Fields of Knowledge." *PMLA* 122, no. 5 (2007): 1377–1388.

———. *Through Other Continents: American Literature across Deep Time*. Princeton, NJ: Princeton University Press, 2006.

Dror, Olga. "Translator's Introduction." In Nhã Ca, *Mourning Headband for Hue: An Account of the Battle for Hue, Vietnam 1968*, ed. Olga Dror, xv–1. Bloomington: Indiana University Press, 2014.

Duiker, William J. *Ho Chi Minh: A Life*. New York: Hyperion, 2000.

Dung, Nguyễn Hữu. "Một Tai Tiếng Lịch Sử." *Văn Học* 56 (March 15, 1966): 3–6.

Duong, Lan P. *Treacherous Subjects: Gender, Culture, and Trans-Vietnamese Feminism*. Asian American History and Culture. Philadelphia: Temple University Press, 2012.

Dutton, George Edson, Jayne Susan Werner, and John K. Whitmore, eds. *Sources of Vietnamese Tradition*. Introduction to Asian Civilizations. New York: Columbia University Press, 2012.

Eckman, Fern Marja. *The Furious Passage of James Baldwin*. New York: M. Evans, 1966.

Edwards, Brent Hayes. *The Practice of Diaspora: Literature, Translation, and the Rise of Black Internationalism*. Cambridge, MA: Harvard University Press, 2003.

Edwards, Penny. "Womanizing Indochina: Fiction, Nation and Cohabitation in Colonial Cambodia, 1890–1930." In *Domesticating the Empire: Race, Gender and Family Life in French and Dutch Colonialism*, ed. Julia Clancy-Smith and Frances Gouda, 108–130. Charlottesville: University of Virginia Press, 1998.

Elias, Amy J. *Sublime Desire: History and Post-1960s Fiction*. Parallax: Re-Visions of Culture and Society. Baltimore: Johns Hopkins University Press, 2001.

Eng, David. "The End(s) of Race." *PMLA* 123, no. 5 (2008): 1479–1493.

Eng, David L., and Alice Y. Hom. *Q & A: Queer in Asian America*. Asian American History and Culture. Philadelphia: Temple University Press, 1998.

Espiritu, Yen Le. *Body Counts: The Vietnam War and Militarized Refuge(es)*. Berkeley: University of California Press, 2014.

Fajardo, Kale Bantigue. *Filipino Crosscurrents: Oceanographies of Seafaring, Masculinities, and Globalization*. Minneapolis: University of Minnesota Press, 2011.

Fanon, Frantz. *The Wretched of the Earth*, trans. Richard Philcox. New York: Grove, 2004.

Fields, Karen E., and Barbara Jeanne Fields. *Racecraft: The Soul of Inequality in American Life*. London: Verso, 2012.

Firpo, Christina E. "Lost Boys: 'Abandoned' Eurasian Children and the Management of the Racial Topography in Colonial Indochina, 1938–1945. " *French Colonial History* 8 (2007): 203–221.

Ford, Gerald. "Address at a Tulane University Convocation," April 23, 1975. American Presidency Project, comp. Gerhard Peters and John T. Woolley. Available at http://www.presidency.ucsb.edu/ws/?pid=4859.

Frow, John. *Genre*, 2nd ed. The New Critical Idiom. London: Routledge, Taylor and Francis, 2015.

Fung, Catherine. "A History of Absences: The Problem of Reference in Monique Truong's *The Book of Salt.*" *Novel* 45, no. 1 (2012): 94–110.

Gardner, Mona. *The Menacing Sun*. New York: Harcourt, 1939.

Gillman, Susan Kay. *Blood Talk: American Race Melodrama and the Culture of the Occult*. Chicago: University of Chicago Press, 2003.

Giraud, Gaston. "Trade with French Indo-China." In *Official Report of the Seventh National Foreign Trade Convention*, 407–410. New York: O. K. Davis, Secretary, National Foreign Trade Convention, 1920.

Goscha, Christopher E. "Courting Diplomatic Disaster? The Difficult Integration of Vietnam into the Internationalist Communist Movement (1945–1950)." *Journal of Vietnamese Studies* 1, nos. 1–2 (2006): 59–103.

———. *Going Indochinese: Contesting Concepts of Space and Place in French Indochina*. Nordic Institute of Asian Studies Classics Series. Copenhagen: Nordic Institute of Asian Studies Press, 2012.

———. *Vietnam: A New History*. New York: Basic, 2016.

"The Gossip Shop." *Bookman* 44 (February 1922): 760–768.

Greene, Harlan. *The Damned Don't Cry—They Just Disappear: The Life and Works of Harry Hervey.*" Columbia: University of South Carolina Press, 2017.

———. "The Multi-talented Harry Hervey." *Gay and Lesbian Review* (May–June 2017): 24–27.

Greene, Harlan, and James M. Hutchisson, "Introduction: The Charleston Renaissance Considered." In *Renaissance in Charleston: Art and Life in the Carolina Low Country, 1900–1940*, ed. James M. Hutchisson and Harlan Greene, 1–18. Athens: University of Georgia Press, 2003.

Groth, Helen. "Kaleidoscopic Vision and Literary Invention in an 'Age of Things': David Brewster, Don Juan, and 'a Lady's Kaleidoscope.'" *ELH* 74, no. 1 (2007): 217–237.

Guillemot, François "Tạp Chí Văn (1964–1975)—Nguyễn Đình Vượng: Un panorama des idées littéraires et philosophiques au Sud Viêt-Nam." *Hypotheses*. Available at http://indomemoires.hypotheses.org/24195.

———. "Tạp Chí Văn Học (1962–1975)—Phan Kim Thịnh (Chủ Trương Biên Tập): Aperçu historique et production éditoriale." *Hypotheses*. Available at https://halshs.archives-ouvertes.fr/halshs-01398942.

Gunn, Geoffrey C. *Rice Wars in Colonial Vietnam: The Great Famine and the Viet Minh Road to Power*. Asia/Pacific/Perspectives. Lanham, MD: Rowman and Littlefield, 2014.

Ha, Marie-Paule. "'La Femme Française aux Colonies': Promoting Colonial Female Emigration at the Turn of the Century." *French Colonial History* 6 (2005): 205–224.

Hansen, Peter. "Bắc Di Cư: Catholic Refugees from the North of Vietnam, and Their Role in the Southern Republic, 1954–1959." *Journal of Vietnamese Studies* 4, no. 3 (1009): 173–211.

Heberle, Mark. "Michael Herr's Traumatic New Journalism: *Dispatches*." In *Vietnam War: Topics in Contemporary North American Literature*, ed. Brenda M. Boyle, 27–45. New York: Bloomsbury Academic, 2015.

Herr, Michael. *Dispatches*. New York: Alfred A. Knopf, 1977.

Herring, George C. *America's Longest War: The United States and Vietnam, 1950–1975*, 4th ed. New York: McGraw-Hill, 2002..

Hervey, Harry. *Congaï*. New York: Cosmopolitan, 1927.

———. *Congaï: Mistress of Indochine*, ed. Kent Davis. Holmes Beach, FL: DatAsia, 2014.

———. *Travels in French Indo-China*. London: Thornton Butterworth, 1928.

———. "The Young Men Go Down." *The Nation* 118, no. 3056 (January 24, 1924): 112–114.

Hitchcock, Peter. *The Long Space: Transnationalism and Postcolonial Form*. Cultural Memory in the Present. Stanford, CA: Stanford University Press, 2010.

Hồ Chí Minh. "Vietnam Declaration of Independence (September 2, 1945)." In *Vietnam and America: A Documented History*, ed. Marvin E. Gettleman, Jane Franklin, Marilyn B. Young, and H. Bruce Franklin. New York: Grove, 1995.

Hoberek, Andrew. "Foreign Objects, or, Delillo Minimalist." *Studies in American Fiction* 37, no. 1 (2010): 101–125.

Holder, Heidi. "Melodrama, Realism, and Empire on the British Stage." In *Acts of Supremacy: The British Empire and the Stage, 1790–1930*, ed. J. S. Bratton, 129–149. Manchester, UK: Manchester University Press, 1991.

Hsu, Hua. *A Floating Chinaman: Fantasy and Failure across the Pacific*. Cambridge, MA: Harvard University Press, 2016

Huang, Betsy. *Contesting Genres in Contemporary Asian American Fiction*. New York: Palgrave Macmillan, 2010.

Huang, Yunte. *Transpacific Displacement: Ethnography, Translation, and Intertextual Travel in Twentieth-Century American Literature*. Berkeley: University of California Press, 2002.

———. *Transpacific Imaginations: History, Literature, Counterpoetics*. Cambridge, MA: Harvard University Press, 2008.

Hubert, Paul. *Ananas*. Bibliotheque Pratique du Colon. Paris: H. Dunod et E. Pinat, 1908.

Hughes, Geraint. "A 'Post-War' War: The British Occupation of French-Indochina, September 1945–March 1946." *Small Wars and Insurgencies* 17, no. 3 (2006): 263–286.

Hughes, William. "Imperial Gothic." In *Historical Dictionary of Gothic Literature*, ed. William Hughes, 141–142. Lanham, MD: Rowman and Littlefield, 2013.

Huỳnh, Kim Khánh. *Vietnamese Communism, 1925–1945*. Ithaca, NY: Cornell University Press, 1982.

Hyslop, Jonathan. "The Invention of the Concentration Camp: Cuba, Southern Africa and the Philippines, 1896–1907." *South African Historical Journal* 63, no. 2 (2011): 251–276.

Jameson, Fredric. *The Political Unconscious: Narrative as a Socially Symbolic Act*. Ithaca, NY: Cornell University Press, 1981.

———. *Postmodernism, or, The Cultural Logic of Late Capitalism*. Post-contemporary Interventions. Durham, NC: Duke University Press, 1991.

Jamieson, Neil L. *Understanding Vietnam*. Berkeley: University of California Press, 1993.

Jeffords, Susan. *The Remasculinization of America: Gender and the Vietnam War*. Theories of Contemporary Culture. Bloomington: Indiana University Press, 1989.

Jennings, Eric Thomas. "Remembering 'Other' Losses: The Temple du Souvenir Indochinois of Nogent-sur-Marne." *History and Memory* 15, no. 1 (2003): 5–48.

Jeon, Joseph Jonghyun. *Racial Things, Racial Forms: Objecthood in Avant-Garde Asian American Poetry*. Contemporary North American Poetry Series. Iowa City: University of Iowa Press, 2012.

Johnson, Barbara. "Apostrophe, Animation, and Abortion." *Diacritics* 16, no. 1 (1986): 28–47.

———. "The Frame of Reference: Poe, Lacan, Derrida." *Yale French Studies* 55, nos. 55–56 (1977): 457–505.

Kelly, Gail Paradise. *From Vietnam to America: A Chronicle of the Vietnamese Immigration to the United States.* Boulder, CO: Westview, 1977.

Kennedy, Edward M. "Refugee Act of 1980." *International Migration Review* 15, nos. 1–2 (1981): 141–156.

Kim, Daniel Y., and Viet Thanh Nguyen. "The Literature of the Korean War and Vietnam War." In *The Cambridge Companion to Asian American Literature*, ed. Crystal Parikh and Daniel Y. Kim, 59–72. New York: Cambridge University Press, 2015.

Kim, Jodi. *Ends of Empire: Asian American Critique and the Cold War.* Critical American Studies Series. Minneapolis: University of Minnesota Press, 2010.

Klein, Christina. *Cold War Orientalism: Asia in the Middlebrow Imagination, 1945–1961.* Berkeley: University of California Press, 2003.

Kneebone, Susan, and Felicity Rawlings-Sanaei. *New Regionalism and Asylum Seekers: Challenges Ahead.* Studies in Forced Migration. New York: Berghahn, 2007.

Koshy, Susan. "The Rise of the Asian American Novel." In *The Cambridge History of the American Novel*, ed. Leonard Cassuto, 1046–1063. New York: Cambridge University Press, 2011.

———. *Sexual Naturalization: Asian Americans and Miscegenation.* Asian America. Stanford, CA: Stanford University Press, 2004.

Kovach, Bill, and Tom Rosenstiel. *The Elements of Journalism: What News People Should Know and the Public Should Expect.* New York: Three Rivers, 2001.

Ku, Robert Ji-Song, Martin F. Manalansan, and Anita Mannur. "An Alimentary Introduction." In *Eating Asian America: A Food Studies Reader*, ed. Robert Ji-Song Ku, Martin F. Manalansan, and Anita Mannur, 1–9. New York: New York University Press, 2013.

Laderman, Scott. "Hollywood's Vietnam, 1929–1964: Scripting Intervention, Spotlighting Injustice." *Pacific Historical Review* 78, no. 4 (2009): 578–607.

Lê, Quang Định. "Vietnamese Geographical Expansion," trans. George Dutton. In *Sources of Vietnamese Tradition*, ed. George Dutton, Jayne Susan Werner, and John K. Whitmore. Introduction to Asian Civilizations, 261–262. New York: Columbia University Press, 2012.

Lee, Josephine D. *The Japan of Pure Invention: Gilbert and Sullivan's "The Mikado."* Minneapolis: University of Minnesota Press, 2010.

Lee, Rachel C. *The Exquisite Corpse of Asian America: Biopolitics, Biosociality, and Posthuman Ecologies.* Sexual Cultures. New York: New York University Press, 2014.

Lentricchia, Frank. "How to Do Things with Wallace Stevens." In *Close Reading: The Reader*, ed. Frank Lentricchia and Andrew DuBois, 136–155. Durham, NC: Duke University Press, 2003.

Levine, Caroline. *Forms: Whole, Rhythm, Hierarchy, Network.* Princeton, NJ: Princeton University Press, 2015.

Li, Tana. "The Eighteenth-Century Mekong Delta and Its World of Water Frontier." In *Việt Nam: Borderless Histories*, ed. Nhung Tuyet Tran and Anthony Reid, 147–162. New Perspectives in Southeast Asian Studies. Madison: University of Wisconsin Press, 2006.

———. "The Late-Eighteenth and Early-Nineteenth-Century Mekong Delta in the Regional Trade System." In *Water Frontier: Commerce and the Chinese in the Lower Mekong Region, 1750–1880*, ed. Nola Cooke and Tana Li, 71–84. Singapore: Rowman and Littlefield, 2004.

———. "Ships and Shipbuilding in the Mekong Delta, c. 1750–1840." In *Water Frontier: Commerce and the Chinese in the Lower Mekong Region, 1750–1880*, ed. Nola Cooke and Tana Li, 119–135. Singapore: Rowman and Littlefield, 2004.

———. "The Water Frontier: An Introduction." In *Water Frontier: Commerce and the Chinese in the Lower Mekong Region, 1750–1880*, ed. Nola Cooke and Tana Li, 1–17. Singapore: Rowman and Littlefield, 2004.

Linh, Lê. "Lời Giới Thiệu." *Văn Học* 56 (1966): 1.

Lipman, Jana K. "A Refugee Camp in America: Fort Chaffee and Vietnamese and Cuban Refugees, 1975–1982." *Journal of American Ethnic History* 33, no. 2 (Winter 2014): 57–87.

Liu, Alan. *Local Transcendence: Essays on Postmodern Historicism and the Database.* Chicago: University of Chicago Press, 2008.

Liu, William T., Mary Ann Lamanna, and Alice Murata. *Transition to Nowhere: Vietnamese Refugees in America.* Nashville, TN: Charter House, 1979.

Liu, William T., and Alice Murata. "The Vietnamese in America: Refugees or Immigrants?" *Bridge: An Asian American Perspective* 5, no. 3 (Fall 1997): 31–39.

Lockard, Joe, and Jillian Sandell. "National Narratives and the Politics of Inclusion: Historicizing American Literature Anthologies." *Pedagogy* 8, no. 2 (2008): 227–254.

Logevall, Fredrik. *Embers of War: The Fall of an Empire and the Making of America's Vietnam.* New York: Random House, 2012.

Louis, Jean. "Note on the Geography of Cochin China." *Journal of the Asiatic Society of Bengal* 6, no. 2 (1837): 737–745.

Lowe, Lisa. *Immigrant Acts: On Asian American Cultural Politics.* Durham, NC: Duke University Press, 1996.

———. *The Intimacies of Four Continents.* Durham, NC: Duke University Press, 2015.

Luciano, Dana. "Conversation: Lauren Berlant with Dana Luciano." January 13, 2013. Available at http://socialtextjournal.org/periscope_article/conversation-lauren-berlant-with-dana-luciano.

Luhrssen, David. *Mamoulian: Life on Stage and Screen.* Lexington: University Press of Kentucky, 2013.

Lye, Colleen. *America's Asia: Racial Form and American Literature, 1893–1945.* Princeton, NJ: Princeton University Press, 2005.

———. "Introduction: In Dialogue with Asian American Studies." *Representations* 99, no. 1 (2007): 1–12.

———. "Racial Form." *Representations* 104, no. 1 (2008): 92–101.

Lyotard, Jean-François. *The Postmodern Condition: A Report on Knowledge.* Theory and History of Literature. Minneapolis: University of Minnesota Press, 1984.

Maa, Gerald, and Lawrence-Minh Bùi Davis. "The World Doesn't Stop for Derek Walcott, Or: An Exchange between Coeditors." In *The Little Magazine in Contemporary America*, ed. Ian Morris and Joanne Diaz, 83–94. Chicago: University of Chicago Press, 2015.

Magosaki, Rei. *Tricksters and Cosmopolitans: Cross-Cultural Collaborations in Asian American Literary Production.* New York: Fordham University Press, 2016.

Malcolm, Janet. *Two Lives: Gertrude and Alice.* New Haven, CT: Yale University Press, 2007.

Malkki, Liisa H. "Speechless Emissaries: Refugees, Humanitarianism, and Dehistoricization." *Cultural Anthropology* 11, no. 3 (1997): 377–404.

Mamoulian, Rouben. "Will Talking Pictures Become 'Talking Paintings'?" In *Celebrity Articles from the Screen Guild Magazine*, ed. Anna Kate Sterling, 70–74. Metuchen, NJ: Scarecrow, 1987.

Manela, Erez. *The Wilsonian Moment: Self-Determination and the International Origins of Anticolonial Nationalism.* Oxford: Oxford University Press, 2007.

Mannur, Anita. *Culinary Fictions: Food in South Asian Diasporic Culture.* Philadelphia: Temple University Press, 2010.

Marchetti, Gina. *Romance and the "Yellow Peril": Race, Sex, and Discursive Strategies in Hollywood Fiction.* Berkeley: University of California Press, 1993.

Marr, David G. *Vietnamese Anticolonialism, 1885–1925.* Berkeley: University of California Press, 1971.

———. *Vietnamese Tradition on Trial, 1920–1945.* Berkeley: University of California Press, 1981.

Matsuda, Matt K. *Empire of Love: Histories of France and the Pacific.* New York: Oxford University Press, 2005.

Mbembe, Achille. "Necropolitics." *Public Culture* 15, no. 1 (2003): 11–40.

McCann, Sean, and Michael Szalay. "Do You Believe in Magic? Literary Thinking after the New Left." *Yale Journal of Criticism* 18, no. 2 (2006): 435–468.

McConnell, Scott. *Leftward Journey: The Education of Vietnamese Students in France, 1919–1939.* New Brunswick, NJ: Transaction, 1989.

McCullers, Carson. *Reflections in a Golden Eye.* New York: Mariner, 2000.

McHale, Shawn. "Vietnamese Marxism, Dissent, and the Politics of Postcolonial Memory: Tran Duc Thao, 1946–1993." *Journal of Asian Studies* 61, no. 1 (2002): 7–31.

McKinley, William. "Executive Order," December 21, 1898. American Presidency Project, comp. Gerhard Peters and John T. Woolley. Available at http://www.presidency.ucsb.edu/ws/?pid=69309.

———. "First Annual Message," December 6, 1897. Miller Center, University of Virginia, Charlottesville. Available at https://millercenter.org/the-presidency/presidential-speeches/december-6-1897-first-annual-message.

Melançon, Jérôme. "Anticolonialisme et dissidence: Tran Duc Thao et *Les Temps Modernes*." In *L'itinéraire de Tran Duc Thao: Phénoménologie et transferts culturels*, ed. Jocelyn Benoist and Michel Espagne, 201–215. Paris: Armand Colin, 2013.

Meyer, Richard. *Outlaw Representation: Censorship and Homosexuality in Twentieth-Century American Art.* Oxford: Oxford University Press, 2002.

Miller, Edward Garvey. *Misalliance: Ngo Dinh Diem, the United States, and the Fate of South Vietnam.* Cambridge, MA: Harvard University Press, 2013.

———. "Roundtable: Logevall's *Embers of War: The Fall of an Empire and the Making of America's Vietnam*." *Journal of American Studies* 48, no. 2 (2014): 1–6.

Miller, Robert Hopkins. *The United States and Vietnam, 1787–1941.* Washington, DC: National Defense University Press, 1990.

Mongin, Olivier, Nathalie Lempereur, and Jean-Louis Schlegel. "What Is Postcolonial Thinking? An Interview with Achille Mbembe," January 9, 2008. Available at http://www.eurozine.com/what-is-postcolonial-thinking.

Montero, Darrel. *Vietnamese Americans: Patterns of Resettlement and Socioeconomic Adaptation in the United States.* Boulder, CO: Westview, 1979.

Morris, Ian, and Joanne Diaz. "Preface." In *The Little Magazine in Contemporary America*, ed. Ian Morris and Joanne Diaz, vii–xviii. Chicago: University of Chicago Press, 2015.

Morrison, Toni. *Playing in the Dark: Whiteness and the Literary Imagination.* William E. Massey Sr. Lectures in the History of American Civilization. Cambridge, MA: Harvard University Press, 1992.

———. "The Site of Memory." In *Inventing the Truth: The Art and Craft of Memoir*, ed. William Zinsser, 83–102. New York: Houghton Mifflin, 1995.

Mufti, Aamir R. *Forget English! Orientalisms and World Literatures.* Cambridge, MA: Harvard University Press, 2016.

Ngai, Mae M. *Impossible Subjects: Illegal Aliens and the Making of Modern America.* Politics and Society in Twentieth-Century America. Princeton, NJ: Princeton University Press, 2004.

Ngô, Diệm Đình. "Statement of June 18, 1954." In *Major Policy Speeches*, 5–6. Saigon: Press Office, Presidency of the Republic of Viet Nam, 1956.

Ngo, Fiona I. B., Mimi Thi Nguyen, and Mariam B. Lam. "Southeast Asian American Studies Special Issue: Guest Editors' Introduction." *Positions: East Asia Cultures Critique* 20, no. 3 (2012): 671–684.

Nguyên, Hoàng Ngọc, "Carson Mccullers, Người Săn Đuổi Cô Đơn." *Văn*, no. 103 (1968): 18–30.

Nguyen, Khai Thu. "Sensing Vietnam: Melodramas of Nation from Colonialism to Market Reform." Ph.D. diss., University of California, Berkeley, 2010.

Nguyen, Lien-Hang T. *Hanoi's War: An International History of the War for Peace in Vietnam*. The New Cold War History. Chapel Hill: University of North Carolina Press, 2012.

Nguyen, Mimi Thi. *The Gift of Freedom: War, Debt, and Other Refugee Passages*. Next Wave: New Directions in Women's Studies. Durham, NC: Duke University Press, 2012.

Nguyen, Viet Thanh. "Just Memory: War and the Ethics of Remembrance." *American Literary History* 25, no. 1 (2013): 144–163.

———. *Nothing Ever Dies: Vietnam and the Memory of War*. Cambridge, MA: Harvard University Press, 2016.

———. "On True War Stories." *Asian American Literary Review* 6, no. 2 (2015): 140–145.

———. "Refugee Memories and Asian American Critique." *Positions: East Asia Cultures Critique* 20, no. 3 (2012): 911–942.

Nguyen-Vo, Thu-Huong. "Epitaphic Nation: The Problem of the South and Necropolitics in Early Modern Vietnamese National Literature." *PMLA* 126, no. 3 (2011): 685–692.

Nochlin, Linda. *The Body in Pieces: The Fragment as a Metaphor of Modernity*. Walter Neurath Memorial Lectures. New York: Thames and Hudson, 1995.

———. *The Politics of Vision: Essays on Nineteenth-Century Art and Society*. New York: Harper and Row, 1989.

Norris, Andrew. "Giorgio Agamben and the Politics of the Living Dead." *Diacritics* 30, no. 4 (2000): 38–58.

Nyers, Peter. "Emergency or Emerging Identities? Refugees and Transformations in World Order." *Millennium: Journal of International Studies* 28, no. 1 (1999): 1–26.

O'Brien, Edward J., ed. *The Best Short Stories of 1924 and the Yearbook of the American Short Story*. Boston: Small, Maynard, 1925.

Okihiro, Gary Y. *Pineapple Culture: A History of the Tropical and Temperate Zones*. California World History Library. Berkeley: University of California Press, 2009.

Oyama, Misa. "The Asian Look of Melodrama: Moral and Racial Legibility in the Films of Sessue Hayakawa, Anna May Wong, Winnifred Eaton, and James Wong Howe." Ph.D. diss., University of California, Berkeley, 2007.

Padoongpatt, Mark. "'Oriental Cookery': Devouring Asian and Pacific Cuisine during the Cold War." In *Eating Asian America: A Food Studies Reader*, ed. Robert Ji-Song Ku, Martin F. Manalansan, and Anita Mannur, 186–207. New York: New York University Press, 2013.

Palumbo-Liu, David. *Asian/American: Historical Crossings of a Racial Frontier*. Stanford, CA: Stanford University Press, 1999.

Parikh, Crystal. *Writing Human Rights: The Political Imaginaries of Writers of Color*. Minneapolis: University of Minnesota Press, 2017.

Peek, Michelle. "A Subject of Sea and Salty Sediment: Diasporic Labor and Queer (Be) Longing in Monique Truong's *The Book of Salt*." *Journal of Transnational American Studies* 4, no. 1 (2012). Available at https://eschoarship.org/uc/item/5kr4j4z1.

Pelaud, Isabelle Thuy. *This Is All I Choose to Tell: History and Hybridity in Vietnamese American Literature*. Asian American History and Culture. Philadelphia: Temple University Press, 2011.

Peters, Erica J. *Appetites and Aspirations in Vietnam: Food and Drink in the Long Nineteenth Century*. Lanham, MD: Altamira, 2012.

———. "Resistance, Rivalries, and Restaurants: Vietnamese Workers in Interwar France." *Journal of Vietnamese Studies* 2, no. 1 (2007): 109–143.

Pfister, Joel. "Glamorizing the Psychological: The Politics of the Performances of Modern Psychological Identities." In *Inventing the Psychological: Toward a Cultural History of Emotional Life in America*, ed. Joel Pfister and Nancy Schnog, 167–213. New Haven, CT: Yale University Press, 1997.

Pham, Minh-Ha T. "Paul Poiret's Magical Techno-Oriental Fashions (1911): Race, Clothing, and Virtuality in the Machine Age." *Configurations* 21, no. 1 (Winter 2013): 1–26.

Pham, Vu H. "Antedating and Anchoring Vietnamese America: Toward a Vietnamese American Historiography." *Amerasia Journal* 29, no. 1 (2003): 137–152.

Phiến, Võ. *Lại Thư Gửi Bạn* [Again, Letters to a Friend]. Westminster, CA: Người Việt, 1979.

———. *Thư Gửi Bạn* [Letters to a Friend]. Des Moines, IA: Nhà Xuất bản Người Việt, 1976.

———. "Vietnamese Americans," trans. Quí-Phiệt Trần. In *Not a War: American Vietnamese Fiction, Poetry and Essays*, ed. Dan Duffy, 68–74. New Haven, CT: Yale University Council on Southeast Asia Studies, 1997.

Phu, Thy. *Picturing Model Citizens: Civility in Asian American Visual Culture*. Philadelphia: Temple University Press, 2012.

Phụng, Vũ Trọng. *The Industry of Marrying Europeans*, trans. Thuy Tranviet. Southeast Asia Program Series, vol. 22. Ithaca, NY: Cornell University, Southeast Asia Program Publications, 2006.

———. *Kỹ Nghệ Lấy Tây and Cơm Thầy Cơm Cô*. Hanoi: Nhà Xuất Bản Văn Học, 2004.

Pitchford, Nicola. "Modernism, Unlikely Postmodernism: Stein's *Tender Buttons*." *American Literary History* 11 (1999): 642–667.

Ponce, Martin Joseph. *Beyond the Nation: Diasporic Filipino Literature and Queer Reading*. Sexual Cultures. New York: New York University Press, 2012.

Povinelli, Elizabeth A. *The Empire of Love: Toward a Theory of Intimacy, Genealogy, and Carnality*. Public Planet Books. Durham, NC: Duke University Press, 2006.

Proschan, Frank. "Eunuch Mandarins, Soldats Mamzelles, Effeminate Boys, and Graceless Women." *GLQ* 8, no. 4 (2002): 435–467.

———. "'Syphilis, Opiomania, and Pederasty': Colonial Constructions of Vietnamese (and French) Social Diseases." *Journal of the History of Sexuality* 11, no. 4 (2002): 610–636.

Quinn-Judge, Sophie. *Hồ Chí Minh: The Missing Years, 1919–1941*. Berkeley: University of California Press, 2002.

Rabin, Jessica G. *Surviving the Crossing: (Im)Migration, Ethnicity, and Gender in Willa Cather, Gertrude Stein, and Nella Larsen*. New York: Routledge, 2004.

Remillard, Horace. "Departure of Governor-General Sarraut—His Colonial Policy, June 6, 1919," ed. U.S. Department of State. Record Group 59, Records of the Department of State Relating to Internal Affairs of France, 1910–1929. U.S. National Archives, Washington, DC, 1919.

Ricoeur, Paul. *Time and Narrative*, vol. 2. Chicago: University of Chicago Press, 1984.

Riley, Wilfred J. "The New Plays on Broadway: Sam H. Harris." *Billboard*, December 8, 1928, 7.

Robbins, Bruce. *The Servant's Hand: English Fiction from Below*. New York: Columbia University Press, 1986.

Robcis, Camille. *The Law of Kinship: Anthropology, Psychoanalysis, and the Family in France*. Ithaca, NY: Cornell University Press, 2013.

Robinson, Court. *Terms of Refuge: The Indochinese Exodus and the International Response*. Politics in Contemporary Asia. New York: St. Martin's Press, 1998.

Rowe, John Carlos. *The Cultural Politics of the New American Studies*. Ann Arbor: Open Humanities Press, 2012. doi:http://dx.doi.org/10.3998/ohp.10945585.0001.001. Available at http://quod.lib.umich.edu/o/ohp/10945585.0001.001.

———. "US Novels and US Wars." In *Cambridge History of the American Novel*, ed. Leonard Cassuto, 813–831. New York: Cambridge University Press, 2011.

Rubin, Andrew. *Archives of Authority: Empire, Culture, and the Cold War*. Translation/ Transnation. Princeton, NJ: Princeton University Press, 2012.

Saada, Emmanuelle. *Empire's Children: Race, Filiation, and Citizenship in the French Colonies*, trans. Arthur Goldhammer. Chicago: University of Chicago Press, 2012.

Sasges, Gerard. "State, Enterprise and the Alcohol Monopoly in Colonial Vietnam." *Journal of Southeast Asian Studies* 43, no. 1 (2012): 133–157.

Saunders, Frances Stonor. *Who Paid the Piper? The CIA and the Cultural Cold War*. London: Granta, 1999.

Schafer, John C. *Võ Phiến and the Sadness of Exile*. Monograph Series on Southeast Asia. DeKalb: Northern Illinois University, Southeast Asia Publications, Center for Southeast Asian Studies, 2006.

Schirmer, Daniel B., and Stephen Rosskamm Shalom. *The Philippines Reader: A History of Colonialism, Neocolonialism, Dictatorship, and Resistance*. Boston: South End, 1987.

Schlund-Vials, Cathy J. "Re-seeing Cambodia and Recollecting the 'Nam." In *Looking Back on the Vietnam War*, ed. Brenda M. Boyle and Jeehyun Lim, 156–174. New Brunswick, NJ: Rutgers University Press, 2016.

Sedgwick, Eve Kosofsky. *Between Men: English Literature and Male Homosocial Desire*. Gender and Culture. New York: Columbia University Press, 1985.

Serres, Michel, and Bruno Latour. *Conversations on Science, Culture, and Time*. Studies in Literature and Science. Ann Arbor: University of Michigan Press, 1995.

Sharma, Sarah. *In the Meantime: Temporality and Cultural Politics*. Durham, NC: Duke University Press, 2014.

Shimizu, Celine Parreñas. *The Hypersexuality of Race: Performing Asian/American Women on Screen and Scene*. Durham, NC: Duke University Press, 2007.

Silverman, Edwin B. "Indochina Legacy: The Refugee Act of 1980." *Publius* 10, no. 1 (Winter 1980): 27–41.

Simon-Nahum, Perrine. "L'évolution de la pensée de Tran Duc Thao, de Sartre à Fanon." In *L'itinéraire de Tran Duc Thao: Phénoménologie et transferts culturels*, ed. Jocelyn Benoist and Michel Espagne, 216–229. Paris: Armand Colin, 2013.

Slaughter, Joseph. "Form and Informality: An Unliterary Look at World Literature." In *The Work of Genre: Selected Essays from the English Institute*, ed. Robyn Warhol-Down, para. 182–226. Cambridge, MA: English Institute and American Council of Learned Societies, 2011. Available at http://hdl.handle.net/2027/ heb.90055.0001.001.

Smith, Leland L. "Department's Instruction No. 623: Monthly Report on Commerce and Industries for November, 1921," ed. Department of State. Washington, DC: National Archives, 1921.

Smith, Sidonie, and Julia Watson. *Reading Autobiography: A Guide for Interpreting Life Narratives*. Minneapolis: University of Minnesota Press, 2010.

Song, Min. *The Children of 1965: On Writing, and Not Writing, as an Asian American*. Durham, NC: Duke University Press, 2013.

Spanos, William V. *Redeemer Nation in the Interregnum: An Untimely Meditation on the American Vocation.* New York: Fordham University Press, 2016.

Stein, Gertrude. *The Autobiography of Alice B. Toklas.* New York: Vintage, 1990.

———. *Lectures in America.* Boston: Beacon, 1985.

Steinbeck, John. *America and Americans and Selected Nonfiction,* ed. Susan Shillinglaw and Jackson J. Benson. New York: Viking, 2002.

———. *Travels with Charley: In Search of America.* New York: Penguin, 1980.

Stepp, Carl Sessions. "The Golden Era of a Magazine with Attitude." *American Journalism Review* (October 1995). Available at http://ajrarchive.org/Article.asp?id=1856.

Stimpson, Catharine R. "'Gertrice/Altrude': Stein, Toklas, and the Paradox of the Happy Marriage." In *Mothering the Mind,* ed. Ruth Perry and M. W. Brownley, 124–139. New York: Holmes and Meier, 1984.

Stoler, Ann Laura. *Carnal Knowledge and Imperial Power: Race and the Intimate in Colonial Rule.* Berkeley: University of California Press, 2002.

———. "Sexual Affronts and Racial Frontiers: European Identities and the Cultural Politics of Exclusion in Colonial Southeast Asia." In *Tensions of Empire: Colonial Cultures in a Bourgeois World,* ed. Frederick Cooper and Ann Laura Stoler, 198–237. Berkeley: University of California Press, 1997.

Stovall, Tyler. "The Color Line behind the Lines: Racial Violence in France during the Great War." *American Historical Review* 103, no. 3 (June 1998): 737–769.

Taft, William H. *William Howard Taft: Essential Writings and Addresses.* Madison, NJ: Fairleigh Dickinson University Press, 2009.

Tai, Hue-Tam Ho. *Radicalism and the Origins of the Vietnamese Revolution.* Cambridge, MA: Harvard University Press, 1992.

Tang, Amy Cynthia. *Repetition and Race: Asian American Literature after Multiculturalism.* New York: Oxford University Press, 2016.

"Thân Gửi Bạn Đọc." *Văn* no. 1 (January 1, 1964): 1.

Thoma, Pamela S. *Asian American Women's Popular Literature: Feminizing Genres and Neoliberal Belonging.* Philadelphia: Temple University Press, 2014.

Thompson, Virginia. *French Indo-China.* New York: Macmillan, 1937.

"Thư Tòa Soạn." *Văn,* nos. 100 and 101 (March 1, 1968): 1–2.

———. *Văn,* no. 102 (March 15, 1968): 1.

Toklas, Alice B. *The Alice B. Toklas Cook Book.* New York: Harper, 1954.

Tompkins, Kyla Wazana. "Consider the Recipe." *J19: The Journal of Nineteenth-Century Americanists* 1, no. 2 (Fall 2013): 439–445.

Tran, Nhung Tuyet, and Anthony Reid. "Introduction." In *Việt Nam: Borderless Histories,* ed. Nhung Tuyet Tran and Anthony Reid, 3–22. New Perspectives in Southeast Asian Studies. Madison: University of Wisconsin Press, 2006.

Tran, Nu-Anh. "South Vietnamese Identity, American Intervention, and the Newspaper *Chính Luận.*" *Journal of Vietnamese Studies* 1, nos. 1–2 (2006): 169–209.

Trần, Phong Giao. "William Faulkner: Con Người Và Tác Phẩm." *Văn* 2, no. 37 (1965): 3–25.

Trần, Thảo Đức. "Le conflit franco-vietnamien." *La Pensée* 22 (January–February 1949): 17–19.

———. "Sur l'Indochine." *Les Temps Modernes* 5 (1946): 878–900.

Trần, Triệu Luật. "Những Người Trẻ Đa Đen Giữa Lồng Giấy Trang." *Văn Học* 56 (March 15, 1966): 18–28.

Troeung, Y-Dang. "'A Gift or a Theft Depends on Who Is Holding the Pen': Postcolonial Collaborative Autobiography and Monique Truong's *The Book of Salt.*" *Modern Fiction Studies* 56, no. 1 (2010): 113–135.

Truong, Monique T. D. *The Book of Salt.* Boston: Houghton Mifflin, 2003.

———. "The Reception of Robert Olen Butler's *A Good Scent from a Strange Mountain*: Ventriloquism and the Pulitzer Prize." *Viet Nam Forum* 16 (Fall 1997): 75–94.

Valladão, Alfredo G. A. *The Twenty-First Century Will Be American*, trans. John Howe. New York: Verso, 1996.

Vang, Ma. "Writing on the Run: Hmong American Literary Formations and the Deterritorialized Subject." *MELUS* 41, no. 3 (2016): 89–111.

Vann, Michael G. "Of Pirates, Postcards, and Public Beheadings: The Pedagogic Execution in French Colonial Indochina." *Historical Reflections/Réflexions Historiques* 36, no. 2 (2010): 39–58.

Vasey, Ruth. *The World According to Hollywood, 1918–1939*. Madison: University of Wisconsin Press, 1997.

Vu-Hill, Kimloan. *Coolies into Rebels: Impact of World War I on French Indochina*. Paris: Les Indes Savantes, 2011.

———. "Strangers in a Foreign Land: Vietnamese Soldiers and Workers in France during World War I." In *Việt Nam: Borderless Histories*, ed. Nhung Tuyet Tran and Anthony Reid, 256–289. New Perspectives in Southeast Asian Studies. Madison: University of Wisconsin Press, 2006.

Vuong, Ocean. *Night Sky with Exit Wounds*. Port Townsend, WA: Copper Canyon, 2016.

———. "Ocean Vuong on Being Generous in Your Work." Interview by Amy Rose Spiegel, Thecreativeindependent.com, May 16, 2017. Available at https://thecre ativeindependent.com/people/ocean-vuong-on-being-generous-in-your-work.

Vũ-Phan, Tri Ngọc Khuê. *Trần Đức Thảo: Những Lời Trăng Trối*. Arlington, VA: Tổ Hợp Xuất Bản Miền Đông Hoa Kỳ, 2014.

Warner, Chantelle. "Speaking from Experience: Narrative Schemas, Deixis, and Authenticity Effects in Verena Stefan's Feminist Confession Shedding." *Language and Literature* 18, no. 1 (2009): 7–23.

Warwick, Alexandra. "Imperial Gothic." In *The Encyclopedia of the Gothic*, ed. William Hughes, David Punter, and Andrew Smith, 338–342. Chichester, UK: Wiley Blackwell, 2016.

Wexler, Laura. *Tender Violence: Domestic Visions in an Age of U.S. Imperialism*. Cultural Studies of the United States. Chapel Hill: University of North Carolina Press, 2000.

White, John. *History of a Voyage to the China Sea*. Boston: Wells and Lilly, 1823.

———. *A Voyage to Cochin China*. London: A. and R. Spottiswoode, 1824.

———. *A Voyage to Cochin China*. London: Longman, Hurst, Rees, Orme, Brown, and Green, 1824.

Will, Barbara. *Unlikely Collaboration: Gertrude Stein, Bernard Faÿ, and the Vichy Dilemma*. Gender and Culture. New York: Columbia University Press, 2011.

Williams, Dana A., and Marissa K. Lopez. "More than a Fever: Toward a Theory of the Ethnic Archive." *PMLA* 127, no. 2 (2012): 357–359.

Williams, Linda. *Playing the Race Card: Melodramas of Black and White from Uncle Tom to O. J. Simpson*. Princeton, NJ: Princeton University Press, 2001.

Williams, Raymond. *Marxism and Literature*. Marxist Introductions. Oxford: Oxford University Press, 1977.

Wilson, Woodrow. "President Woodrow Wilson's Fourteen Points," January 8, 1918. Lillian Goldman Law Library. Available at http://avalon.law.yale.edu/20th_cen tury/wilson14.asp.

Witt, Doris. *Black Hunger: Soul Food and America*. Minneapolis: University of Minnesota Press, 2004.

Wolfe, Tom, and E. W. Johnson, eds. *The New Journalism*. New York: Harper and Row, 1973.

Woloch, Alex. *The One versus the Many: Minor Characters and the Space of the Protagonist in the Novel*. Princeton, NJ: Princeton University Press, 2003.

———. "Partial Representation." In *The Work of Genre: Selected Essays from the English Institute*, ed. Robyn Warhol-Down. Cambridge, MA: English Institute and American Council of Learned Societies, 2013.

Wong, Sau-ling Cynthia. *Reading Asian American Literature: From Necessity to Extravagance*. Princeton, NJ: Princeton University Press, 1993.

Woolley, John T., Gerhard Peters, and University of California. Santa Barbara. "Bills Concerning Indochina Refugees and Prisoner Transfers with Mexico and Canada Remarks on Signing H.R. 7769 and S. 1662 into Law." October 28, 1977. American Presidency Project, comp. Gerhard Peters and John T. Woolley. Available at http://www.presidency.ucsb.edu/ws/?pid=6855.

Zafar, Rafia. "Elegy and Remembrance in the Cookbooks of Alice B. Toklas and Edna Lewis." *MELUS* 38, no. 4 (Winter 2013): 32–51.

Zinoman, Peter. *The Colonial Bastille: A History of Imprisonment in Vietnam, 1862–1940*. Berkeley: University of California Press, 2001.

———. *Vietnamese Colonial Republican: The Political Vision of Vũ Trọng Phụng*. Berkeley: University of California Press, 2014.

———. "Vũ Trọng Phụng's *Dumb Luck* and the Nature of Vietnamese Modernism." In *Dumb Luck, a Novel by Vũ Trọng Phụng*, ed. Peter Zinoman, trans. Nguyễn Nguyệt Cầm and Peter Zinoman, 1–30. Southeast Asia: Politics, Meaning, Memory. Ann Arbor: University of Michigan Press, 2002.

INDEX

Page numbers in *italics* refer to illustrations.

anticolonialism/anti-imperialism (*continued*)
periodical forms and, 101, 102; in Truong's *Book of Salt*, 60, 77–80, 82, 83, 84; U.S. rhetoric of, 41; U.S. rhetoric of, vs. colonial acts, 20, 25, 39, 58, 83; U.S. rhetoric of, vs. exceptionalism, 47, 56; World War I and, 178n59. *See also* decolonization
anticolonial violence, 100–101, 102
Apocalypse Now (film), 86, 112
archive(s): alternative, 163; ethnic, 143; expanding, 142–144; imperialism's censoring of, 71; in progress, 8; South Vietnamese journals as, 164, 166; under-examined/newly released, 5, 18; unofficial, 20, 123
Arendt, Hannah, 154; "We Refugees," 128–129
Asian American Literary Review (journal), 162, 200n2
Asian American literary studies: genre in, 6–7; links to Southeast Asia studies, 20; recontextualization of, 147; subjectivity in, 169n24
assimilation: vs. integration, 124, 128; refugee camps and, 132, 133, 135; refugees and imperatives of, 124, 127, 129, 136; salad bowl metaphor for, 126; Steinbeck's views on, 125–126; Võ Phiến on, 124, 126–128, 129
Auden, W. H., 154
Austin, Oscar P., 56

Bakhtin, Mikhail, 140
Baldwin, James, 155, 201n43
Baraka, Amiri, 182n103
Barry, Lynda (*One! Hundred! Demons!*), 142–143
Barthes, Roland, 95, 191n41
"Be American" (Bulosan), 143
Behaine, Pigneau de, 171n52
Berlant, Lauren, 27
Berrong, Richard, 181n88
Bhabha, Homi, 123, 142
black culture, South Vietnamese journal issues devoted to, 155–158, 159–160
Black Hunger (Witt), 60
Blackmur, R. P., 201n28
"Black Orpheus" (Sartre), 159
Blum, Hester, 12
body/bodies: American imperialism personified in, 39, 42, 43; Asian woman's, hypersexualization of, 33, 44; attraction to, in Hervey's *Congaï*, 37, 44; biracial, colonialism's devaluation of, 26, 28, 33–34, 35; fragmented, as facet of empire, 100; labor-

ing, in *The Alice B. Toklas Cook Book*, 65; laboring, in Truong's *Book of Salt*, 59–60; mixed-race, as limit figure, 133; refugee, victimization and pathologization of, 132, 133–134, 135, 140; as sartorial object, 38–39, 92. *See also* Vietnamese body
body-jewel, 37, 38
The Book of Salt (Truong), 21, 59, 67–72, 74–80, 83–84; ambiguous ending of, 84; decolonizing theme in, 60, 77–80, 82, 83, 84; Eng's reading of, 68, 168n12, 185n28, 185n30, 185n33, 187n54; food objects as material traces of history in, 71–72, 74; Hồ Chí Minh as character in, 68, 77–80, 82, 188n65; language of Vietnamese servants in, 69–70; layered narratives in, 71; postmodernist appraisal of history in, 68–69; queer representation in, 67–68, 76–77, 187n54; subversion of American loyalty in, 83; title of, 74; Vietnamese servitude in, 59, 68, 69–70, 84, 185n36
Borri, Father Christoforo, 72
Boublil, Alain, 49
Bourdet, Edouard, 55
Bradley, Mark, 173n4, 184n15
Braestrup, Peter, 107
Brantlinger, Peter, 91
Braudel, Fernand, 4, 168n12
Brewster, David, 15–17
British imperialism: French imperialism compared to, 29; in southern Vietnam, 192n58
Broadway, Hervey's *Congaï* on, 20, 23, 52, 55, 56
Brooks, Peter, 27
Brown, Dean, 134
Brown, Jerry, 134
Bulosan, Carlos ("Be American"), 143

Calmette, Albert, 73
camps. *See* refugee camps in United States
Camus, Albert, 148, 155, 159
capitalist economy: conditions of labor in, Hervey's *Congaï* on, 35–37; critique of, in South Vietnamese literary magazines, 149–150, 152–153, 157–158, 159; fractured Vietnamese body in, 94; literary critics on, 150; and literary representation, sensationalism in, 112, 152–153; miscegenation as form of exchange in, 33, 34; Vietnamese labor in, Truong's *Book of Salt* on, 74
capitalist expansion, U.S., in Asia, 42, 57
Caplan, Jane, 38
The Captive (Bourdet), 55
Carter, Jimmy, 134–135

Marguerite Nguyen is an Assistant Professor of English at Wesleyan University.

E. San Juan Jr., *The Philippine Temptation: Dialectics of Philippines–U.S. Literary Relations*

Carlos Bulosan and E. San Juan Jr., eds., *The Cry and the Dedication*

Carlos Bulosan and E. San Juan Jr., eds., *On Becoming Filipino: Selected Writings of Carlos Bulosan*

Vicente L. Rafael, ed., *Discrepant Histories: Translocal Essays on Filipino Cultures*

Yen Le Espiritu, *Filipino American Lives*

Paul Ong, Edna Bonacich, and Lucie Cheng, eds., *The New Asian Immigration in Los Angeles and Global Restructuring*

Chris Friday, *Organizing Asian American Labor: The Pacific Coast Canned-Salmon Industry, 1870–1942*

Sucheng Chan, ed., *Hmong Means Free: Life in Laos and America*

Timothy P. Fong, *The First Suburban Chinatown: The Remaking of Monterey Park, California*

William Wei, *The Asian American Movement*

Yen Le Espiritu, *Asian American Panethnicity*

Velina Hasu Houston, ed., *The Politics of Life*

Renqiu Yu, *To Save China, To Save Ourselves: The Chinese Hand Laundry Alliance of New York*

Shirley Geok-lin Lim and Amy Ling, eds., *Reading the Literatures of Asian America*

Karen Isaksen Leonard, *Making Ethnic Choices: California's Punjabi Mexican Americans*

Gary Y. Okihiro, *Cane Fires: The Anti-Japanese Movement in Hawaii, 1865–1945*

Sucheng Chan, *Entry Denied: Exclusion and the Chinese Community in America, 1882–1943*